THE MORMON COLONIES IN MEXICO

El Paso

T E X A S

Rio Grande

Col. Morelos
Col. Oaxaca
Col. Juarez
Bavispe
La Ascención
Col. Diaz
Col. Dublán
Casas Grandes
Pacheco
Garcia
Chuichupa

Gulf of California

Gulf of California

S O N O R A

Chihuahua

C H I H U A H U A

S I N A L O A

D U R A N G O

C O A H U I L A

Rio Grande

Monterrey

Gulf
of
Mexico

San Luis Potosi

Gudalajara

Mexico City

Mormon Colonies
Mexican Cities
State Boundaries

Pacific Ocean

The Mormon Colonies in Mexico

By

Thomas Cottam Romney, Ph.D.
Director Logan L.D.S. Institute

The University of Utah Press
Salt Lake City, Utah

This book is lovingly dedicated
to my devoted wife, who has shared with
me many of the experiences recorded herein,
and who has been an inspiration to me
under all conditions.

Introduction © 2005 by The University of Utah Press. All rights reserved.

09 08 07 06 05   5 4 3 2 1

 The Defiance House Man colophon is a registered trademark of the University of Utah Press. It is based upon a four-foot-tall, Ancient Puebloan pictograph (late PIII) near Glen Canyon, Utah.

LIBRARY OF CONGRESS CATALOGING-IN-PUBLICATION DATA

Romney, Thomas Cottam, 1876-1962.
  The Mormon colonies in Mexico / by Thomas Cottam Romney.
    p. cm.
  Originally published: Salt Lake City, Utah : Deseret Book Co., 1938.
  ISBN-13: 978-0-87480-838-4 (pbk. : alk. paper)
  ISBN-10: 0-87480-838-3
  1. Church of Jesus Christ of Latter Day Saints—Mexico. 2. Mormon Church—Mexico. I. Title.
  BX8617.M4R6 2005
  289.3'72—dc22

                        2005015070

Printed on recycled paper with 50% post-consumer content.

CONTENTS

ILLUSTRATIONS
(following page 148)

FOREWORD

Some years ago, when captivated by Dr. Romney's tales of pioneer days on the vast plains of Chihuahua, in the semi-tropical valleys of Sonora, and in the formidable Sierra Madre that lies between—regions always of high romance to me—I urged him to write his personal experiences during that life, so full of adventure and of human significance. Now, in this book, he has fulfilled my wish, and in it has gone beyond to write a full-length account of the migration and settlement in which he took part. The book is most welcome, for the history of the Mormon colonies in northern Mexico during the last half century forms an important chapter both in the activities of the Latter-day Saints and in the relations of the two peoples who live on opposite sides of the international boundary.

Dr. Romney writes of events in which he himself participated. Having gone to Mexico as a youth and lived some twenty-five active years in the Mormon colonies of Chihuahua and Sonora, in both peaceful and troublous times, he writes with the vividness of an eye-witness, and for those years he draws his story in considerable part from personal experiences, that circumstance which made a book by Bernal Diaz del Castillo the most lasting work on another episode in the colorful history of Mexico. On the other hand, Dr. Romney's book reflects free access to official and unofficial Mormon sources of information regarding his subject, and intimate personal contacts with the most important men who participated in the events of which he writes. His account covers the history to the present time.

A loyal Mormon, Dr. Romney manifests in this work the same tolerance and generosity of spirit which is so characteristic of his daily contact with his fellow men, and his narrative reflects a deep affection for the land where he spent the golden years of early manhood. Of necessity he treats some topics that may be controversial, but always with fair-mindedness. His primary aim is to set forth for general readers the human aspects of his subject. Some other eye-witness, it is to be hoped, will some day treat the subject in the same spirit, and with as free access to the archives of Mexico as Dr. Romney has had to Mormon sources.

One thing is plain from this book. The Mormons in Mexico have shown the same sterling qualities that made them the great colonizers of the Interior Basin of the United States.

Dr. Herbert E. Bolton.

PREFACE

This book was written at the suggestion of a number of my friends, among them being Dr. Herbert E. Bolton, head of the History Department of the University of California, and beloved teacher, and Dr. Carl O. Sauer, head of the Department of Geography at the same institution.

The purpose of the volume is to tell the story of the founding of the Mormon colonies in Chihuahua and Sonora in northern Mexico; their growth and development, and the exodus of the Mormon colonists to the United States, resulting from the chaotic conditions after the Madero revolution. A chapter has been devoted to an evaluation of the progeny of the founders of these colonies, and some space has been given to a narration of conditions since the return of some of the refugees to re-establish themselves in their homes. The chapter relating to Mormon doctrines was written primarily for the benefit of those into whose hands the book might come, who are unacquainted with the fundamental religious tenets of the Church of Jesus Christ of Latter-day Saints. Such information will give a clearer understanding of the motives underlying the migration of the Mormons to Mexico, and of their varied experiences in that land.

This is the only printed volume dealing with the Mormon colonies in Mexico that has ever appeared, and this knowledge has made me doubly careful in sifting the material that has come into my hands, with the view to including in the narrative only that which is true and will be of general interest. If any errors have crept in, I assume all responsibility for them and assure the readers that they have not been intentionally included.

I acknowledge a debt of gratitude to all who have rendered service in the preparation and publication of this volume. Especially am I grateful for the service rendered by Dr. Herbert E. Bolton, head of the History Department and Director of the Bancroft Library at the University of California, Berkeley, California, who read the entire manuscript and offered corrections that are of immeasurable value to the book; to the Committee on Church Publications, Stephen L Richards, Melvin J. Ballard and Dr. John A. Widtsoe, member of the Council of the Twelve, who read the manuscript and recommended its publication; to President Joseph Quinney, Jr., of the Logan Temple, who also read the manuscript; to President J. Reuben Clark, Jr., of the First Presidency of the Church, and who, as a prominent attorney of Salt Lake City, collected much valuable material, to which I have had access; to attorneys Vernon Romney and Don Skousen for materials collected and to Junius Romney, Mrs. Theresa S. Hill, Mrs. Bertha Spencer, Mrs. Lea Ivins Cardon, President Antoine R. Ivins, D. V. Farnsworth and Theodore Martineau for freely contributing valuable information and illustrations used in the book; and finally to Dr. Milton R. Humler for his work on the map of the Mormon colonies.

While historical accuracy has been the keynote of the book, an attempt has been made to present the facts, not as a mere chronicle of events, but in a style which will be interesting to the general reading public. If this has been accomplished I am content.

THOMAS COTTAM ROMNEY.

Logan, Utah.
November 15, 1938.

INTRODUCTION

MARTHA SONNTAG BRADLEY

In traditional narratives of LDS church history, historians usually portray the Mexican colonies as a sort of safety valve for Utah polygamists, a place where family life and community building could continue unabated or undisturbed by legal restrictions placed on plural marriage by federal law. But that's only part of the story. A far more rich picture of devotion to church and family, community and country, lies just beyond this familiar view.

After the United States Congress passed the Edmunds Act of 1882 it became evident that if plurality was to continue it would have to be kept out of sight. This subterranean practice of polygamy forced men and women into hiding, required that women either deny the paternity of their children or keep them hidden, and demanded huge compromises and sacrifices of the families involved—compromises and sacrifices that tried already complicated family systems and pushed them to the limit. Moving such families to Mexico was one solution to some of those difficulties.

A possible location for establishing Mormon colonies in Mexico was identified in 1875, when the first Mormon expeditionary party traveled from Arizona over the Mexican border. Apostle Orson Pratt told the members of the expedition "to look out for places where our brethren could go and be safe from harm in the event that persecution should make it necessary for them to get out of the way for a season." But it was not until after the Edmunds Act that colonization began in earnest. In 1884, LDS Church President John Taylor sent Stake President Christopher Layton instructions to take his Saint Joseph, Arizona, ward to Mexico. The next year, Taylor visited northern Mexico and southern Arizona with other church leaders, encouraging polygamous men and women to escape into the safety provided by Mexican territory. [1]

President John Taylor, his counselor Joseph F. Smith, and a company of other church leaders, a decade earlier traveled to southern Arizona evaluating the suitability of Mexico both as a place for settlement and a set of political conditions for the practice of plurality, and intending to identify available land. Their most important criterion for determining suitability, however, was a stable or favorable political climate which would allow the polygamists to practice their peculiar type of marriage without threat of legal action. The visit was disrupted, in part, by the threatened arrest of Taylor when the party reached California. Ironically, at that time he said he would be willing to submit to arrest, "if the law would only be a little more dignified." Instead, he returned to Salt Lake City on January 27, 1885, not long after preaching his last public sermon, and later that day withdrew from public view and went underground.

Congressional passage of the Edmunds-Tucker Act in 1887 brought severe penalties against the church for its failure to comply with the earlier act. More members were forced to go underground and the church desperately sought alternate landscapes in order to continue a practice many believed was fundamental to their religious way of life. The economic, societal, and political impact of the underground period on the church was profound and sweeping. Church leaders sat on the boards of most important Salt Lake City businesses, such as Zions Cooperative Mercantile Institution (ZCMI); they ran most city and territorial government operations; and as bishops or other church leaders managed local resources, social relationships, and exchanges between individual members of the church. When these men and their wives went on the underground these activities—at the heart of community—ceased or were severely impeded by the loss of leadership. Some church activities such as general conferences, which typically were held in the tabernacle, moved to areas outside the church center. Federal officers were known to haunt such events, circling the periphery of the crowds, hoping for a sight of a leader on the run. A familiar sight throughout the territory during the 1880s were federal marshals on horseback scouting out for "polygs" hiding from federal arrest. The constant pressure placed on the church and individual polygamist members was unrelenting, and despite the vigilant efforts of many to outsmart or at least outlast the threat of arrest, many church leaders served prison terms in the territorial penitentiary.

Tiring of the endless pressure he and other polygamists felt from the federal marshals, George Q. Cannon suggested to President Taylor that the polygamists might all surrender at the same time, overwhelming the government with the proposition of jailing them all, saying ironically, "the laws of congress conflict with my sense of submission to the will of the Lord, I now offer myself, here, for whatever judgment the courts of my country may impose."[2] Short of such a drastic measure, the location of another home for the Mormons in yet another remote refuge, isolated from public view, seemed the only solution.

Mormons felt it was their moral obligation, imposed on them by God, to continue in the practice of plural marriage. Stopping the practice was not at that point an option, while relocation was. This was nothing new, but was in fact one of the most persistent patterns of church settlement. In addition to settlements throughout Utah territory, outlying settlements had already been established in many areas of the region, including Colorado, Nevada, Wyoming, and Arizona. Some of these became havens to those on the run during the underground period, while colonies in Mexico extended the church's influence beyond the borders of the United States.

It would have been impossible for the church to look toward expansion into Mexico without considering the immense missionary opportunity it provided. Given the significance of proselytizing and the missionary programs to the church, such opportunities would have added to the appeal. Finding suitable land for colonization could also include preaching the gospel to native populations.

Thomas Cottam Romney moved to Mexico with his polygamist family in 1885 when he was nine years old and stayed for the next twenty-seven years. When as an adult two of Romney's academic friends, Herbert E. Bolton and Carl O. Sauer, urged him to write a book about his experience, they most likely were responding enthusiastically to years of shared stories about life in the Mexican colonies. Recognizing that these stories were too good to be lost, and that Romney's account had the value of firsthand knowledge, they encouraged Romney to put pen to paper and record his memories, reflect on their meanings, and document this important moment in the Mormon past. *The Mormon Colonies in Mexico* is the result.

Romney's unique vantage point is the strongest draw of this narrative, as Romney and his family lived much of their life in the Mexican Mormon colonies. But the narrative's value is much broader and deeper than just that. Romney's insights into Mexican politics and personalities, and his view of the course of history from inside rather than from outside, are fascinating, colorful, and opinionated. He was clear in who he admired and why, and who he did not. While the book is a record of his own impressions and analysis, it is also likely a reflection of the opinions that he shared with others. While it is his private understanding of Mexican life at this particular moment in time, it also represents a distinctly Mormon "read" as well.

When *The Mormon Mexican Colonies* appeared it was the first and only story of the Mexican colonies, but it has enduring interest and value beyond this. His telling of the story is fresh and clear headed. Neither sentimental nor nostalgic about "how it used to be," it is a forthright and candid telling of what worked in Mormon community building and what did not. Romney's portrayal of the unique challenges of living in a foreign country and maintaining American and Mormon values is suggestive of larger human realities. It is difficult, even under the most favorable of circumstances, to stand true for what one believes. Sometimes in the Mexican colonies life was good, it could be easy and even productive. But more often it was not. Instead, the typical challenges of agricultural life and the complications of providing for large numbers of people building new homes and communities was magnified by turbulent politics and a cultural life not fully understood by these outsiders.

Romney's telling of the diplomatic acts and the research and exploration embedded in the process of colonization complete his picture of the settlement efforts. Though schooled in important ways by successful colonization throughout the Great Basin, the Mormons found that Mexico presented unique challenges. Romney describes the colonies as both a place and as a way of community life, with its specific code of ethics. He demonstrates the evolution of a settlement through a series of stages and accompanying problems by telling stories, showing the applicability of knowledge gained from irrigation or planning endeavors, for instance, and how that knowledge was transplanted from one environment to another. According to Romney's account, Mormons traveled to Mexico not only to escape persecution, but also "in order to shape their social and religious life in harmony with their own peculiar ideals. There was no exception made to this rule by those who sought homes in Mexico."

Mormon institutions were clearly portable and duplicable, made over again and again regardless of the locale. A Mexican Mormon town resembled those built by Mormons elsewhere, and regardless of where they sprang up they featured straight streets which met at right angles, cooperative industries and irrigation systems, a central focus on church and school, and a group of people striving to live in accordance with their understanding of God's will. This narrative places particular doctrines such as plurality and matters of religious authority in real world situations and tests their viability in the lives of human beings. How difficult was it to live plurality in a foreign place under extreme poverty while feeling persecuted by the law? What personal costs came with accepting the prophetic authority of one man who claimed to speak with God? What were the human costs of the federal government's clampdown on polygamists? Romney suggests some answers.

While colonists fled to Mexico to escape federal prosecution for the violation of antipolygamy legislation, when they arrived they built homes and towns that indicated they planned to stay. Sturdy adobe brick homes and impressive churches and school buildings gave indication that the Mormon settlers were making the Mexican landscape into their home turf, and that they believed their children would stay as well. Romney shows how they went about the process of making this their new home. He discusses the Latter-day Saint version of the Good Society, with branches of ZCMI and other church businesses, the willingness of members to work together, their continued ties to the central church, and their desire to maintain a certain standard of living regardless of the privation of their neighbors. For the Mexican colonists, each challenge that came along—whether drought, conflict with the native populations, political chaos, or poverty—was interpreted as a test placed on

their shoulders by God. Making good had religious significance and impacted their chance at salvation.

Romney's portraits of President Porfirio Diaz, Henry
Eyring, Isaac Stewart, and Franklin Harris, among many
others, are richly human: they are real people whose ambi-
tions and hopes sometimes intruded on their ability to succeed. Many of these men were impeded by forces beyond
their control as they attempted to find straight answers to
complicated questions about how best to live in the world.
Men such as Anthony W. Ivins or Moses Thatcher are heroes in this narrative, because of the strength of character they modeled, as well as the kindness and intelligence
they exemplified through their approach to dealing with
individuals and institutional problems. Romney described
Anthony Ivins as a gentleman who was "never rugged and
his method of discipline and direction was always characterized by a quiet gentleness and gentlemanliness usually
typical of the truly great." An excellent model for men raising children in the colonies, Ivins was a tremendous support to both community-building efforts and righteous living. Romney identified goodness within both the Mormon
world and its leaders, and the Mexican landscape and the
native Mexicans who supported the church's effort to create
a place of refuge for its people, helped them build homes
and communities, and carve out livings in the diverse environment of the Mexican countryside. Moreover, Romney's
account fleshes out the picture of the Mormon effort—the
prosperity and wealth gained at various times, and the de-
spair and failure that drove certain groups from one part of
the Mexican state into another.

Romney positions the story of the Mexican colonies
within the persistent persecution narrative of the church,
which carried the LDS Church from the Midwest to the

Far West, and after the 1880s onto foreign soil, telling the story through the particular lens of the nineteenth century church and the Mormon point of view. Describing how the church's history looked to him and to others at that moment in time, before it had been interpreted and analyzed by generations of church historians, Romney felt that the Mormons went to Mexico because they had been tested yet again and had felt persecution.

But when the political situation shifted in Mexico and the colonists were no longer favored visitors but intruders, Romney's account demonstrates the way one nation protected its own at the expense of outsiders, a case study in the flexibility or fluidity of notions about law and human rights—who is protected by law and who is not. Both the church itself and the Mexican government watched and monitored closely the connection between the colonies and Salt Lake City.

Thomas Romney's volume is social history in the truest sense, presenting a view from the bottom up. It portrays the way LDS doctrine and leadership, kingdom building and devotion, played out in varied environments. It is of its time in particular ways in terms of its attitude toward matters of race, ethnicity, and gender. Romney read the significance of difference through contrasts in traditions and habits, in temperament and attitude, in education and relationships. Examined through the lens of turn-of-the century Mormonism, Romney's understanding of the gap between the Mexican people (including Mormon converts) and the colonists from Utah reflects a particular moment in time. His depiction of Mexican politics and social conditions captures the erratic and sometimes precarious climate that surrounded the Mormon colonists, threatening their lives and livelihood and placing them in a vulnerable, confusing state of anomie. He shows how lives were tossed out of balance by the threat of war and how negotiations for the movement of the group either into or out of Mexico took on a similar complexity. He captures the confused ambiguity of identity that resulted from living in a foreign land so different than their home, but a land that many had begun to consider their home. He writes,

> But the natural longing of man to return to his old haunts persisted even in the breasts of the most skeptical of the refugees, who felt that it would be impossible for them ever again to return to the land of their choice. The climate, the soil, the grandeur of the Sierras, the finny myriads in the crystal streams, the droves of deer, the flocks of wild turkey, the screaming parakeets, the romanticism of the people, the moon-lit sky, the soul-stirring yet dreamy music of the Mexican orchestra, the promenades at the plaza, the half playful and bewitching smile of the Spanish maiden, the fiesta, the bull fight—all these had a charm whose grip even the passing of a quarter of a century cannot efface.

While Romney suggests this was the longing of "other men," it is most likely that this passage and many others in the text reveal his own heart and his nostalgia for the landscape of his new home, a place he loved and learned from as a boy. He poignantly speaks of the power of place to both evoke memory and identity, but also to encourage what is best in human beings to emerge. "No wonder, then," he writes, "that the lure of the southland finally wove its magic spell about certain ones of the exiled band and gave them faith and courage to again return to the land of their adoption to rebuild and reinhabit a region war-torn and made desolate by the tramp of dusky feet." Mexico had become more than just another backdrop to the Mormon experiment, for many it had become their home.

Thomas Romney's account of life in the Mexican Mormon colonies tests Frederick Jackson Turner's frontier thesis, which identifies the uniquely independent, highly individualistic American character, and which for Romney rang true. For he saw the way the frontier forged character and stimulated independence and creativity. He believed that the men and women who emerged from Mexico were different, and were "known for their sobriety, their healthy outlook upon life, their religious fervor and for their unusual qualities of leadership." Again, the value of this narrative is that Romney witnessed this transformation in his own family and community.

Since Romney first published this text in 1938, a number of important scholarly articles and books have examined the Mexican Mormon colonies, most notably LaMond Tullis's *Mormons in Mexico*.[3] But Romney's personal account retains its charm and its importance as a firsthand narrative. His unique vantage point, which allowed him to assess the value and importance of these experiences, makes this an invaluable and rich document that enlarges our understanding of this moment in the Mormon past, a moment when the boundaries between countries and families, between heaven and earth, acquired new meaning.

NOTES

1. Jessie Embry, *Mormon Polygamous Families: Life in the Principle* (Salt Lake City: University of Utah Press, 1987), 23.

2. Richard Van Wagoner and Steven C. Walker, *A Book of Mormons* (Salt Lake City: Signature Books, 1982), 53–54.

3. F. LaMond Tullis, *Mormons in Mexico: The Dynamics of Faith and Culture* (Logan: Utah State University Press, 1987).

THE MORMON COLONIES IN MEXICO

CHAPTER I

PRESIDENT DIAZ, THE DICTATOR

President Diaz, ruler of Mexico when the Mormons first entered that territory, was a man of consummate ability in the field of military strategy. His skill as a general had been tested scores of times upon the blood soaked battle fields of his country during the decades when the sons of Montezuma were struggling for independence against the foreigner foe and the native insurrectionists. His courage was never questioned and his loyalty to his country stands unimpeached, though at times he vigorously opposed the policies of the foremost Mexican leaders.

Born in the State of Oaxaca, of Mestizo parents, Diaz was subjected to all the hardships common to this class. But unlike the masses who permitted adversity to enslave them in the toils of ignorance and grinding routine, Porfirio Diaz capitalized on these struggles and made them the stepping stones to a most brilliant career. He developed a strong, active body in which was a mind just as vigorous and a will as adamant as the frowning cliffs and rugged canyons so oft traversed by him in his native habitat. With such a rugged nature and an unbending will it is not strange that the masses stood in awe of him. Neither is it to be marveled at that millions paid homage at his shrine in contemplation of his many victories upon the field of battle. Those were the days when the military man was the idol of the people; when the man of peace, however talented, was given little recognition by the side of the man with the brass buttons. This comment is not intended as an insinuation against the character of the man who guided the destinies of his country for over a quarter of a century, but as a partial explanation for the high regard in which he was held by the Mexican people whom he dominated as absolutely as did the Czar of Russia his subjects before the World war.

When President Diaz came to the head of the Mexican government in 1876, Mexico contained less than half the number of square miles of territory held by her before the revolt of Texas. She had shrunken as a result of American intrigue and diplomacy to the point that her northern boundary line extended to the mid-stream of the Rio Grande River. No further shrinkage of domain occurred during the rule of President Diaz but there was a very decided preference shown for foreigners in the distribution of national gifts of land, timbers and minerals, and in industrial concessions.

There is no other country of similar size in the world that surpasses Mexico in natural wealth as represented in variety of climate, extent and richness of minerals, fertility of soil and timberland areas, covered with forests of pine, mahogany, and rosewood. Neither is there a country whose general populace has benefitted less by such inexhaustable wealth than has the citizenry of the Mexican republic. In discussing the economic inequalities of this period usually favorable to the foreigner and unfavorable to the Mexicans, a well known writer has epitomized the situation in the rather ironical statement, "Mexico, the mother of foreigners and the step-mother of Mexicans." In confirmation of this expression Mr. Gruening in his volume on Mexico cites numerous examples of the high handed and discriminatory policy of the Diaz regime. At the outset Diaz sought to perpetuate himself in power indefinitely by drawing to himself representatives of all groups by means of special privileges, or by assassinating those who would not conform. Recalcitrant newspapers were suppressed and editors and writers who dared voice sentiments in the least degree unfavorable to the government were put to death. Should the ill-favored attempt to maintain his rights, one of three disgraceful penalties was sure to overtake him—A jail sentence extending into months and perchance years or still worse he would be ingloriously subjected to the position of a soldier-convict or tragically meet his death under the "Ley Fuga," whereby the prisoner would be shot in the back by a group of soldiers while on the march, the inference being that the culprit was trying to make his escape from the hand of justice. A veritable massacre occurred at Vera Cruz in which nine young men were shot without trial for anti-Diaz political demonstrations. It has been reliably affirmed that during the Diaz regime fully ten thousand Mexicans were slain under the pretext of ridding the country of bandits, while it is a well known fact that they were merely political offenders.

Something less than a decade before the close of the nineteenth century, Porfirio Diaz had succeeded in putting through "indefinite" re-elections, and had established his power supreme throughout the national as well as the state governments.

The freedom of the press had completely disappeared. Congress was appointed by the President or incumbents held their positions by virtue of his consent. By him a citizen of the state of Mexico was designated a senator from Chihuahua and a life-long resident of Sonora was appointed a deputy from Yucatan. The judiciary was "hand-picked" and according to Mr. Gruening the whole machinery of government including the 27 governors of states, the 295 Jefe Politicos, 1798 presidents of municipalities, 4574 justices of the peace and members of the state legislatures was dependent on the will of one man.

Reference has been made to the favoritism shown foreigners but the history of this period likewise reveals the fact that a few of the Mexican born who were politically dangerous or potentially serviceable, fed fat from the coffers of the state, and in a few cases received monopolies and concessions from Mexico's dictator that made them independently rich and politically great. A few examples will suffice: General Bernardo Reyes not only became the great

Cacique of the frontiers but the Jefe de Operaciones over four of the Mexican states and civil governor of Nuevo Leon as well. Generals Carlos Pacheco, Rafael Cravioto, Manuel Mondragon, and a few others rose from poverty to become multi-millionaires. The Corral-Torres families controlled the state of Sonora and the Cravioto brothers took over the state of Hidalgo while Don Luis Terrazas monopolized in large measure the resources of the state of Chihuahua. Terrazas became the individual land and cattle king of the world and controlled the political as well as the financial interests of his state. At one time he was governor and when he got ready to retire he handed the position over to his son-in-law, Enrique Creel.

Millions of acres of land were virtually given away, including the "ejidos" or communal grounds cultivated by the native inhabitants since the conquest of Mexico by Cortez in the early sixteenth century. Much of this land fell into the hands of rapacious foreigners who had taken leading parts in the political campaigns favoring the election of Diaz and who otherwise curried the favor of the president.

To a Spaniard was given the Laguna (lake) of Xico which with other concessions freely bestowed, netted him the prodigious sum of eight million pesos, while to another Spaniard, Jose Sanchez Roms, and an American partner were given a monopoly on the production of paper. Parasitic foreigners fed fat on 50 million dollars spent by the federal government on financing railroads.

While special privileges corrupted the social and political life of the nation, it must not be assumed that Mexico was making no progress industrially. Foreign capital was flowing into the republic, much of it finding its way into the various enterprises such as railroad building, textile manufacturing, mining and smelting, farming and cattle raising, all of which tended in the direction of great federal prosperity.

Diaz increased the national income from something

like nineteen millions of dollars to one hundred millions. The imports of the country were increased eightfold while the exports were greatly multiplied. The number of miles of railroad throughout the Republic was increased 400 per cent and telegraph lines from 4,420 to 20,000 miles. In 1876 when Diaz came into power the postal service carried nearly five million pieces of mail at an outlay of over four hundred thousand dollars; thirty-three years later (1909) five million pieces of mail were carried at a cost of about five million dollars. When Diaz was installed as president there were no manufacturing plants. Today there are 146 mills manufacturing more than forty million dollars worth of fabrics and furnishing employment for nearly forty thousand workmen. The tobacco industry has made rapid strides likewise. Four hundred and thirty-seven factories operate, producing annually over 81 million cigars and 500 million cigarettes. In addition there are silk industries, woolen mills, iron works, smelters, paper mills, soap factories, breweries and meat packing plants established.

The gold and silver mines turned out fabulous wealth and the credit of Mexico was such that she could borrow all the money needed at a reasonable rate of interest. The genius who was largely responsible for this national prosperity was Jose I. Limantour, secretary of the Treasury, (the Alexander Hamilton of Mexico) who came into power at a time when his country was facing bankruptcy and when it seemed impossible to even pay the interest on its foreign debts.

Unfortunately, agriculture, the basic industry of the country, did not receive the same economic support and encouragement as had been given to other vocational and industrial enterprises. As a result, agriculture languished. The land areas remained practically in the same state of semi-cultivation in which they had been since the coming of Cortez. The wooden plough, an implement as old as historic man, continued to function as the chief farming

2

tool except on a few of the larger haciendas owned and operated by foreigners or wealthy Mexicans. The sickle remained the chief harvesting implement and the oxen continued to tread out the grain as they had done from the beginning of time.

The living conditions of the masses were appalling. Filth and squalor stalked the land and poverty was the common lot of all except a mere handful who reigned as feudal lords holding in jeopardy the bodies and souls of the 15 millions of people. The houses of the masses were usually of adobe, consisting of one or two rooms, or they might be of wattle, or even a dugout in the side of a hill. Articles of furniture were conspicuous for their absence. There were few tables or chairs and the bedstead was usually a mat spread upon the floor. In most instances the roofs and the floors were of mud and the smoke from the fire must find its way out as best it could. Pigs, chickens and dogs frequently slept and ate with the members of the family—truly a communal society of animals. The food was of the coarsest. Beans and tortillas were the principal articles of diet, supplemented occasionally by vegetables and meat. Milk and butter, except on the haciendas, were limited and of poor quality. Due to the unsanitary conditions and the lack of proper nourishing foods, outbursts of contagious diseases infested the land taking a heavy toll annually. Smallpox and malignant fevers, such as typhoid and malaria, were especially common and since there were no serums and few doctors, the mortality was great.

Wages were low for all kinds of labor. The common farm hand was paid the stingy sum of from thirty-five to fifty centavos per day with which he must feed, clothe and shelter himself and family. And families of the common class in Mexico were usually not restricted to one or two children but ranged in number from five to twelve. Even more galling than the mere pittance of a wage was the peonage system which held the masses in a thralldom as absolute and inextricable as did the slave system of the

Pharaohs of Egypt the Israelites more than three thousand years ago. Theoretically it was possible for a peon to free himself from economic bondage imposed upon him by his master, but actually such a boon was seldom if ever achieved. Personal freedom could be purchased by liquidation of all debt but the landlord saw to it that the peon was always in his debt. *Such were the political, social and economic conditions when the Mormon colonists settled in Mexico.*

Chapter II

MORMONISM

That the reader may be able to appreciate the problems of Mormon colonization in Mexico and the methods employed in their solution, a retrospect of early Mormon history would seem imperative.

Mormonism holds a unique position in the family of religions in America; unique in the sense that it is neither Catholic nor Protestant, and yet it is Christian; unique also in that it had its birth in America while the Catholic church as well as most of the Protestant churches were transported from European countries to America. In their claims for authority the Catholics and Mormons have some ideas in common, both insisting that their priesthood goes back to Peter to whom Christ gave the "keys of his kingdom." They differ, however, in their belief regarding the perpetuity of the priesthood, the Catholics maintaining that their present Pope holds his position by virtue of an unbroken line of succession from Peter whom they contend was the first Pope of Rome. The Mormons, on the contrary, believe that there was an apostacy from Christ's Church following the tragic death of the Jewish apostles making it necessary for the Priesthood to be restored in the Latter-days. This restoration occurred in the year 1829 when Peter, James and John appeared to Joseph Smith, Jr., and Oliver Cowdery, likely on the banks of the Susquehanna River in Pennsylvania and conferred upon them the Melchizedek Priesthood. The Aaronic Priesthood had been conferred upon them a few months earlier on the banks of the same stream by John the Baptist. The Protestants go to the Bible for their source of authority.

The founder of Mormonism, Joseph Smith, Jr., was born in the State of Vermont in the year of 1805. His parents like most of the New England farmers, were not overburdened with worldly goods. Neither were they num-

bered with the destitute or shiftless. While Joseph was
yet a lad his parents were swept by a westward wave of
migration that carried them beyond the Alleghanies to the
western part of the state of New York, mid-way between
the villages of Palmyra and Manchester. This was one
of the cheap land areas on the western frontier of America
that proved inviting to land hungry people, and people
of limited means, who saw here opportunities to provide
themselves and their posterity with inheritances that would
insure them an economic standing, not to be had in the
more thickly settled regions along the Atlantic seaboard.

It was here that Joseph, at the early age of fourteen,
received his first vision that was soon to be heard around
the world. As on other frontiers in westward expansion,
a religious contagion was sweeping the land and but few
of its inhabitants escaped its impressive attack. Protracted
meetings became the order of the day, and thousands of
penitents made confession of sin and were admitted into
the churches of which there were legions. Young Smith
caught the contagion and sought the Lord to know which
of all the churches was of divine origin. While thus engaged in earnest prayer he was surrounded by a heavenly
light, in the midst of which stood two celestial personages,
the Father and the Son. Joseph was informed that none
of the churches were right and that "the ministers were
corrupt, having a form of godliness but denying the power
thereof." Thus in its very beginning Mormonism was
arrayed against the various religions of the day.

Three years had elapsed from the time of his first vision
when the young Prophet was again visited by a messenger
divine, who said his name was Moroni, an ancient Nephite
prophet. His mission was to reveal the whereabouts of gold
plates containing a record of his people and kindred races
long since passed away. Joseph was informed that if he
proved faithful he would be the instrument favored of the
Lord to translate the record and present it to the world.
After four years had expired, during which time Joseph

was annually visited by the Angel, the plates were put into the hands of the youth. This was in 1827 and by the close of 1829, the translation was completed and the book was ready for publication under the well-known title, "The Book of Mormon." On the last leaf of the book appear the names of eleven witnesses, all of whom testify to the world that they saw the plates and the engravings thereon and that the characters were translated "by the gift and power of God and not of man." Three of the witnesses certify that an Angel of the Lord showed them the plates, while the remaining eight were shown them by Joseph Smith, Jr., the translator.

The Church of Jesus Christ of Latter-day Saints, contrary to the opinion of many, makes no claims for the Book of Mormon that in any way detracts from the sacredness of the Jewish Scriptures. The Book of Mormon does not supercede the Bible but merely supplements it. Its doctrines are confirmed by the teachings of the Book of Mormon. Both teach the existence of a God whose power is supreme and whose wisdom is boundless. Christ is the Son who came to earth to reveal the Father and to atone, through His death, for the sins of the world, and to bring to pass the resurrection and redemption of man. The pre-existence of man is attested by both, and man's mortal life is merely a stage in his development in which he is to prepare himself through a life of service to return to his Father to be crowned with immortality and eternal life. The principle of faith is the foundation of religion and the doctrines of repentance and baptism are necessary as a means of purification and to place man in a position to receive the companionship of the Holy Ghost.

As the Bible is the record of Israel in the Ancient Eastern world, the Book of Mormon is the story of the ancient peoples of America who inhabited this continent from about 2200 B. C. to 420 A. D., and from whom sprang the various tribes of American Indians of today. These ancient peoples were "white and delightsome," possessing a

culture and refinement comparable to that found among
the most advanced races of the ancient near East.   Confirmatory evidence of their superior enlightenment is found
in recent archaeological discoveries throughout America.
The pyramids and temples uncovered in Mexico and Central America rival the mighty pyramids and temples of
Egypt in quality of material and construction, and the
cities of Yucatan, Uxmal, and Palenque in the heyday
of their glory were not surpassed in grandeur or extent
by Thebes, Memphis or even Akhetaton in the golden days
of the Egyptian Empire ruled by the Thutmoses and Amen-
hoteps.

On the sixth of April, 1830, the Church of Jesus
Christ of Latter-day Saints was organized at the Whitmer
home in Fayette, Seneca County, New York. Joseph Smith,
Jr., and five others constituted the total membership on the
day of its organization, and on the same day Joseph was
designated the "first elder of the church" and Oliver Cowdery the "second elder." Such were the humble beginnings
of a church which today, in spite of violent opposition, has
a membership of over seven hundred thousand souls and
ranks tenth among the Christian churches of America at
the present time.   Truly a remarkable achievement!

Before the church was a year old the missionary movement was begun which was destined to become one of the
greatest factors in the growth of the church numerically,
and in the spiritual and mental development of the lives
of thousands who since that time have accepted calls to fill
missions abroad.   The first missionaries were called to
preach the gospel to the tribes of Indians on the western
frontiers, principally in the state of Missouri.   While this
mission resulted in failure so far as making converts among
the natives was concerned, it bore fruits in other directions,
that had a decided influence upon the future growth and
development of the church.   Scores of Anglo-Americans
were converted and baptized by the four Indian missionaries in and about Kirtland, Ohio, several of whom became

prominent officials of the church a few years later. The church membership thus augmented in this region, it was only a short time, indeed the following year, when the headquarters of the church was moved to Kirtland. Simultaneous with the building of Kirtland, settlements of Latter-day Saints were being established in Jackson County, Missouri, that spot by this time having been designated, "The land of Zion." It is not my purpose to narrate in detail the development of this region by the Mormons, suffice it to say, their activities were cut short by an open conflict between the Mormons and their neighbors, that resulted in the expulsion of the former from Jackson County, in 1833 and finally in 1838, from the entire state of Missouri.

Various reasons have been assigned by both friend and foe for the expulsion of the Mormons from Missouri, but time and space forbid a discussion of this matter. An analysis of the various reports of both factions leads to the inevitable conclusion that the fundamental and basic cause of the trouble was "a suspicion, dislike, and fear of the religious claims and pretensions of the Saints." Subsidiary causes were likely first, political fear due to the rapid increase of the Mormon population in Jackson County, and second, fear that the Indians might be used as tools in the hands of the Mormons to punish their enemies.

Driven from their homes in Missouri, and dispossessed of practically all their material means, the exiles sought refuge within the boundaries of another state. With Joseph, the Prophet, and several others of the leading brethren in Missouri dungeons on a charge of treason, the Saints would have been as "sheep without a shepherd" but for the leadership of Brigham Young, who as President of the Twelve, took control of the situation and conducted his people to a temporary place of safety on the east bank of the Mississippi in the state of Illinois.

The reception accorded them by the people of their newly adopted state was most cordial. In the course of a few months following their expulsion from Missouri, the

number of Mormons that found refuge in Illinois amounted
to fifteen thousand souls, and the testimony of a non-Mor-
mon writer was to the effect that they were, "a pre-emi-
nently industrious, frugal, and painstaking people."

Due to their thrift and the extraordinarily liberal
charter under which they lived, the Mormons, in the course
of three years, had made of Nauvoo (formerly Commerce)
not only the most pretentious city of the state, but one
of the best of the entire West. A traveler who beheld
Nauvoo for the first time in 1844 thus expressed his astonishment: "When I was told that this place was five years
ago a wilderness, I could scarce believe my senses. On
every side I saw extended around me the beautiful cottages,
the smiling flowers, and the well cultivated gardens of the
enterprising inhabitants. Over the whole of the vast city
of four square miles I saw the beautiful mansions, mostly
of brick, of its twenty thousand inhabitants," but that
which especially attracted his admiration was the "neatness,
cleanliness and comfort of their abodes, and the intelligence,
industry, and good order of the inhabitants."

But the Mormons were not long to enjoy in sweet
tranquility the bounteous gifts which nature and themselves had provided. Already the rumblings of an on-
coming storm could be heard which, coming ever nearer
and nearer, finally in 1844, burst with fury upon their
heads. In the frightful maelstrom the Mormon Prophet
and his brother Hyrum lost their lives in Carthage jail and
the body of the church was driven at the point of the
bayonet, to seek an asylum in the wilderness of the West.

The first company to cross the Mississippi left Nauvoo
early in February, passing over on flat boats. On the
thirteenth of the month the river was frozen hard so that
the heaviest wagons could cross over in safety. Two days
later Brigham Young and others of the apostles with their
families, passed over and proceeded a few miles west of
the river, where the exiles who had preceded them had
formed a camp.

By the middle of May, it was estimated that sixteen thousand Mormons had crossed the Mississippi and were ready to take up their line of march with their personal property, their wives and little ones, westward over the continent. But a thousand were left behind and this group comprised only those who had as yet been unable to dispose of their property or who, having none, were too poor to get away.

And now begins the great trek of the Mormons as they turn their backs upon their beloved Nauvoo to search for a home in the wilderness where they can be free from the persecutions which have followed them since they first became known as an organization. It was a flight primarily from persecution, but in addition, it was a call of the West —that great free, open country of endless plains and rugged mountains—the call which had gripped scores of brave and adventurous frontiersmen before them and gave them courage to brook the lurking dangers of the great unknown. It was the same spirit that impelled the founder of Mormonism to appeal to the general government in March, 1844, for permission to conduct a body of one hundred thousand armed volunteers to march into the western territory for the purpose of opening "the vast regions of the unpeopled West and South to our enlightened and enterprising yeomen." Thus it appears that early in the history of Mormonism the leaders of the church had the spirit of the West, and had Joseph Smith, Jr., been permitted to live a few years longer, there is no doubt that he, instead of Brigham Young, would have been the one to lead the Saints into the Great Basin and found an inland empire.

The first camp of exiles was at Sugar Creek, west of the Mississippi River and just a few miles from Nauvoo. Here they remained for nearly a month during which time the weather was extremely cold, the thermometer dropping to twenty degrees below zero, and to add to the distress of the camp, a heavy fall of snow occurred. On the first night of the encampment nine children were born and

from then on mothers gave birth to offspring under all
conditions imaginable except those affording comfort.

On the first of March the exiles broke camp on
Sugar Creek and the caravan of five hundred wagons began
to move slowly toward the setting sun. Travel over the
plains of Iowa was retarded at times, due to the heavy rains
and the boggy nature of the ground. "Teams fed on browse
obtained from felling trees became very weak," recorded
Eliza R. Snow, "and when crossing the lowlands where
spring rains had soaked the mellow soil, they frequently
stalled on level ground. In some instances a cow and ox
and frequently two cows were yoked together and these
poor animals after helping draw wagons through the day,
at night furnished the milk with which the family was
supplied."

Organization and discipline have always been cardinal
principles of Mormonism and in no period of its history
were these things more in evidence than upon the plains.
On the twenty-seventh of March Brigham Young was
unanimously elected President over the whole "Camp of
Israel." The entire group was then split into units of hundreds, fifties and tens over each of which was placed a
captain. In addition to these officers a historian was appointed, as well as a clerk over the whole camp and a clerk
for each fifty.

Wayside stations were established at Garden Grove,
Mount Pisgah and at Winter Quarters and grew so rapidly
that by January 6, 1847, Brigham Young reported that
there were more than seven hundred houses in Winter
Quarters, mostly of logs, and that the city was divided
into 22 ecclesiastical wards over each of which a bishop
was called to preside.

During the winter of 1846-47 preparations were being
made to send a band of pioneers to blaze a path across the
plains and mountains for the main body which was to follow, and to select a new home for the Saints. When made
up, the company consisted of one hundred and forty-three

men, three women and two children, making a total of one hundred and forty-eight souls. Brigham Young was sustained as Lieutenant General and next to him in authority, were five captains of fifties, and below them were captains of tens.

The route traveled from the Missouri river to the Rocky Mountains was much the same as that followed by emigrants bound for the Pacific Coast, except that the Mormons kept on the north side of the Platte river until Ft. Laramie was reached, while the general highway of travel had been on the south side of that stream. On their journey westward the pioneers met up with several noted pathfinders, among them being Major Moses Harris, Jim Bridger, and Thomas L. Smith, from whom they obtained considerable information relative to the Great Basin.

On the twenty-third of July, 1847, the noted Mormon leader got his first glimpse of the Great Basin, upon which occasion he feelingly remarked, "The spirit of the Lord rested upon me and hovered over the valley, and I felt that there the Saints would find protection and safety." On the following day the pioneer band led by Brigham Young entered the valley of the Great Salt Lake.

The twenty-fourth of July, 1847, is a red letter day in the history of the Church of Jesus Christ of Latter-day Saints because it marked the advent of the pioneer leader into the Great Basin. It was the day before when the water was diverted from its channel and spread over the thirsty land. Thus was introduced into the Great Basin for the first time, by Anglo-Saxons, the beginning of a vast and successful system of irrigation that has played such an important part in the converting of the great western wilderness into a fruitful garden.

Two days after the arrival of Brigham Young in the Salt Lake Valley, ten men were called to explore the region, among whom were Brigham Young and eight others of the Apostles. This was the beginning of exploration and colonization in the Great Basin that ultimately led to settlements being established by the Mormons, not only in the vicinity of the Great Salt Lake, but to the remote parts of the inter-mountain region and even to the Pacific Coast.

By the twenty-eighth of July President Young was so confirmed in his impression, "This is the place," that he called a council of the members of the twelve then in the valley for the purpose of making a plan for the city. Walking out to a plat of ground between the two forks of what is now "City Creek," and where the Salt Lake Temple now stands, the President said, "Here is the place for the temple to be built." The plans formulated upon that occasion subsequently materialized and upon that spot of ground has arisen a modern city, whose beauty is second to none among the cities of the West and whose fame has circled the globe.

The key note of President Young's economic and social policy in the founding of settlements was sounded by him on the Sunday following his advent into the Great Basin. He told the people that they must not work on Sunday, that they would lose five times as much as they would gain by it. None was to hunt or fish on that day and there should not any man dwell among them who would not observe these rules. He also said that no man who came to the Valley could buy land since he had none to sell, but that every man should have his land measured out to him for city and farming purposes. He might till it as he pleased, but he must be industrious and take care of it. Later announcements stipulated that there should be community ownership of the streams of water as well as of the forests. "The value of these three fundamental economic principles dealing with land, timber, and water," declares one writer, "can not be over estimated in their bearing upon the successful establishment of colonies in the Great Basin." In the passage of such measures can be seen the wisdom and foresight of the great colonizer in caring for the interests of the fifteen or twenty thousand who were shortly to come into the Great Basin to make homes.

President Young's plans for colonization were conceived on a large scale as is evident from a statement he made in March, 1849, "We are about to establish a colony of about thirty families in Utah Valley about fifty miles south. We hope soon to explore the valley three hundred miles south and also the country as far as the Gulf of California, with a view to settlement and to acquiring a seaport." That this was no idle boast is proved by subsequent developments. The first permanent settlement in the present state of Idaho was founded by the Mormons as was also the first settlement in Nevada. San Francisco can almost be said to have been founded by the Mormons since it contained only a few white families when Sam Brannan arrived with his two hundred and thirty-eight Saints on July 31, 1846, being the first sea-faring Americans to land on the Coast of California. Shearer, in his eulogy of Brannan says, "Sam manages to turn up first in nearly everything. After performing the first marriage and occasioning the first jury trial in the lonesome hamlet to which he brought such exuberance he set up and operated the first flour mills and gave his town the first newspaper, 'The California Star.' His company brought with them a printing press, a variety of agricultural implements, flour mill machinery and text books."

In 1851 President Young purchased the Rancho de San Bernardino, consisting of thirty-five thousand acres of fertile land with an abundance of water and timber, and in March, 1852, the city of San Bernardino was founded. Soon thereafter Mormon settlements were springing up in Arizona, Colorado and Wyoming.

It is interesting to note the ingenious method employed by President Young in securing the services of men in building up these remote colonies. The call came to them in much the same manner as that to a foreign mission. One who would disregard such a call would be considered lacking in faith and unworthy of the fellowship of the Saints. Men were selected on the basis of fitness to meet the needs of a particular situation. Illustrative of this is the proclamation issued by the Church Presidency anticipating the founding of a settlement later to be known as Parowan, in Iron County. "Brethren of Great Salt Lake and vicinity who are full of faith and good works are informed by the Presidency of the Church that a colony is wanted at Little Salt Lake this fall; that fifty or more good, effective men with teams and wagons, provisions, and clothing are wanted for one year."

Then follows a list of things to be taken, among which should be an abundance of seed grain and tools in all variety. The work to be done was, "to sow, build and fence, erect a saw and grist mill, establish an iron foundry as speedily as possible and do all other things necessary for the preservation and safety of an infant settlement among the Indians." Soon thereafter the Deseret News published the names of fifty men selected to accompany Apostle George A. Smith, the leader of the expedition.

Anson B. Call, a prominent pioneer in early Utah history, was called to help establish settlements in Southern Utah as follows: "Brother Call," said President Young, "I want you to go and make some new settlements in the southern part of this territory. Will you go?" "I answered," said Call, "Yes, I will." Brigham then said, "If you will go and do as I tell you, you shall right here add farm to farm and have wives, children, houses and lands to your heart's content." (Utah Sketches, Ms. No. 10, Bancroft Library.)

My father was called in a similar manner to supervise the building operations of the "United Order" in the early history of Saint George, in the extreme southern end of Utah. Levi Edgar Young makes the following observation relative to the quality of men chosen by Brigham Young to found colonies: "Brigham Young in founding the infant settlements, carefully selected the best and strongest for the pioneer work. No weaklings could conquer the desert, the Indians, the wild animals, the extremes of climate and live and develop the country."

In the early settlement of the Great Basin, the Mormons lived under a government of their own called by some writers "a Theo-democracy." Under this form of government, Church and state were one. The same men who held positions in the church as High Councillors and Bishops had jurisdiction in municipal affairs as well. Tullidge, Utah's early historian, says: "Under the government of the Bishops, Utah grew up, and, until the regular incorporation of Great Salt Lake City in 1851, they held what is usually considered the secular administration over the people." This statement he modifies by saying that Brigham Young was their director "for he formulated and constructed everything in those days." "Salt Lake," he further observes, "was analogous to a county and the High Council is a quorum of judges at the head of which is the President of the Stake with his counsellors." That this sort of government met well the exigencies of the times seems evident in the light of comments coming down to us from such unbiased witnesses as Captains Stansbury and Gunnison of the United States Army. The former stated that, "The jurisdiction of the State of Deseret had been extended over all and was rigorously enforced upon all who came within its border, and justice was equitably administered to Saint and 'Gentile,' as they term all who are not of their persuasion." He further stated that the courts were constantly appealed to by companies of passing emigrants and that "the decisions were remarkable for fairness and impartiality." Captain Gunnison referred to their fundamental law as being tolerant of conscience in religion and their criminal code as applying "to their peculiar situation and feelings." Impartial writers justify the Mormon people for setting up a government of their own on the grounds that the Federal Government of the United States failed to give them any form of government, thus leaving them exposed to the attacks of the red man and without recourse in case of infringement on their rights by bands of outlaws who frequented their territory.

The Mormons have always been strong believers in education. How could they be otherwise when their doctrine teaches that "the glory of God is intelligence" and that "it is impossible for a man to be saved in ignorance." In harmony with this doctrine the Mormon pioneers, immediately following their entrance into the Valley of the Great Salt Lake, made provisions for educating their progeny by establishing a school for primary children in October, 1847. This school was taught by Mary J. Dilworth and was held in a military, cone-shaped tent furnished with rough logs for seats and an old camp stool for the teacher's desk. A few weeks later a school for older children and adults was established in which all the common branches of learning and Latin were taught. From these humble beginnings education grew apace until in 1852 Captain Gunnison, then in Utah, could say, "In Utah or Deseret, the arrangements for the cause of education are upon an extensive scale." Two years earlier than Gunnison's observation, the Deseret News announced that common schools were beginning in all parts of the city for the winter and that plans for the construction of school houses in every ward were being made, with the view to establishing a general system throughout Salt Lake City. On February 28, 1850, less than three years subsequent to the arrival of the first band of pioneers into the Valley, the legislature of Deseret passed an ordinance incorporating the University of the State of Deseret (now the University of Utah). Thus was launched the first University west of the Missouri River. The love for education has not weakened with the passing of years and today the state of Utah, largely Mormon, is among the foremost of the states of the Union in her educational facilities and in the literacy of her people.

An admirable quality of these early colonists was their
3

ability betimes to cast aside the grinding cares of life and submerge their troubles in a sea of mirth. Together the old and young, with playful spirit would beguile away the time in dancing to the music of the accordion, organ or flute or perchance to the musical strains from a well trained orchestra or band. Dramatics also had a conspicuous place on the program of entertainment. Home troops sprang up in the larger centers that produced plays of merit. Later, traveling troops on their way to and from the Pacific Coast, found it convenient and even profitable to stop off at Salt Lake City and present their offerings to large and critical audiences of the drama.

"In social life (said Stansbury) the Mormons are pre-eminent. In their social gatherings and evening parties, patronized by the presence of prophets and apostles, it is not unusual to open the ball with prayer and then will follow the most sprightly dancing in which all join with hearty good will from the highest dignitary to the humblest individual."

A Brief Summary of Fundamental Mormon Doctrines

The Church of Jesus Christ of Latter-day Saints, while admitting the reality of change in the Universe (a self-evident fact) denies the mutability of truth. Once a truth always a truth is, according to the Mormon belief, axiomatic. Conditions may change rendering necessary the rejection of one set of truths and the substitution of a new set.

The children of Israel in Moses' time and for several centuries thereafter lived the carnal law; Jesus introduced a new and higher order of things. Why? Not that truth had changed but that the social order of things had changed. The carnal commandment code was still a truth in the days of Jesus but its application had become obsolete in an age when Israel had achieved a state of ethical and spiritual excellence that they could appreciate and live a higher law. The carnal law, as Paul observed, had served as a "school master to bring the people to Christ."

The law of consecration (having all things in common) is a divine truth and will always be such, but only at intervals in the world's history have people been righteous enough to live it. The law of tithing is a truth, also, but the conditions of its application to society are not identical with the conditions under which the law of consecration can be lived. A tithing of one's income represents a tenth of that income, nothing more and nothing less. Its immutability is as fixed as that two times two are four.

The Latter-day Saints accept as being fundamental and unchangeable a belief in a personal God who, though He is constantly progressing, yet the reality of his personal existence is as enduring as his Godhood. Mormonism has its roots in a concept of a personal God who holds absolute power over the universe and unto whom all things pertaining to the universe can be known by Him.

An acceptance of a Divine Redeemer fashioned after the image of God the Father, whose only Begotten Son he is, is indispensable to the belief of a fully converted Latter-day Saint. He accepts the fall of man as a reality and the Redemption of Christ as being necessary to overcome the effects of man's transgression. This Redemption will bring to pass a resurrection from the dead of a fleshy tabernacle and vouchsafed to all men irrespective of their merits. Through this Redemption of our Savior eternal life is also made possible to man through obedience to a gospel plan, formulated before the foundations of this world were laid.

The chief corner stones of this plan are faith in God and in the plan of salvation; repentance from sin, followed by a baptism of the water to symbolize a burial and resurrection and whose chief function is the remission of sins, and finally a confirmation of the Holy Ghost by the imposition of hands. These are called "initiatory rites" and if properly subscribed to admit people into Christ's kingdom.

Having been admitted into the kingdom, man's duty and privilege is to observe the laws of the kingdom which will lead him Godward.

The Bible is accepted by the Mormon people as being a divine book written in the beginning by inspired men of God but, with such acceptation, they are not unmindful of the presence therein of human elements. They believe also in the Book of Mormon, alluded to in the early part of this chapter, as well as in continuous revelation through God's holy oracles.

A pre-existent state is accepted as a reality, as well as a tangible post existence, this life representing merely a segment of eternity appointed unto man as a testing period to determine his future destiny.

CHAPTER III

THE FIRST MORMONS IN MEXICO

The first Latter-day Saints known to have set foot
upon Mexican soil were members of the famous Mormon
Battalion who had volunteered their services to fight in
the Mexican War. The call came through Captain Allen
while the exiles were encamped upon the plains between
the Mississippi and Missouri rivers, they having been
driven from the State of Illinois and now in quest of a new
home in the far West. Captain Allen visited the several
camps in June 1846 and asked for the services of 500 men.
The quota was raised immediately, consisting chiefly of
comparatively young men, who were organized and soon
thereafter set out for Fort Leavenworth to receive arms
and other necessary equipment preparatory to marching
to Santa Fe and thence to California. From Fort Leavenworth to Santa Fe, much of the way over a desert, the
journey was characterized by considerable suffering from
intense thirst and, at times, the scarcity of food reduced
the men to meager rations. Many were sick when they
arrived at Santa Fe, making it necessary for them to go to
Pueblo under the command of Capt. James Brown, to spend
the winter. These and others who had preceded them to
Pueblo because of illness, made their way to the Valley of
the Great Salt Lake, some of them entering the Basin just
a few days after the advent of Brigham Young and his
pioneer band. The main body of the Battalion pushed on
toward California, their journey taking them exclusively
through Mexican territory. The only fight participated
in by these Mormon boys was on the San Pedro River a few
miles southwest of the present city of Douglas, Arizona.
This fight was not between Americans and Mexicans but
American troops and wild Mexican bulls—incensed over
the intrusion of a foreign element into their territory.
Victory finally perched on the banner of the Americans

but not until a few injuries had come to their numbers, and several of the foe lay dead upon the battle field. The Battalion was disbanded soon after its arrival in California.

Subsequently several members of the Church passed over the boundary line into the States of Chihuahua and Sonora but no definite steps were taken to colonize or even engage in missionary work until the year 1874. In the summer of this year President Brigham Young called upon Daniel W. Jones and Henry W. Brizzee to prepare for a mission to Mexico. As a feature of their mission these men, both of whom spoke some Spanish, were asked by the President to translate certain "Book of Mormon" passages into Spanish that they might be used by the missionaries in their work among the natives. A few months following their appointment, Jones and Brizzee had the good fortune to meet a Spanish officer from the Phillipine Islands by the name of M. G. Trejo. This man had come in search of the Mormons in response to an impressive dream he had received and which later resulted in his receiving baptism at the hands of Brizzee. Without delay Trejo, assisted by Jones, began making translations of certain Book of Mormon passages and by the following year (1875) a book of 100 pages had appeared in print, the price of publication being met by contributions from devotees of the church.

In the fall of 1875 a relatively large group of men was called to serve as missionaries to Mexico, several of whom later became prominent in business and Church affairs. Most prominent of these was Anthony W. Ivins, later to become an Apostle of the Church and finally a counselor to Heber J. Grant, President of the Church of Jesus Christ of Latter-day Saints. Others called were Daniel W. Jones, James Z. Stewart, Helaman Pratt, a son of Apostle Parley P. Pratt, Wiley C. Jones, Robert H. Smith and Ammon M. Tenney.

This mission was of dual character—first, to preach the gospel to the native population of Mexico and second, to locate suitable lands for future Mormon colonies in Arizona, New Mexico and in Old Mexico. President Young instructed them to keep a record of their travels and labors and to report to him any places which might be suitable to establish settlements, giving a careful description of each and the advantages offered. Orson Pratt, a member of the Quorum of the Twelve, admonished the members of the expedition "to look out for places where our brethren could go and be safe from harm in the event that persecution should make it necessary for them to get out of the way for a season." If any member of the company was in doubt at the time as to the significance of this message later developments made the meaning perfectly clear.

This mission was sufficient to try the faith of less faithful men for all of them were almost destitute of material goods. Indeed, without help from outside sources, it would have been most difficult if not quite impossible to raise the necessary equipment for such an extended journey. Elder Ivins in referring to the situation said that he was under the necessity of selling everything he had to procure the necessary outfit and even then he was assisted by several of his personal friends. Anticipating the dire financial straits of these brethren, President Young had in the meantime authorized the sending of a circular letter to certain members of the Church, soliciting funds to aid the expedition. In response the Saints generously contributed cash, tithing orders, factory orders, dried meat, merchandise and other such things as they could spare.

In the middle of September, 1875, Wiley C. Jones, Helaman Pratt, J. Z. Stewart and Robert H. Smith bade adieu to their families and friends in Salt Lake City and vicinity and began their journey toward the South. At Nephi, about 90 miles south of Salt Lake City they were joined by Dan W. Jones and at Toquerville and Kanab in Southern Utah, the party was further strengthened by the addition of Anthony W. Ivins and Ammon M. Tenney. By this time the missionaries were well equipped for the journey, having

seven mounts and seventeen pack horses. They were fer-
ried across the Colorado River at Lee's Ferry and then made
their way to the Moqui Villages in Arizona, passing en route
through Moencopie, Navajo Springs and Willow Springs.
At the seven Moqui Indian villages the missionaries paused
for a seven days' visit with the Indians and then pursued
their way in the direction of the Salt River Valley. They
arrived in Phoenix on November 24, 1875, and found it
to be a prosperous town consisting of several stores and
shops and surrounded by fertile land with abundant water.
At Tempe, a few miles further on, they were kindly greeted
by Judge C. T. Hayden, who furnished them with letters
of introduction to Governor Safford and other leading
men of Arizona. In a report sent to President Young of
the Salt River Valley, the members of the expedition called
attention to the fine opportunities for settlement. At the
village of Sacaton on the Gila River was held their first
public meeting with the Indians. Their meeting they
reported as being well attended. Twenty-four miles further up the river brought them to Florence. From this
point they made their way without incident to Tucson, a
distance of 65 miles, where they were kindly received by
the governor of Arizona. The day following their arrival
being Sunday, the missionaries were tendered the use of the
Court House in which to hold a religious service. The
invitation was gladly accepted. At a military post near
Tucson, the party sold some of their animals and purchased
a spring wagon. It appears to have been their intention
to cross over the boundary line into Sonora near this point
but their plans were changed when they heard of the unsettled condition of the Indians in that region. They decided, therefore, to push on to El Paso before passing into
Mexico. Much of this country through which they journeyed was fine for grazing, particularly San Bernardino on
the San Pedro River, as well as in the vicinity of Sulphur
Springs. At the latter place they met a wealthy rancher
who furnished beef for the Indian reservations in Arizona

and New Mexico and who was reported to have 45,000 head of cattle. Arriving at El Paso, the members of the expedition with the exception of Tenney and Smith, who had remained in New Mexico to preach to the Pueblos and Zunis, decided to push on to the city of Chihuahua, the capital of the state of the same name. They followed down the Rio Grande River for three days to San Ignacio and then left the river, travelling due west. At Contaraccio where they camped for the night, they had the experience of having their horses driven off either by civilians or members of a troop garrisoned there. The act was perpetrated ostensibly for the purpose of reward for recovery. There was joy in camp when the horses were found the following day. From this point the journey took the travellers through Carrisal, Guachinera to Carmen where they arrived on the 28th of March. Carmen is described as being suitably located in a valley one-half mile wide by eight or ten miles in length with fertile soil and abundant water.

On April 2 they arrived at Sacramento where General Doniphan with a company of United States soldiers defeated a larger body of Mexican troops during the war of 1846-47. Twenty-two miles further on brought them to the city of Chihuahua whose appearance at that time was very impressive. The streets were paved either with flag or cobble stones and many fine buildings adorned the city. The visitors were impressed by the great number of churches to be seen on every hand, the most imposing structure of this sort being a big stone cathedral whose front was elaborately decorated with carved figures representing the twelve apostles and the Virgin Mary. Governor Luis Terrazas having given the Mormons permission to hold religious services in Chihuahua, a meeting was held on the 12th of April, 1876, in a large building known as the "Cock Pit." This was the first meeting held by the Mormons in the interior of Mexico and since there were more than 500 in attendance the future looked bright for the spread of the doctrines of the Church.

A short time later the elders arrived at La Villa de Concepcion in the Canton de Guerrero, where they remained for twelve days holding religious services almost daily. Their message was welcomed by several who applied for baptism but the request was not granted, the missionaries likely feeling that the candidates were hardly prepared to receive the sacred ordinance.

About the middle of May the expedition arrived at Casas Grandes, famous for its prehistoric ruins and for being the birth place of many political disturbances that shook Mexico from center to circumference. Leaving Casas Grandes the party followed down the Casas Grandes River passing through Barrancas and Corralitos, thence to Janos where they arrived May 16. This was the last Mexican town before passing over the boundary line into the United States. One month later they reached Kanab after an absence of about nine months. The Deseret News for July 5, 1876, reported the return of this Mexican Missionary Party and optimistically declared, "We understand there is a prospect for good work being done in Mexico."

This was merely the beginning of a vast missionary labor to be sponsored by the Latter-day Saints in far off Mexico. On October 17, 1876, another group of elders consisting of Helaman Pratt, James Z. Stewart, Isaac Z. Stewart, George Terry and Louis Garff departed from Salt Lake City on a second mission to Mexico. Later they were joined by M. G. Trejo. Their journey was over much the same route as the previous one as far as Tubac, Arizona. At this point the elders separated, Pratt and Terry going into Mexico by way of Altar, the other missionaries by way of Magdalena. The Stewarts soon returned to El Paso while Garff and Trejo continued to Hermosillo, the capital of the state of Sonora, where they were kindly received. During a period of three months, four of the missionaries were continuously engaged in preaching and teaching in the

cities and towns of Sonora. Pratt and Terry did considerable traveling about the state, their business taking them
as far as Guaymas near the mouth of the Yaqui River. There
they visited the American Consul as well as a Yaqui Governor. Their return trip to the United States led them
through Hermosillo and up the Sonora River by Arispe
to Santa Cruz, Sonora. They arrived in Tucson on July
4, 1877.

The question of establishing Mormon colonies in Mexico was discussed by President Young in a letter of April
11, 1877, addressed to J. Z. Stewart and his companion
missionaries. The President instructed them to get in touch
with J. W. Campbell, residing in Texas, to ascertain if
conditions in Mexico would justify such a movement. At
a conference held shortly thereafter, relative to this matter,
it was decided inopportune to attempt colonization in the
immediate future because of the frequent raids of Apache
Indians in the northern states of the Mexican Republic.
The death of President Young resulted in the missionaries
being released to return home in the fall of 1877.

In the summer of 1879, Dr. Platine Redakanaty, a
cultured gentleman of Mexico City, accidentally came into
possession of a Mormon doctrinal tract which so impressed
him that immediately he addressed a letter to the First
Presidency of the Church, requesting that a missionary be
sent to enlighten him still further. The Presidency responded by sending three missionaries to the Mexican Republic with explicit instructions to establish a mission for
the spread of Mormonism in that southern land. The chief
responsibility of this mission was placed upon Moses
Thatcher, an Apostle of the church. His associates were to
be James Z. Stewart and M. G. Trejo who had previously
been on a mission to Mexico.

On October 10, Apostle Thatcher was set apart for
his mission by John Taylor, the successor of Brigham
Young as President of the Church, and on November 1,

Thatcher left for Mexico City by way of Chicago, New Orleans and Vera Cruz.

Upon his arrival at the Mexican capital in the middle of November, the Apostle established temporary headquarters at the hotel Iturbide. The welcome extended the Mormon elders by Dr. Rodakanaty was most cordial and he invited them to hold religious services at his home. Needless to say the invitation was gratefully accepted and a fine group of investigators met to hear the Apostle expound the doctrines of his Church, his discourses being translated into Spanish by M. G. Trejo. Before the year had expired, 16 converts had become identified with the Church through baptism, and a branch of the Church had been established in Mexico City with Dr. Rodakanaty as the presiding elder. On January 25, Elder Thatcher dedicated the land of Mexico to the spread of the gospel among the natives of the land and the establishment and growth of Mormon settlements throughout the Republic. He prayed that as the Spanish conqueror had foreshadowed bondage, the coming of the Gospel might foreshadow deliverance through the proclamation of divine truth.

Soon after his arrival in Mexico, Mr. Thatcher formed the acquaintanceship of Emelio Biebuyck, a Belgian gentleman of considerable influence in Mexico and familiar with Utah affairs, he having been in Utah upon three different occasions. Mr. Biebuyck had a most liberal concession from the Mexican government, granting him permission to establish colonies in any of the states of Mexico, the public land to be given free, together with a subsidy of $80.00 for adults and $40.00 each for children. Colonies were also to be exempted from taxes and from military duty for a period of twenty years. They could also bring into the country, free of duty, teams and wagons, agricultural implements, building materials, and provisions, pending the establishment of the colony or colonies. In casting about for colonists Mr. Biebuyck concluded that "the Mormons were the best colonists in the world." "With the Mormons in Mexico," he said, "will come stable government and consequent peace and prosperity, and thereafter success to my business, and that is all I ask."

Mr. Thatcher was sufficiently taken up with the proposition that he left for Salt Lake City on February 4, to place the matter before the Presidency of the Church and the Quorum of Twelve. Mr. Biebuyck also appeared in person before the Council of the Church and laid before it his concession from the Mexican government. The Council, following a careful consideration of the matter, reached the conclusion "that the colonization of the Latter-day Saints in Mexico at this time, even under the generous concessions of the contract mentioned, would be premature." Biebuyck was visibly disappointed.

In October, 1880, Elder Thatcher accompanied by a talented young man by the name of Feramorz Young returned to Mexico City. Soon after his arrival, through the courtesy of General Greenwood, formerly of Roanoke, Va., the Apostle was accorded an interview with several of the Cabinet officials of the country, among them being Senor Zarate, Minister of Foreign Affairs, Fernadez Leal, Minister of Fomento (public works and colonization) and Carlos Pacheco, Minister of War.

Leal had previously visited Utah and greatly admired the pluck of her enterprising and prosperous communities whom he regarded as the best colonizers of the world. To such people he said he would extend the hand of fellowship and hoped many of them would come to Mexico to make their homes. The one-legged hero of Puebla, General Pacheco, and the most powerful man in Mexico next to President Diaz, granted audience to Mr. Thatcher while scores of army officers stood without, waiting to be heard. The General was Courtesy itself and without solicitation presented Mr. Thatcher with letters of introduction and recommendation to the chief executives of the various states of the Mexican union. Later the Apostle interviewed Senor Ignacio Mariscal, who had come to the head of

Foreign Affairs. Of him, Mr· Thatcher had this to say:
"A brainy man of brilliant attainments and a perfect gentleman, the master of several languages. He is familiar
with the Saints from the beginning."

The year 1881 looked promising for the spread of
Mormonism in the Southern Republic. On April 6, exactly
fifty-one years after the organization of the Church, Mormon elders, under the leadership of Moses Thatcher, held
the first conference of their Church in Mexico on Mount
Popocatapetal. This mountain lies fifty miles southeast
of Mexico City and is one of the highest mountains in the
Republic, having an elevation of 17,000 feet. The devotees
of the Church were a day and a half reaching the top but
the inspiration that came to them above the clouds fully
compensated them for the struggle they made. In August,
Elder Thatcher was able to report 61 baptisms since the
establishment of the Mexican Mission. In the fall of 1881,
he received his release to return home and accordingly
made immediate preparations for the homeward journey.
Accompanying him were Feramorz Young and Fernando
Lara, a native convert, but the former took sick and died
of typhoid pneumonia, aboard the vessel, and was buried
at sea when within twenty miles of the Florida coast.

With the release of Moses Thatcher as President of the
Mexican Mission, August Wilcken was exalted to that position. In May, 1882, Elder Anthony W. Ivins and Milson
R. Pratt arrived in Vera Cruz as missionaries and on the following day left for Mexico City. Soon after arriving in the
city, Elder Ivins received a letter from his cousin, Heber
J. Grant an Apostle of the Church, asking him to look
out for suitable places for colonization in Mexico and also
to ascertain how the Mexican government would feel regarding the establishment of Mormon colonies near the
boundary line. A short time previous to this President
Wilcken had been instructed to investigate the San Bernardino Ranch which lay partly in Cochise County, Arizona, and partly in Mexico, with the view to purchasing it.

The ranch belonged to Juan Mariscal and he had offered to sell it for $13,500. Later he dropped the price to $11,000, Mexican silver, but the property was never purchased by the Church.

In the spring of 1883 Wilcken was released from his position and Moses Thatcher was again sustained as President of the Mexican Mission wtih Anthony W. Ivins as acting President. Two new elders, Helaman Pratt and Franklin R. Snow, arrived from Utah to augment the limited number of missionaries. But their arrival was offset by the departure in the following spring of Anthony W. Ivins and Milson R. Pratt who had been released with the request that they arrive in Salt Lake City in time for the April conference. The mission of Elder Ivins had been unusually successful, as evidenced in the fact that fifty-seven natives were brought into the Church under his personal administration.

After the release of President Ivins, Helaman Pratt was called to serve as the President of the Mexican Mission. Associated with him in the ministry were Franklin R. Snow, Isaac Stewart, Horace H. Cummings and William W. Cluff, but on July 23, 1885, Franklin R. Snow was released to return home, leaving but four elders to carry on the work. It was a small force but the elders were energetic and their work proved effective, judging by the numbers who were added to the Church.

Up to this time the Mormon missionaries had confined their labors chiefly to the territory in and near the city of Mexico, but in November, 1887, A. M. Tenney, Peter J. Christofferson, Charles Edmund Richardson and Gilbert D. Greer were called on a mission to the State of Sonora. Their home was at Springerville, Apache County, Arizona, and their journey to their mission field was rather an arduous one, but they cheerfully engaged in the work, feeling that they had been divinely called. On February 9, 1888, they baptized fifteen converts, the first to accept Mormonism in what was called the "Sonora Mission." In May of the same year the missionaries crossed over the boundary line into Arizona, but early in June they recrossed again into Sonora to visit their recent converts. Late in June they returned again to the United States after having added a few more to the fold. Since leaving his home in Springerville, Elder A. M. Tenney reported that he had traveled over 2,000 miles, which is no mean distance when account is taken of the method of travel in those days.

The name of A. M. Tenney stands high among the valiant ones who gave of their services to the converting of the Lamanites (Indians). For about a quarter of a century he dedicated his life to that service and, like the faithful Catholic Fathers before him, who endured all to bring enlightenment to the aborigines of this continent, he suffered almost untold hardships and brooked the dangers of the deserts and mountains, wild animals and savage Indians to bring the Gospel of the Master to a benighted people. A report of his labors from November, 1887, to September, 1890, shows that Elder Tenney travelled 5,000 miles by team, horseback and on foot. During that time he preached 137 times and baptized 111 souls. The missionary work among the natives of Mexico continued until the turbulent times following the Madero Revolution when the Mormon elders were withdrawn because of intense opposition to all foreign ministers. At the time of the withdrawal of the Mormon elders, Rey L. Pratt was the President of the Mission. President Pratt was the son of Helaman Pratt and the grandson of Apostle Parley P. Pratt, one of the first group of Mormon missionaries to be called to preach to the Indians in this Dispensation.

Chapter IV

THE MORMONS SEEK MEXICAN LANDS TO COLONIZE

While the doctrines of the Church were being preached with vigor by the Mormon elders in the city of Mexico and its environs, a movement was being launched by the Church toward the purchase of lands in Mexico on which to plant colonies. Such an exigency arose because of the widespread opposition to polygamy—a social institution of the Mormons.

Now this order of marriage should not be confused with the marriage commonly in vogue among the membership of the Mormon Church. I refer to Celestial marriage. Before ever plural marriage was revealed, Joseph Smith had received a revelation (May 16 and 17, 1843) dealing with "Celestial" marriage, referred to, also, as the "everlasting covenant of marriage." In this revelation it was revealed that in the Celestial glory there are three degrees and that in order to attain to the highest of these a man must enter into the new and everlasting covenant of marriage; "if he does not, he cannot obtain it."

A compliance with this law merely means that a man in full harmony with the Church of Jesus Christ of Latter-day Saints takes a woman to the temple and in the presence of witnesses has her sealed to him over the altar as a wife for time and all eternity. The sealing must be performed by one authorized of the Lord, and according to the Mormon belief there is only one man on the earth at one time who holds that authority. The President of the Church is that man, but since it is not feasible or even desirable for him to perform all the temple marriages of the Church, he has the power to delegate others to act in his stead. The marriage ceremony, unlike the civil ceremony or even that of other churches, unites a couple not only for this life but its binding force is perpetuated beyond the grave. Under this order of marriage all children born under this covenant will belong to the couple so united, eternally.

This doctrine is based, obviously, on the assumption that the family organization consisting of father, mother and children will continue on in the metaphysical world, or what we ordinarily think of as the "spiritual world."

Now "plural marriage" connotes all this and more. More, in the sense only that instead of a man having but one wife sealed to him he will have two or more thus united with him in wedlock.

The doctrine of "plural marriage," commonly known as "polygamy," from the days of Nauvoo, had been one of the cardinal doctrines of the Church. It is a historical fact, not generally known, that but few of the male members of the Church at any one time entered into that order of marriage. Yet the vast majority of the devotees of the Church believed it to be a divine principle. Brigham Young usually has been accredited, by the uninformed, with having first introduced polygamy into the Church, but such is not historically true. Joseph Smith, Jr., the founder of Mormonism, was responsible for its introduction among his followers. The revelation setting forth the principle of "plurality of wives" and commanding its practice was given to the Prophet in Nauvoo, Illinois, July 12, 1843, less than one year before his death at Carthage jail. The Revelation appears to have come as a result of a query in the mind of Joseph Smith, Jr., as to why the Lord justified the practice of polygamy by the Patrirachs of the Bible including Abraham, Isaac and Jacob, Moses, David and Solomon. Adultery is condemned in the strongest terms in the Revelation but the doctrine of "plurality of wives" entered into in the spirit of righteousness is declared holy. If a man is given "ten virgins" in marriage for time and eternity by the law of the Lord, the Revelation declares that " he cannot commit adultery, for they belong to him, and they are given unto him, therefore is he justified."

Joseph, the Prophet, lived the principle as well as having taught it if the testimony of his most intimate friends can be relied upon. A number of women of known veracity testified to having been sealed to the Prophet in Nauvoo as his wives.

Long since, the Church discontinued the practice of polygamy, yet, in the days of which I write, those who had contracted plural marriages felt they had neither broken the laws of God nor of man and, to their credit be it said, many of them would have stood by their families to the death.

A bitter war was on against the practice by enemies of the Church and, in instances, devout and well meaning men and women denounced the doctrine in most vigorous terms. Even the Government joined in the fight. Legislative enactment by Congress, known as the Edmunds-Tucker Act, against the practice of plural marriage, resulted in the prosecution and imprisonment of scores of devout believers in the doctrine of polygamy. Many who had not yet come to trial or imprisonment were in constant hiding in order to escape the clutches of laws deemed by them to be unconstitutional as well as tyrannical in the extreme. Husbands were separated from wives and children in many instances from their parents. Homes that had known nothing but contentment and peace were broken up and terror reigned throughout the land.

This state of affairs induced John Taylor and George Q. Cannon of the First Presidency of the Church to address a letter to President Layton of an Arizona Stake suggesting that an effort be made to obtain "a place of refuge under a foreign government to which our people can flee." The letter was dated Dec. 16, 1884, and in part is as follows, "A general attack is being made upon our liberties throughout all the territories where our people reside. It is said that prosecuting officers in making this raid are acting under instructions from the department at Washington. Whether this be true or not, there can be no question that there is apparently a concert of action on their part to push our people to the wall and to destroy our religious liberty and with it our religion itself. Even the Utah Commissioners in making their report to the government recommend measures not to punish polygamy alone but to destroy our religion. In Utah Territory God-fearing men, whose only offense is that they have obeyed a command of the Almighty, are thrust into prison while appeals are pending in a higher court, being refused bail, a boon which should be granted to every person not guilty of a capital offense. These men are incarcerated in the penitentiary in the midst of a crowd of the vilest criminals, one of whom is a convicted murderer. In Arizona we learn that the same course is being pursued, that to be accused before any of these courts is equivalent to being convicted. The usual rule is entirely reversed. Under a proper system of jurisprudence an accused man is presumed to be innocent until proof of his guilt is furnished. Our counsel has been and is to obtain a place of refuge under a foreign government to which our people can flee when menaced in this land. Better for parts of families to remove and go where they can live in peace than to be hauled to jail and either incarcerated in the territory with thieves and murderers and other vile characters, or sent to the American Siberia in Detroit to serve out a long term of imprisonment. * * * The Saints in your various Stakes should contribute of their means to form a defense fund so that our brethren who are assailed will not in addition to the anxiety and annoyance which they have had to endure, be compelled to bear the brunt of defending themselves alone. This should be vigorously pushed and the fund be made available at once. We send this by the hand of Elder Seymour B. Young who will also be able to state to you our feelings more in detail than the limits of this letter will permit."

In a letter addressed to Seymour B. Young these same correspondents wrote: "You will see from what was said to you and from our letter how important we think it is that there should be a place of refuge obtained for our people, a place to which the eyes of those who are in jeopardy and who are oppressed may turn with some hope of finding some peace and liberty which are denied in their own land."

Ante-dating the above letter, exploring expeditions had gone into Mexico for the purpose of locating suitable places for Mormon settlements, but with little success. In 1881, A. F. Macdonald, David Kimball, C. I. Robinson and one or two others made a trip into Sonora, and in 1882 a party of thirty-two moved to a ranch on the San Bernardino river at a point where the boundary lines of the two Mexican states, Sonora and Chihuahua and Arizona and New Mexico meet with the intention of establishing the first Mormon colony in Mexico, but due to a scarcity of farming land, the group was counselled by Apostles Snow and Thatcher to abandon the project. No further moves were made in the direction of settlement until 1884 when Apostles Brigham Young, Jr., and Heber J. Grant, accompanied by parties from the Salt River and St. Joseph settlements of Arizona, attempted to make a treaty with the Yaqui Indians to settle in southwestern Sonora. The party of twenty-four went by train from Nogales, Arizona, to Hermosillo, Sonora, and arrived there on December 3rd. Elders Young, Grant and Macdonald called at the state capitol to pay their respects to the Governor but he was absent. They therefore called upon the Secretary of State who gave them an enthusiastic welcome. He counselled them, however, against going into the Yaqui country as the Indians were on the warpath. The following day, December 4th, members of the expedition visited the Governor upon his return to the capital and from him they received the same advice as had been given them by the Secretary of State. The Governor offered to give them an escort into any part of the State into which they wished to go.

At two o'clock in the afternoon a group of seven men under the leadership of Brigham Young, Jr., left by train for Guaymas, located near the mouth of the Yaqui river, and arrived at their destination on the evening of the same day. The following morning they called on the American Consul, Mr. Willard, from whom they received encouragement to pay the Yaqui Indians a visit. For the sum of fifteen dollars they chartered a boat to take them down the Yaqui river to its mouth and return. When ready to embark a multitude of natives, including a Catholic priest, congregated on the river bank to witness the departure of the boat and to warn the members of the expedition of the urgent need of confessing their sins and making restitution for the same before entering upon their perilous journey. Even their guide, Valenzuela, fearful of the undertaking, refused to accompany them. A terrific gale was blowing and for several hours it seemed that the boat would be dashed to pieces by the angry waves. Without accident, however, they finally reached the port for which they were headed, but imagine their dismay when they learned that to reach the Yaqui village they must wade knee deep through the water for a distance of five miles. Undaunted, they pushed forward to their destination and were rewarded by a kindly welcome from a race of Indians whose war-like reputation had spread terror throughout northern Mexico. The Mormon elders were glad of the privilege of bearing testimony to the Christian faith but no conversions were reported. The exposures and hardships of the trip proved disastrous to the health of the Mormon Apostle, Brigham Young, Jr. Attacked by yellow fever he left for Salt Lake City accompanied by Heber J. Grant, his fellow Apostle, who was also ill. As soon as the report of the expedition to Mexico was made public the press agents throughout the country sought to stir up strife by circulating a scurrilous tale which reflected upon the loyalty of the Latter-day Saints toward the United States. The story was to the effect that the Mormons were in collusion with the Yaqui Indians to make war upon the American Union. With the thought of forestalling further trouble the President of the Church advised against colonization in the Yaqui territory, for the time being at least.

Pursuant to instructions from the Presidency of the Church, A. F. Macdonald and Christopher Layton left St. David, Arizona, on January 1, 1885, in further quest of land in Mexico. At the station of San Jose on the Mexican Central Railroad, the travellers found a group of Mormons engaged in hauling salt. The personnel of the party consisted of John W. Campbell, Joseph Rogers, John Loving and Peter McBride. They had gone into Mexico to seek employment but principally to locate a home. Macdonald and Layton did considerable scouting in various parts of the country but principally along the Casas Grandes River in northern Chihuahua. In this region they visited Corralitos, Janos and La Ascencion and were impressed with the facilities offered for making a livelihood. At Corralitos 300 acres of fertile land were rented which were soon thereafter planted to crops by Mormon colonists. Leaving the Casas Grandes Valley, Macdonald and companion pushed westward into the tops of the Sierra Madre Mountains and explored the Corrales Basin, beautiful for situation and offering splendid opportunities for grazing and agricultural pursuits. From this point the two explorers went directly to their homes in Arizona. In the meantime small companies of home seekers came pouring in from different parts of Utah and Arizona and established themselves along the banks of the Casas Grandes River. Among the first to arrive was a band from Arizona, most prominent of whom were Jesse N. Smith, George C. Williams, Lot Smith, William B. Maxwell and William C. McClellan. These pioneers had arrived sometime in February, 1885. On the 4th of March of the same year this group was joined by a company led by Apostle Moses Thatcher and A. F. Macdonald who had left St. David, Arizona, February 23, and had come by team by way of Dragoon Pass, Bowie Station, San Simon Station and Mesquite Springs. On March 6, others arrived headed by John H. Earl, Joseph H. James, Israel Call and, a few days later, these companies were strengthened by the arrival of other colonists, chiefly from Snowflake, Arizona, among whom were Chas. W· Merrill, Levi M. Savage, Charles Whiting, Sullivan C. Richardson, Ernest L. Taylor, Joseph and Philip Cardon and Sixtus E. Johnson. This was the beginning of Mormon Colonization in Mexico that finally resulted in the establishment of eight permanent Mormon settlements, six of which were located in the state of Chihuahua and the other two in Sonora.

Practically all of the early arrivals were of very limited means; not that they were a class devoid of financial ability, but their accumulations had largely been dissipated during the years of persecution that had preceded their advent into Mexico. The question of a livelihood in a strange land was therefore one of prime importance. To secure lands sufficient and suitable for cultivation the colonists established themselves in several small communities stretching along the Casas Grandes River for a distance of more than 60 miles. The first camps organized were adjacent to La Ascension, a typical Mexican village about ninety miles South of Deming, New Mexico, and not far from the spot on which later arose Colonia Diaz, one of the largest Mormon settlements in Mexico. The other important camps in this early period, were one at a point five miles north of Casas Grandes on the Casas Grandes River and from La Ascencion about 60 miles, and one at Corralitos, about twelve miles north of Casas Grandes. There were about 350 colonists in Mexico six weeks after the arrival of the first group. In the latter part of April, 1885, an exploring party consisting of George Teasdale, an Apostle of the Church, A. F. Macdonald, Miles P. Romney and others were sent out in quest of other suitable lands for settlements. The journey took them up the Janos River as far as Casa de Janos, where they discovered a level tract of land of 1000 acres in extent, but nothing tangible resulted

from their trip.   In the month of May, Moses Thatcher
went to Paso del Norte (Cuidad Juarez) across the Rio
Grande from El Paso to negotiate for the purchase of a
tract of land offered by R. J. Garcia for $10,000 but the
deal was not made due to the owner changing his mind
relative to the price of the property.

The influx of Mormon refugees into Mexico and their
increasing activity aroused the suspicion and dislike of
certain local Mexican officials, foremost of whom were the
Jefe Politico of the Canton de Galeana.   In a letter addressed to the Secretary of the State of Chihuahua, he announced that an armed force of Mormons had come into
the state without declaring their intentions, the implication
being that they had come for conquest.   In reply the Secretary of State declared that the Mormons must be ordered
out of the country at once or as soon as it was possible for
them to comply with the orders.   On April 9, a letter was
received by A. F. Macdonald from the chief magistrate
of Casas Grandes in which reference is made to the expulsion order of the Secretary of State.   The letter con-
cludes with the following: "According to the foregoing
which I have transcribed for your information, I hereby
command you, together with the other families which you
represent, to leave the state within the period of 16 days
from this date, April 9, 1885."

Immediately upon receipt of the letter, Macdonald
went to the camp Corralitos to confer with George Teasdale, the Ecclesiastical head of the colonists in Mexico
since the return of Moses Thatcher to Salt Lake City. The
situation was truly grave.   The band of Mormon exiles
were facing deportation to a land from whence they had
fled to escape the wrath of their enemies.   To forestall
such an eventuality steps must be taken at once.   On the
11th of April, Teasdale, Macdonald, Turley and Moffatt
left by train for Chihuahua City to intercede with the governor of the state for an annulment of the expulsion edict.
They arrived at San Jose on the Mexican Central Railroad

and left by rail for the city of Chihuahua at once, arriving there on the 15th of the month. Their conference with the Governor proved disappointing. He was adamant to their supplication and strongly insisted that the Mormons must quit the State. A letter was written at once to Moses Thatcher at Logan, Utah, relative to the matter, and the following day a telegram was dispatched to him by Church authorities asking him to go to the City of Mexico to intercede with the federal officials in behalf of the colonists. A letter was received from Moses Thatcher in answer to the message sent him, April 27th, in which he stated that Helaman Pratt, then a missionary in Mexico City, had been asked to request of the head of the government a stay of proceedings until Moses Thatcher and Brigham Young, Jr., could arrive at the Capital. Upon receipt of the telegram, Helaman Pratt, in company with a fellow missionary, Franklin R. Snow, called upon a prominent lawyer of Mexico City for assistance in getting the matter properly before the heads of the government, but he demanded $100 in advance, an amount the elders could not reach. They therefore repaired to the national capitol to lay the matter before Senor Carlos Pacheco, Minister of Colonization, but were requested to call the following day when an interview would be granted. The following day, April 28, Pratt and Snow were admitted to the national palace and had an interview with Senor Fernandez Leal, subminister, who promised to use his influence in favor of the Mormons. On May 9, Apostle Brigham Young, Jr., and Moses Thatcher arrived in Mexico City. Reporting their visit by letter to A. F. Macdonald from the Humboldt Hotel, May 15, 1885, they stated that they had met Helaman Pratt, Franklin R. Snow and Isaac J. Stewart, who "are quite hopeful of the future for Mexico and her people. We found that your application for a stay of proceedings was acted upon and the document highly spoken of by the Federal officials. Brother Pratt had also been busy and we have experienced the results of their labors. We have met

Secretary of State Mariscal, who received us warmly and manifested an honest desire to forward our interests by his influence with the President and Cabinet. We have had two interviews with Senor Don Carlos Pacheco, Secretary of Public Work, and Governor of Chihuahua. He expressed personal regards for our people and in all our conversation, when opportunity afforded, expressed the hope that the Mormons would conclude to colonize within the Mexican borders." He said he was astonished and could not understand why the Mormons had received such abusive treatment as he had given orders to the acting governor to treat them courteously. He explained that he was Governor of Chihuahua, but had not had time to go to the state to give the matter his personal attention, but if a letter were addressed to him, enclosing the acting Governor's order, he would act upon it officially. The result was that the acting Governor was finally removed from office by Minister Pacheco, and another man put in his place.

In an interview with President Diaz, the Mormon Apostles were informed that the Mormons were not only welcome as colonists in Mexico, but that the Government was anxious to have them help in the development of the country. Should they find suitable locations in Sonora and Chihuahua, they could settle there or they would be equally welcome any place else they might choose to live in, except in what was known as "Zona Prohibida." Those of the colonists who had located on such lands were ordered to vacate such holdings immediately after the harvesting of their crops and to seek another location. The expulsion edict was annulled. The Mormons remained in Mexico.

CHAPTER V

FURTHER EXPANSION

The assurance from the Federal officials that Mormon colonization in Mexico would receive encouragement from both the national and state governments served as an impetus in the fields of exploration and colonization. Francis M. Lyman of the Council of the Twelve left Salt Lake City July 5, 1885, to join Senor Ignacio Gomez del Campo of the City of Mexico in making an inspection of certain lands in northern Chihuahua with the idea of purchase should they prove to be satisfactory. The regions to be explored had been the habitat of Geronimo, the Apache chief and his hostile band, since forced to flee from the boundaries of the American Union, as a result of atrocious acts committed against her citizens. To protect the exploring party against a probable attack from this band of savages, Gomez dispatched Colonel Angel Boquet with orders for a company of Mexican troops to accompany the expedition. In the meantime, equipment was being collected, suitable for a company of twelve men, consisting of mounts, pack animals, provisions, arms and ammunition. The men selected to make the trip were for the most part outstanding frontiersmen, inured to the dangers and hardships encountered in unsettled regions. For the safety and comfort of the party an efficient organization was effected, with F. M. Lyman, President, George Teasdale, Chaplain, and recorder, and George C. Williams (Parson Williams), Captain of the Guard. Other officers were appointed to look after the Commissary department and still others to supervise the care of the animals.

On the 18th of July, 1885, the group left Corralitos, having decided not to wait for the Mexican troops. Their route led them fifteen or twenty miles up the fertile Casas Grandes Valley to the town of Casas Grandes. At this point they left the river and traversed a semi-mountainous region for a distance of sixteen miles to a narrow valley on the Piedras Verdes river, a tributary of the Casas Grandes. On this spot, later to become Colonia Juarez, the party camped the first night. The following morning they began their journey up the Piedras Verdes river which finally led them into the well-timbered and picturesque vales and canyons of the Sierra Madre Mountains. Two of the outstanding valleys through which they passed were Cave Valley and Corrales Basin where a few years later two Mormon colonies were planted. At the latter place a pause was made to celebrate the 24th day of July, the anniversary of the entrance of the pioneers into the Salt Lake Basin. Upon this occasion the American flag was raised at half mast from one of the tallest trees, out of respect to the death of ex-President U. S. Grant, in whose honor flags were at half mast over the whole of the United States. From here the expedition moved forward in a westward direction passing over the mountains into the state of Sonora.

The country over which they traveled is described by a member of the group as being rugged and of very little account for settlement.

The return trip led them down the San Pedro and Janos rivers to Casa de Janos where they beheld vast stretches of grass lands well adapted to the raising of cattle and horses. Upon the arrival of the expedition at Corralitos, from whence it started, a meeting of the entire camp of Saints was called to hear the report of the explorers. It was decided upon this occasion to purchase some of the land explored and lying along the banks of the Piedras Verdes river. Their decision, as will be noted later, was carried into effect.

A few months later Brigham Young, Jr., of the Council of the Twelve, in company with others, explored much the same territory as that covered by the group above referred to. Speaking of his explorations, particularly in Sonora, Mr. Young observes: "My journey to Sonora was very satisfactory. Governor Torres and other state officers were anxious that we should settle in their state as being quite equal in facilities for settlement and the people were more civilized than in Chihuahua." Due to the "indefiniteness" with respect to the purchase of land the colonists were advised by their ecclesiastical leaders to rent lands for the time being and to proceed at the opportune time with all diligence with the planting of their crops.

In the middle of January, 1886, A. F. Macdonald was given the power of Attorney by 31 colonists to purchase for them a tract of irrigable and pasture land adjacent to the San Diego grant, owned by Don Luis Terrazas, a multi-millionaire and ex-Governor of Chihuahua. George Teasdale accompanied Mr. Macdonald on this business trip to the City of Mexico where they arrived January 21. Here they went into conference with General Campo, Elder Helaman Pratt acting as interpreter. Several days were spent in the examination of the deeds and other documents pertaining to the property and finally, on the 12th of February, a contract was drawn up and signed for the purchase of 20,000 hectares, or 49,400 acres, of land on the Piedras Verdes River, on which later was built Colonia Juarez. In addition, they negotiated for 7,000 acres near La Ascension on which Colonia Diaz was later planted, and 60,000 acres chiefly of timber land, in the Sierra Madre Mountains on which was to arise Colonia Pacheco. The Trustee in Trust of the Church, President John Taylor, furnished twelve thousand dollars of Church money to go toward the purchase of these tracts.

In the apportionment of these lands it was decided by a vote of the group that they should be held in common, but to be leased by the colonists for a nominal sum, with the understanding that the sales or transfers of leases should be made only with the consent of a company, later to be organized. The company was to consist of representatives of the several stakes of the Church that had contributed toward the purchase of the lands and representatives of the colonists. Erastus Snow, a member of the Council of the

Twelve, was to act in an advisory capacity as an agent of the President of the Church. This company was soon thereafter organized, but a little later it developed into, or was supplanted by the Mexican Colonization and Agricultural Company formed under the laws of Colorado. Moses Thatcher was made the President and A. F. Macdonald the manager of the company.

To obtain the use of any of this property one must furnish a recommend from the bishop of his ward certifying that he was honest and honorable and in full standing in the Church of Jesus Christ of Latter-day Saints. So long as the holder of the land observed the rules laid down by the company he could remain in possession of it, but should he prove recreant in any respect he was liable to a forfeiture of his stewardship. In case he were dispossessed of his holdings an arbitration committee would place a price upon the improvements he had made and he would receive due compensation for the same. It will thus be seen that the early Mormon colonists in Mexico held property under the same restrictions as did the early settlers of the Great Basin. In both cases only the devotees of the Mormon Church in full standing were entitled to possession and in both instances possession merely implied a stewardship—the titles being held by the Church while the tiller of the soil held his concession only during good behavior. The purpose of such a policy was to insure against the influx of non-members of the Church and other undesirables into a community whose aim was to control absolutely its social and religious life, and not for the purpose of materially enhancing the coffers of the Church. Indeed, investments in lands in Mexico by the Church subtracted from rather than added to its revenues. In the course of a few years the economic policy of stewardship was supplanted by individual ownership. From what has been said relative to the general land policy it must not be assumed that lands could not be purchased by Mormon settlers in Mexico independently of the agents of the Church as represented by the Mexican Colonization and Agricultural Company. In some instances colonists purchased their lands direct from individuals or companies owning tracts of land. In a letter addressed to the Deseret News September 11, 1890, Mr. Macdonald said with reference to this matter: "The colonists who live on the company lands have chosen individual title for their benefit and security of possession. Some living at Casas Grandes and La Ascencion acquiring individual title but enjoying the benefits of contract, the same as colonists on the Company's land, the inhabitants of each town electing their own committee, who, in connection with the Company's manager adopt such rules as are needful for the welfare of the Community agreeable with the principles of stewardship, yet in harmony with the law of the land." The report continues with the statement that persons of limited means can buy a farm or a few acres of improved land with water rights in towns or municipalities at, from $2.50 to $20.00 per acre and obtain title. Range and pasture lands in large tracts can be purchased for 25 cents American money per acre. At the close of the 90's a report was issued by George M. Brown representing a committee of Mormons residing near Casas Grandes to the effect that at Colonia Huller (Colonia Dublan) there was a tract of 73,000 acres for sale. Of this amount 20,000 acres was first class farming land on which could be raised all kinds of fruit and grain. Near the foothills to the eastward the committee reported the existence of several large depressions in the earth having the appearance of ancient reservoirs. The remains of an ancient canal leading from the Casas Grandes River to the reservoirs was visible. Farm lands under the reservoir were offered for 75 cents per acre and other lands for from 40 to 50 cents. Town lots, 1¼ acres in size, were offered at prices ranging from $2.50 to $10.00 each. Twenty acres were to be given free to the head of each family who would settle and reside in the colony for a period of five years—the offer was good only for the first one hun-

dred families. Titles were to be issued to those purchasing
lands guaranteed to be as good as any that "could be found
in the Republic." The prices quoted were in terms of
Mexican money and it is well to observe that only those
who could present recommends from their bishops were
eligible to make purchases. Mr. Huller, from whom the
land was purchased, was a German-Mexican and at one
time bore the evidence of being financially prosperous but
soon after contracting with the Mormons to sell them the
above mentioned land, financial disaster overtook him and
the deal fell through. By 1891, 380 people had assembled
at Colonia Huller to procure land under the Huller grant,
some of them having paid in advance for their land. With
the refusal of Mr. Huller's creditors to let the Mormons
settle on the tract, the money advanced by the colonists
was refunded and they invested in lands held by Mexicans
for which they got quit claim deeds with the prospect of
getting regular government deeds later. Incidentally it is
interesting to know that the Huller property fell into the
hands of the Mormons later, a considerable portion of it
coming under cultivation, made possible by the flow of
water passed through the ancient irrigation system of reservoirs and canals.

Increased agricultural opportunities came to the colonists with the purchase by John W. Young (a son of
President Brigham Young) of 150,000 acres north of Colonia Diaz and watered by the Casas Grandes River. The
price paid for the land was $110,000 and was to be rented
to the Mormon settlers on easy terms. In 1889, the
Mexican Colonization and Agricultural Company bought
from Mr. Young 28,000 acres of the tract adjacent to
La Ascencion and this became a possession of the settlers
of Colonia Diaz.

Other significant land deals negotiated for in the interests of Mormon Colonization in Chihuahua before the
close of the century was the Cave Valley purchase made by
Moses Thatcher, Erastus Snow, G. C. Williams, Helaman

5

Pratt and the Mormon Church. This tract lay along the banks of the Piedras Verdes River, thirty-five miles west of Colonia Juarez and five miles north of Colonia Pacheco and was especially valuable for its wealth of saw timber and grazing facilities. Its agricultural possibilities were somewhat limited, the land suitable for such purpose varying from five yards to six miles in width and was ultimately divided among the purchasers according to the amount invested by each. Round Valley, commonly known as Garcia, consisted of about 1300 acres and was situated ten miles south of Pacheco and thirty-eight miles from Colonia Juarez, while Chuichupa, meaning "The Place of the Mist," was valuable land located near the western boundary line of the State of Chihuahua, about eighty-five miles south of Casas Grandes and forty-five miles south of Pacheco. The region was well adapted for dairy purposes and abounded in great stretches of timber such as pine, juniper, and oak. Notwithstanding its altitude averages 8262 feet, the climate is sufficiently moderate that oats, potatoes and corn can be profitably raised. All told there were more than 6000 acres in the tract. In the midst of this mountain area, game of all kinds such as wild turkey, bear and deer was plentiful and the region became the mecca for hunters from all over the United States and from some foreign countries.

In the year 1892, steps were taken toward the fulfilment of a long cherished dream of Mormon expansion into the state of Sonora when Los Horcones (Colonia Oaxaca) was purchased by George C. Williams and John C. Naegle. The grant contained about 200 square miles and extended north and south for a distance of about 20 miles along both banks of the Bavispe River, a tributary of the Yaqui, which flows into the Pacific Ocean. Los Horcones was 25 miles north of the city of Bavispe and a hundred miles south-east of Bisbee, Arizona. The farming land, though limited, was extremely fertile, and cut into small parcels by the winding river, no piece containing more than 200 acres. There was considerable timber on the property for fuel purposes such as mesquite, cottonwood, sycamore, ash and walnut. The sale of the tract of land was negotiated by Generals Kosterlitzky and Fenokio, who had been given the tract by the government, for the sum of $35,000, Mexican currency, the amount to be paid in three equal installments.

Soon after his appointment to the presidency of the stake in Mexico, Anthony W. Ivins, representing the Mexican Colonization and Agricultural Company as President, consummated a deal for the purchase of 9,000 acres of heavy mesquite land in the Batepeto Valley for the sum of $10,000. The tract was located 60 miles south of Douglas, Arizona, and down the Bavispe River from Los Horcones about twenty miles. The deal resulted not from the desire to speculate but to furnish opportunity for several hundred home-makers to establish themselves in a land of peace and opportunity.

With the purchase of thousands of acres of choice lands in two of the northern states of Mexico and with the influx of nearly three thousand souls in a trifle more than a decade after the first Mormon colonists came to Mexico the permanence of Mormon expansion into the Southern Republic seemed assured.

Yet the difficulties confronting the colonists in these years of initiation into a foreign land were sufficient to baffle spirits less courageous. Few of them could understand the tongue of their adopted country and, as a result, misunderstandings and even disagreements between the natives and the late comers were not unknown. But the greatest handicap of all was the galling grind of poverty. I have pointed out elsewhere that a vast majority of the immigrant Mormons into this foreign land were near the borderline of penury, their substance having been depleted during the years of persecution that drove them into hiding and placed a goodly number behind prison bars. To add to their financial strain and mental discomfiture, were the hateful duties that must be paid in passing over the international boundary line. Only those who have had such experience can fully sympathize with these pilgrims as they approached a foreign custom house and were made aware of the fact that everything they possessed must undergo the searching scrutiny of revenue officers in quest of dutiable articles. Even the rolls of bedding must be inspected to ascertain if by chance or otherwise goods subject to duty had been tucked away within their folds, or perchance some of the suspicious looking indivdiuals might be brusquely ushered into the inspection room to undergo the humiliation of being stripped by customs officials in quest of bolts of cloth or surplus clothing. But worst of all was the seizure of personal effects and their confiscation because the owners had not the wherewith to pay the duty charges.

But duties were in a constant state of flux. A statement of duty charges on a tabulated list of commodities or even luxuries usually varied from year to year, but the following list submitted from the year 1888 will furnish the reader with a fairly reliable notion of the burdens imposed upon the foreigners by the Mexican government. Wagons, 3 cents per pound, harnesses, 15 cents per pound, saddles, $1.00 per pound, gelding horses, $40.00 each, wagon covers, 91 cents each, window glass, 12 cents per pound, boots, $1.25 to $2.50 per pair, shoes, 85 to 90 cents, hats, 29 cents to $1.00 each, tents, 10 cents per pound, furniture, 7½ cents per pound, flour 5½ cents per pound, bacon 12½ cents, sugar, 7½ cents, coal oil, 35 cents per gallon, sewing machines, $1.25 to $2.50, cutlery, 10 cents per pound, glass ware, 10 cents, potatoes, 1½ cents and soap 9 cents. On all kinds of unmade fabrics the duty was from 40 to 100 per cent of the original cost. As if to add to the expense and discomfiture of the colonists it was not an unusual experience to be held at the custom house for several days awaiting the completion of the long drawn out inspection of the goods and a corresponding delay in preparing papers for the release of the cargo.

It would be unfair to the Mexican government, however, to omit mention of the fact that rather early in the history of Mormon colonization, prospective colonists were permitted to enter Mexican territory on what was termed a "free list," that is to say, commodities such as horses and wagons, farm machinery, household goods, food and clothing could be admitted free of duty. To enjoy this concession the individual had to certify that he intended becoming a permanent resident of the country and in addition must submit in writing a list of the articles upon which he desired exemption from duties. This material must be in the hands of the government officials at least 60 days before the date set for crossing the international boundary line.

An excerpt from a letter written by President Ivins "for the benefit of prospective settlers," dated May 30, 1898, will suffice to make clear this matter: "Persons desiring to colonize to any of these places can do so under concessions granted the Mexican Colonization and Agricultural Company. * * * The colonist should appear before a notary and obtain a certificate in the following form: 'I hereby certify that John Doe is personally known to me to be a moral, industrious man, his occupation being a farmer, etc. He declares it to be his intention to leave the United States and go as a colonist to Mexico, and to establish himself at Colonia Juarez, or elsewhere, in the state of Chihuahua.' The certificate will be sent to the secretary of state who will certify to the signature and seal of the notary. In addition the names and ages of the family, their nationality as well as a description of property, brands of horses and cattle should be sent two months before the colonist desires to start from home." Exemptions granted colonists and to be in force for a period of ten years are enumerated by President Ivins: "(1) Exemption from military service; (2) from all taxation and imports, except stamp and municipal taxes; (3) from payment of customs duties on wagons, harnesses, saddles, tools, machinery, agricultural implements, breeding and work stock, furniture, materials for construction of houses and personal effects, including clothing, dishes, bedding, etc., etc."

To what extent this tax exemption contract on the part of the government was adhered to cannot be definitely known but as early as 1897 it is recorded that Anthony W. Ivins and Henry Eyring called on the Governor of Chihua-hua, Ahumada, requesting that the colonists be not taxed who had not yet completed a ten year's residence in Mexico. In response, the Governor stated that the rights of the colonists would be protected in harmony with the terms of the government concession.

Wage earners in Mexico were very poorly paid, resulting in another hardship to the new comers since many of them must hire out as mechanics or farm laborers as the only means of support for themselves and families. A report submitted by M. Romero, the Mexican Minister, in February, 1892, shows that the highest average wage per day was in Coahuila, being 53½ cents. The lowest average wage was in Nuevo Leon and Aguas Calientas, where 18¼ cents per day was paid. These wages apply to farm laborers. The employees of the railroads and of the mines were paid as much as $1.50 per day. Had the cost of goods corresponded with the low wages paid, the living conditions would have been tolerable, but many of the commodities could be obtained only by paying relatively exorbitant prices. In Mexico for example, sugar was selling for 21 cents per pound, while the same quality of sugar in New York could be purchased for 5 cents; cotton in Mexico was 19 cents per pound, in the United States it was 10 cents; flour cost 5 cents in Mexico while in the United States it could be had for 1½ cents per pound. It will be noted that these articles generally were not produced in northern Mexico in large quantities and must therefore be imported largely from the United States. Produce raised in Mexico such as corn, beans, wheat and beef gave a return to the producer barely sufficient to pay for the cost of production. In 1888 wheat sold for 1¼ cents per pound, corn for ¾ cents, beans for 2 cents and beef for 6 cents.

Notwithstanding the many discouragements financial and otherwise which confronted the Mormon colonists in the Southern Republic, they had by 1891 made considerable headway both in numbers and in prestige. The Mexican Financial Review reported that "The Mormons are rapidly settling in the state of Chihuahua, especially along the line of the Mexican Northwestern Railroad now building from Deming, New Mexico, to the City of Chihuahua. Hundreds of industrious Mormons have purchased lands and they have everywhere built neat and comfortable adobe cottages, and windmills for raising water for home use as well as for irrigation. They have built and are building barns and their vineyards and orchards are rapidly coming in bearing. In fact, they have changed the once wild and almost uninhabitated region into comfortable and productive farms. So far the Mormons in the State of Chihuahua have proved good immigrants."

The Revista Internacional, published at Ciudad Juarez said: "Without any exaggeration whatever, it may be said that among the 3,000 souls from the colonies of Diaz, Pacheco and Dublan there is not a single drunkard, gambler or vagabond. The efforts of all are concentrated for their mutual welfare. * * * They have worked like the ants ardently and constantly. * * * They are not land speculators in disguise but people accustomed to the field,—laborers,—and among them are some artisans who are masters of their professions. They arrive in the Republic with one wagon or two as the case may be, each with its respective team, animals and with their tools and implements of agriculture and industry which constitute the only capital that many of them possess. But they bring with them something of more value than gold or bank notes and that is the love of labor. * * * On the arrival of the colonists the superintendent apportions to each the land needed. Immediately work is begun and the land cleared off and labor continues incessantly. While the seed is deposited in the ground all help, the wife, the elder children and even the little fellows who drop the seed in the ground. * * * At first they live in a rude hut, but this is replaced in a few years by a commodious house surrounded with flowers and fruit trees and amply furnished, wherein reigns the most complete tranquility. * * * They don't squander the money they have earned by the sweat of their brow. They practice true economy and only provide the necessaries and they use their surplus means to increase the productiveness of their land, to purchase more, always being careful not to go beyond their means. The oldest colony is the Colony Diaz which contains nearly a thousand souls, with clean streets, lined with shade trees on either side. Diaz has several industrial establishments, a church, school, and drug store, but they have neither a saloon, billiard hall, nor any place whatever, where mescal is sold. Consequently they have no need of a jail, nor have they one in any of the colonies. There are seldom any complaints or quarrels and scandals are entirely unknown in any of the colonies."

Further proof of the growing prestige of the Mormons is seen in the report appearing in the Deseret News, March 10, 1896, in which the writer says: "The colonies have come to the front of late by sending some specimens, the result of their industry to the Coyoacan fair at the City of Mexico. * * * The Mormon exhibition, we are told, was very attractive, exciting general admiration and the views of the residences, schoolhouses, etc., were much admired. I am happy to inform you that eleven medals and the same number of diplomas were awarded to our colonists."

Speaking of the same event, Joseph C. Bentley, who went to the City of Mexico to look after the Mormon exhibit, reported: "They had no idea that our colonies could make such an excellent showing, and when President Diaz and Minister of Fomento, Leal, and other government officials saw the photographs of our principal residences, schoolhouses, and views of the colony, together with the products of cheese, canned fruits, jellies, candy, molasses, roller mill flour and potatoes all put up in American style they were delighted. President Diaz said it appeared to him to be the thrift and energy of 50 years rather than the few years the colonies had been established. * * * President Diaz instructed the Minister of Fomento to address a note to our agent requesting him to take back to the colonists his personal thanks for the excellent manner in which they had colonized into Mexico and for the industry and good example exhibited since coming."

In the same year a report of the American Consul Buford appeared in the "Deming Headlight," concerning the Mormons in which he said there were "ten colonies, nearly all Americans. Their buildings are in the finest portions of Northern Mexico. The soil is very rich and productive, and with the advance of railroads from the nearest of which they are removed from 120 to 200 miles, these lands will greatly enhance in value * * * the Mormons are exceedingly prosperous and highly regarded."

Chapter VI

COLONIA DIAZ—THE FIRST PERMANENT
MORMON COLONY

From the inception of Mormonism its adherents have tended to settled in communities of their own in order to shape their social and religious life in harmony with their own peculiar ideals. There was no exception made to this rule by those who sought homes in Mexico. Though possessing no lands of their own for nearly a year following their advent they adhered as far as possible to the community plan of living. Obviously, however, their settlements had no permanent status assured them so long as the colonists were dependent upon others for the lands they tilled. At any time they were in danger of being uprooted. But with the purchase of lands by the Church, a feeling of security and permanence was born that manifested itself in the founding of colonies that became famed throughout the Republic for their beauty and charm.

Colonia Diaz, established in the early part of 1885, is justly entitled to be known as the first permanent Mormon Colony planted in the Southern Republic, since its founders were among the first groups to enter the country in quest of homes. They had previously settled in temporary camps adjacent to the plat on which Diaz was later built and when that townsite was laid off they rushed in and became permanent residents of the newly founded colony.

Colonia Diaz, as was true of all the Mormon settlements in Chihuahua, was situated on the Casas Grandes River and was located nearly 200 miles southwest from El Paso, Texas, and northwest of the City of Chihuahua about 250 miles. The valley in which it is situated is about 25 by 70 miles in extent and has an elevation of about 5000 ft. above sea level. The soil is fertile and well adapted to the production of beans, corn, potatoes, squash, sugar cane, small grain, and even fruit, common to the temperate zone, did well. By the middle of 1890, 2,000 shade trees had been planted on the town site, as well as 15,000 fruit trees and 5,000 grape vines. For the grazing of cattle, the country surrounding was excellent. Wind mills became common with the growth of population and proved to be profitable since there was plenty of wind and an abundance of water of good quality, from eight to ten feet beneath the surface of the ground. The water thus pumped furnished culinary water for the housewife and assisted in keeping the gardens growing. Additional water was added for town and fields in 1888 with the completion of a canal tapping the river four miles south of the colony at a cost of $2,000, and somewhat later, another canal, twenty-five miles in length which conveyed the water from a series of magnificent springs whose water was constant and the size of a "mill stream." But little timber of value grew in the valley and it was to be found only along the banks of the river. This limited supply consisted chiefly of cottonwood and willow. Far to the west could be seen the Sierra Madre range with its majestic peaks piercing the blue gray atmosphere to lofty heights. The only other elevations to be seen could sacrcely be termed mountains. They were little more than hills and even they stood afar off like sentinels guarding the passes that led into the peaceful and fertile valley of the Casas Grandes.

The ground on which the colony stood and the lands adjacent thereto had belonged to two separate tracts as has been previously indicated. One of them, comprising 7,000 acres, was bought by the Church in the early part of 1886, from General Campo while the other one was purchased from John W. Young, a few years later (1890) and consisted of 28,000 acres.

The land was later classified under instructions from President Anthony W. Ivins, into pasture, meadow and farming lands and sold and deeded to the individual members of the community in harmony with their desires and on easy term payments. The pasture land was sold at the nominal sum of $2.50 a hectara (2.471 acres); the meadow land for $5.00 a hectara and the farming land for from $8.00 to $12.00 per hectara. But the first cost of the farming land was meager compared to the expense of clearing the ground. A large part of it was covered with a heavy growth of mesquite that must be grubbed and cleared away before it could be plowed and planted to crops. And, then, in that semi-arid region where the rainfall was insufficient to mature the crops, dams must be constructed, and canals dug to convey the irrigation water to the thirsty soil. The task in the beginning was truly collossal and a less heroic people would have weakened under the burden, but they manfully toiled on and were, in the course of a few years, rewarded by seeing arise from the plain homes of comfort and beauty.

The first dwellings to appear on the town site were usually nothing but tents or wagon boxes supplemented with arbors of cottonwood and willow as a protection against the burning rays of the sun. Later, stockade and adobe houses, with their mud roofs, supplanted the tents and wagon boxes. These were an improvement in some respects but during the rainy season the water trickled through the relatively flat mud roofs for a day or two after the rain had ceased falling without. The first shingled house to be built in Colonia Diaz was the home of Bishop William D. Johnson, completed in the winter of 1886. It is also reputed to be the first shingled house ever to be erected in the state of Chihuahua. I have no evidence to verify or refute the claim but shingled houses in those days in Mexico were certainly a novelty. It must be born in mind that lumber and shingles were difficult to obtain, colonists from Colonia Diaz being compelled to freight them in by team and wagon from Deming New Mexico, a distance of one hundred and eighty miles the round trip, or from saw mills owned and operated by the colonists in the Sierra Madre, a distance of from seventy to one hundred miles from the colony. The duties on these materials as on other foreign importations made the goods from the States almost prohibitive. Fortunate were those who could bring them in on a "free list."

The house furnishings in these early days generally were scant and of rude quality, the chairs usually consisting of dry goods boxes, or perchance homemade benches fashioned by the hand of the home owner. The table would likely be a large goods box or it might be constructed of pine boards nailed together and supported by four rough legs. In some instances, the floors would have a covering of rough boards or portions of the mud floor might be adorned with one or more braided rugs, the handiwork of the cultured and art loving wife and mother. The beds usually were of straw or cornhusks within a covering of factory or denim over which were spread a quilt and a counterpane that hinted of better days. Not all the homes were thus rudely furnished, for some of the colonists brought with them their house-furnishings from their former homes in Utah and Arizona, but even these articles showed signs of wear. The food was coarse, consisting mainly of frijoles (beans), cornbread and molasses with an occasional piece of bacon thrown in, but what was lacking in variety of food was made up in appetite.

The religious and social life of the people of Colonia Diaz was not neglected because of the grinding toil and unrelenting drudgery required to wring from the elements a meager existence. Though poor in purse the colonists were rich in spirit. Scarcely had they arrived at the town site when the people were united under an ecclesiastical organization known as a ward. The one chosen to be their Bishop was William Derby Johnson, a man not lacking in experience and of pleasing personality, who was ordained by Apostle Teasdale on November 9, 1886. Martin P. Mortensen and Joseph H. James were chosen to be his counselors. Later Charles Whiting and Peter K. Lemon filled these positions. The Relief Society, Sunday School, Mutual Improvement and Primary Associations were also organized with efficient officers to preside over them. At all of the temporary camps, similar organizations had existed since the beginning of Mormon colonization in Mexico except that the chief presiding officer of each camp was merely a "presiding elder" and not an ordained Bishop.

In the matter of recreation the Mormons have always been most liberal and, at the same time, conscientious in furnishing ample entertainment for all, irrespective of age or sex. Extremely orthodox Church people have in some instances criticized them because of their favorable attitude toward certain forms of amusement, as for example, the theatres and the dances. Down through the middle ages and even in modern times many church people have looked upon such forms of recreation as being entirely antagonistic to the true spirit of Christianity and have often placed a ban upon church members who would indulge therein, but the protagonists of Mormonism have, from the beginning, recognized no such conflict when the recreation was conducted in an orderly and chaste manner. If anything, Mormonism is practical. It does not differentiate between the worship of God in the dance and His worship on Sunday. All things that are beautiful and ennobling are to the Latter-day Saint, religious and worthy of acceptation. Before beginning a dance or the presentation of a drama or a concert it has always been customary for the Mormon people to open such entertainment with prayer. Such procedure has usually so clothed the participant with a feeling of social and moral responsibility as to stimulate him to do his best and to act his best toward the social group.

Soon following the organization of Diaz into a ward, a home dramatic troop was organized whose duty was to place before the community dramatic productions on a high plane of excellence both in content and presentation. That these theatricals were approved and enjoyed by the masses is attested in the fact that as a usual thing the play houses would be crowded to the door. Dancing parties were of frequent occurrence especially during the winter months. Both old and young would usually participate and it was not an unusual sight to witness the father dancing with the daughter and the mother with her son. Even the mother-in-law would come in for her share of attention. In the early days of Colonia Diaz, as was the case in the other Mormon colonies, no round dancing of any sort was permitted, the Church authorities feeling that close contact of the sexes might induce improper thought and action. Sex irregularities of any sort were looked upon by these pioneers as being deadly in their effects and extreme sex impurity as being second only to the shedding of blood in the category of crimes. Every precaution was taken therefore to guard the chastity of the youth. The dances considered appropriate included cotillions, the lancers, the Virginia reel, the Scotch reel, and the French Four. The ability to call the various changes was not easily attained but he who could master the art was in great demand and was held in high esteem. The music for the dances would not, today, be considered classic, yet there was something in the tone and volume that fairly electrified the nervous system and gave rhythm to every muscle and fibre of one's being. Instruments of most common use were the organ, the fiddle and the flute, though the accordion and even the Jew's harp and harmonica were not uncommon.

Other recreational functions that were also popular and of not infrequent occurrence were the holiday festivities such as the 24th of July, Cinco de Mayo, Mexican Independence Day, (16 September), and Christmas. Then occasionally an outing would be arranged for by the Sunday School or some other auxiliary of the Church when old and young would cast aside the irksome toil for a day and hie to some shady grove by the river's brink and spend the succeeding hours in athletic contests and in listening to a program of speech and of song, but most important of all was the feasting to the full on the choicest dainties that could be provided by mothers and sweethearts in their efforts to please.

A brief report of a characteristic program held in honor of Mexican Independence is herewith presented. "In the early part of the day a great parade was staged, consisting of floats that would have been a credit to a people of greater opulence and wealth. Striking was the float representing the 28 states of Mexico by as many little girls appropriately dressed. Then followed floats representing the various auxiliaries of the Church and finally floats representing the industrial organizations of the community. The program that followed was intensely patriotic both in speech and in song. As an opener the Mexican National air was sung by ten charming young ladies attired in white and wearing the national colors. The struggle to gain Mexican independence was dramatically told in the tongue of the foreigner and of the natives as well. At night a torch light meeting was held in the park. The illumination was made by the pitch pine bonfire, the glare of which lit up the heavy branches of the foreground and obscured in more intense gloom those in the distance, making a picture to remind one of the Druids who were wont to assemble for rites and ceremonies in just such temples of nature."

The educational needs of the people were similarly provided for. Among the first buildings to be constructed were school houses for both grade and high school instruction. The cost of the school buildings was met largely by the several communities, a pro rata tax usually being levied for that purpose with the consent of the tax payers. The maintaining of the schools, aside from a relatively small tuition fee, was in major part assumed by the Church as a whole, made necessary in the first place by the financial limitations of the local inhabitants and, in the second place, by a desire on the part of the people to maintain their own schools entirely independent and apart from the Mexican system of schools. In that event no help could be expected from the local or federal government. In addition to the grade schools a Church Academy was founded in

Colonia Diaz in something less than a decade after the town was established. Referring to the educational opportunities of Colonia Diaz a reporter of the Deming Headlight, Oct. 18, 1895, said: "At Colonia Diaz is a large commodious schoolhouse which has lately been finished outside and in, at considerable cost by the colonists. It is built of adobes and has a beautiful hard finish on the outside. The inside has nicely painted woodwork and has wainscoting throughout the entire building. * * * It is acknowledged to be the largest and best school house in the state of Chihuahua." At the Diaz Academy, not only were the usual secular subjects taught, but theological and religious subjects as well, the aim being to establish the young men and women firmly in the doctrines of the Church.

A steady but not a phenomenal growth in population occurred at Colonia Diaz in the first years of its existence. By 1900 the statistician recorded a total membership of 623. A growth was also noted in the number of splendid homes and in places of business. The colony was given over largely to farming and stock raising but some trade was carried on in flour and some other forms of merchandise.

In the winter of 1887-88 a candy factory was established by Bishop Johnson and several thousand pounds of candy were made from Mexican sugar. By 1894, a prosperous candy business was reported.

The first grist mill to be built in Diaz (1891) was owned by John Rowley. The burrs were home-made and the mill was run by wind power. In the following year, Charles E. Richardson built a small mill run by water power. In 1893, Joseph James and William D. Hendricks constructed a burr mill, having a turbine wheel. The machinery was shipped from Cache Valley, Utah. Later, French burrs, a cleaner, elevator and other up-to-date fixtures were added. A broom factory was also put into operation.

6

For the purpose of advertising and consolidating the farming, stock and trade interests of the community an Agricultural and Manufacturing Association was organized. In the fall of 1896, a fair was held at Colonia Diaz, to which President Diaz and Governor Ahumada of Chihuahua were invited to be present. At the same time those two distinguished officials were made honorary members of the Association. Replying to the letter of Bishop Johnson, conferring the honor, President Diaz replied, "Esteemed Sir: I am very thankful as well for the distinction which you have conferred upon me in making me an honorary member of the Agricultural and Manufacturing Association of which you are the honored president, as well as for the invitation which you are pleased to make me, which although I am not able to accept, because of a multiplicity of official duties, I esteem highly, and I will send at once to Governor Miguel Ahumada asking him to represent me in the ceremony of the inauguration of the fair."

The Governor and a party of distinguished state officials arrived in Diaz in the forenoon of the 23rd of October, 1896, and found the Sunday School children lining the Main Street on one side and on the opposite side were the adults. He was much impressed with this exhibition of hospitality and deference as well as with the various exhibits at the fair, such as grains, fruits, and vegetables and the handiwork of the colonists. In his public address he stated that he had long heard of the thrift of the Mormon people and he felt they would be a great asset to the country. "I shall give an account to President Diaz of what I see and hear that he may also form more extended ideas of your condition and prospects. * * * The sight before me is a very pleasing and interesting one, of so many bright and healthy children born on the soil of Mexico. It promises well for your future growth and development in the country of your adoption." In conclusion he promised to do all he could to promote the material and intellectual development of the colonists. These fairs became quite a regular feature in the economic life of the colony and did much to stimulate prosperity and trade.

Retarding factors in the growth of population and in material and social prosperity of Colonia Diaz as well as of the other colonies were the frequent outbreaks of malignant diseases such as typhoid, malarial fever, diphtheria, and smallpox. Lack of skilled medical help and serums and sanitary devices resulted in widespread mortality, and otherwise unnecessary suffering. I recall that a promising son of Bishop Johnson of Diaz was bitten by a mad coyote upon the plains of Mexico. It occurred just after he and his youthful companions had retired for the night, their beds having been spread upon the ground. A few days later the youth was writhing in agony, a victim of hydrophobia, while his family and friends with blanched and tear-stained faces stood nervously about the room waiting the tragic but certain end. A few years later another youth was bitten by a mad dog; he was rushed immediately to the City of Mexico for treatment and returned home little worse for his experience. Such are the marvels of science, unknown to the first Mormon colonists of Mexico.

Life was not only rendered unsafe from diseases but assassinations took their toll of human life. One example for the present will suffice. Young Wesley Norton of Colonia Diaz, a sewing machine agent, bade goodbye to his parents for a trip up the Casas Grandes River hoping to dispose of some sewing machines to improve his financial condition. About two days later, a colonist beheld a team still hitched to a light wagon, without a driver, wandering aimlessly about. Suspicion of foul play was aroused. A search was begun, resulting in the finding of young Norton's body (March 4, 1894) in an old building at Barrancas, four miles south of Corralitos and forty-one miles from Colonia Diaz. The evidence favored the theory that he had entered a room of the building, had built a fire and was in the act of warming himself when he was struck a blow on the head that resulted in his death. The murderers then took his money and escaped. This was the first of a series of assassinations suffered by the Latter-day Saints, extending over a series of years.

Bishop Johnson presided over Colonia Diaz from its founding until July 11, 1911, when he was succeeded by Ernest Romney as bishop with Alma Fredrickson and Junior Rallinson as his counsellors. Romney presided until the time of the Exodus in 1912. Soon after the Mormons left, the town was entirely destroyed by fire and up to the present has never been rebuilt.

CHAPTER VII

THE FOUNDING OF COLONIA JUAREZ

The temporary camps that furnished the pioneers of Colonia Diaz, sent a stream of colonists still further up the Casas Grandes River where other temporary settlements were located at intervals, one of the most important being at San Jose, five miles northwest of Casas Grandes. From this camp a group of families proceeded to a point on the Piedras Verdes River, a tributary of the Casas Grandes, and laid the foundations of Colonia Juarez. The first to arrive on the spot were George Sevey, George C. Williams and family, Isaac Turley and family, Peter Nelson and family, Ira B. Elmer and family, Joseph A. Moffat, William G. Romney, Hyrum C. Nielson, Peter N. Skousen, Hyrum Judd and Ernest L. Taylor. This was on the 7th of December, 1885. Two days later Miles P. Romney and Thomas Hawkins and families joined the camp and on the 16th of the month, John Bloomfield and Joseph Hancock arrived. Before the close of the year the townsite was surveyed by Joseph C. Fish. Town lots were apportioned the heads of the several families and soon some sort of a shelter was provided for the winter. For the most part they consisted of wagon boxes and dugouts in the side of the river banks. Miles P. Romney has the honor of building the first dugout and in that humble abode was born to his wife the following spring the first child of the new colony, a boy. Picture if you can the courage of a woman who, under such adverse conditions will consent to bring into the world offspring. No doctor, no comforts, no shelter from the elements except a mere hole in the ground. All honor to those self-sacrificing pioneer mothers.

The first death to occur in the camp was that of Peter Nielson who passed away of pneumonia on the 23rd of January, 1886. Miles P. Romney preached the funeral sermon and dedicated the grave.

In the early part of the year 1886, A. F. Macdonald returned from his trip to the City of Mexico, where he had been to negotiate for land on which the Saints could settle permanently. On March 6th, he reported his trip at a Priesthood meeting and announced that he had purchased from the government through Minister Gomez del Campo, 20,000 hectares of land, or approximately 40,000 acres. At another priesthood meeting held on the 19th of the same month a vote was passed unanimously "That we hold the lands with all upon them as a company cooperation and that no title pass to individuals, but that our Church is to unite in a common agreement for united protection and benefit." For a number of years this policy of common ownership was adhered to, each man having apportioned to him his possession as a stewardship. As time passed, however, the sentiment grew in favor of individual ownership, resulting in the abolishment of the cooperative plan and the issuance of titles to the holders of the lands.

The soil was fertile but in a region such as this the natural precipitation must be supplanted by artificial means to mature the crops. This would involve the expenditure of considerable time and labor but fortunately very little cash would be required. With a determination that knows no defeat these hardy pioneers entered upon their task and in the course of a few months had completed a system of irrigation that insured water for their townsite and the adjacent lands as well. The thirsty soil drank ravenously of the life giving stream and in return abundantly rewarded the husbandman for his gift.

A spirit of restlessness and uncertainty gave way to a feeling of permanence and calm. At last the pilgrims had reached the promised land. Beautiful for situation was the newly founded colony. The valley at this point was nearly two miles in width and extended several miles along the picturesque Piedras Verdes River. Off to the west a low range of grass-covered hills skirted the valley. From the crest of these hills and extending westward for several miles

was an undulating expanse of territory, admirably adapted
for grazing purposes, which ended abruptly at the foot of
the Sierra Madre chain. Bordering the east side of the valley and paralleling the river was another bulwark of hills,
beyond which was a broken country with a gradual slope
toward the fertile valley of the Casas Grandes.

Scarcely had the Saints halted at this new townsite
when they began to make preparations to care for the
social, religious and educational needs of the group. The
first step taken, looking toward that end, was the calling
of a public meeting where it was unanimously agreed to
erect at once a community building that would serve the
needs of the people in all of these lines of activity. A committee was appointed to draft a plan for the building and
to supervise its construction. These preliminaries were
attended to on the 9th of January, 1886, and on the 30th
of the same month the structure was ready for use, for
the records show that upon that date the first meeting
was held in the "New meeting house." The brief time
required for its completion by a mere handful of people,
consisting of thirty families, is indicative of the crudeness
of the structure as well as of its dimensions. It was a stockade building with the walls formed of logs set on end,
the interstices being filled with mortar, while the roof and
floor were of dirt. It was diminutive in size, being 18 by
28 feet. The only furniture within were rough benches
made of slabs supported by four legs and having no backs,
a small table and a chair or two.

In this age of palatial structures when school houses
are mainly of brick and marble, an affair such as I have
depicted would to the masses seem contemptuous, but to
those of the frontier whose early years were spent in schools
of adversity, to whom the bare necessities seemed heaven-
sent, that old stockade building calls forth tender memories.

It was within its hallowed walls that many of Life's
best spiritual lessons were taught and found lodgment in
youthful hearts. It was under the shade of that old dirt

roof that some received their first lessons in the funda-
mentals of arithmetic, reading and spelling, but best of all,
within its sacred precincts, there came into the lives of
the pupils an inspiration to push on to higher levels of
intellectual and moral living. As I recall those boyhood
days spent in that stockade building in happy communion
and fellowship with the group of barefoot boys and girls
and under the inspiration of a sympathetic and competent
teacher, I am forcibly reminded that buildings nor equipment make a school. The first teacher to be employed at
Colonia Juarez was Annie M. Romney, a matronly woman
of rare attainments and of considerable experience in the
teaching profession. She had no thought of amassing great
wealth from the position, for she engaged to teach for the
paltry sum of thirty pesos per month and a considerable
portion of her pay was to be in food products and such other
materials as could be produced by the patrons.

The school had an auspicious beginning, all things considered. The records show that there were enrolled at the
outset, sixty pupils—a commendable registration in a community of thirty families and in a country with open win-
ters that will admit of work the whole year round. I may
be pardoned for a slight digression to relate briefly an impressive incident connected with the school: Students were
absorbed with their several duties when suddenly and without warning the walls of the school house began to rock
like a drunken man at sea. To most of the students, unused
to such phenomena, the experience was thrilling and
fraught with terror, but the teacher, preserving her com-
posure, at least outwardly, hurried the children without
to a place of safety until the effects of the shock had
passed. Fortunately the building did not collapse and
when the danger had passed, timidly the pupils followed
their teacher within to supplement their practical experience with a theoretical lesson on the phenomena of earth-
quakes. I presume it is true, at any rate the older heads
declared that the hand of God must have been in the shock,

for the water supply in Piedras Verdes was measurably increased as a result of the physical disturbance.

The recreational activities of the new colony were marked by the usual simplicity and zest characteristic of all the western frontiers. There was no class distinction because there was but one class. The dancing parties largely attended by old and young were scenes of gaiety which might be interpreted by the fastidious as bordering upon levity, but how otherwise could they be when the music, the dirt floor and even the very atmosphere seemed surcharged with wild freedom that gave motion to the feet and unsubdued rhythm to the body. Soul stirring, indeed, were the patriotic celebrations commemorating the achievements of Mexican national heroes. Their valor was extolled both in song and in speech. Honored was he who was called to deliver the principal oration of the day and what a thrill was felt by the young maidens who were so honored as to be appointed to render the national anthem! Not uncommon was it to invite the political officials and other dignitaries of the adjoining municipality to the function and most certain would one of their number find an important place on the patriotic program. The first such festivity recorded, occurred in the month of March a few months following the founding of the colony. Among the visiting guests were the Jefe Politico of Casas Grandes and the Catholic priest. To the Jefe was given the honor of raising the Mexican flag accompanied by hearty cheers from the assembled multitude. Then followed a procession. An oration on Benito Juarez was delivered by Miles P. Romney and other speeches were made by Apostle Erastus Snow, the Jefe, Don Urbano Zubia, Senor Patricio Gomez del Campo, the Padre of Casas Grandes, and A. F. Macdonald. Upon this occasion an event of great significance took place, namely, the dedication of the townsite and the bestowal of its name, Colonia Juarez, in honor of Benito Juarez, the Abraham Lincoln of Mexico. Following the program, the visitors were served a sumptuous repast.

Needless to say the distinguished guests left for home with a fine taste in their mouths for the new founded colony.

The summer of 1886 betokened a glorious future for the settlers on the Piedras Verdes. The crops planted in the early spring had responded vigorously to the enticements of the fertile soil, watered by the refreshing waters of the river and gave promise of well-filled granaries in the fall. The cattle feeding on the luxurious gramma grass covering "a thousand hills," were beginning to look sleek and fat. At this juncture, and in this state of exultation over the prospects of material prosperity, the colonists received the startling news that they were located on a tract of land belonging to the multi-millionaire and ex-governor of Chihuahua, Don Luis Terrazas, and that they must pull up their stakes and remove two miles further up the river.

In their financial distress they had built a dam and dug a canal costing them many hundreds of dollars; they had plowed their ground and planted it to crops and they had erected a number of respectable dwellings and a public building or two. To leave all this without one cent of remuneration except the promise of harvesting their crops was most disheartening, but worst of all they must move up the river to a point where the river valley narrowed down to little more than a canyon, less than one-half mile in width. Whether the occasion of the disappointment resulted from a defective survey or from the consummate selfishness of a dictator whose word was law in Chihuahua, because he claimed the greater part of it, is perhaps not definitely known, but move the colonists must.

As a preliminary to the removal, A. F. Macdonald began the survey of the new townsite on November 3, 1886, and on the 6th of the same month he initiated the survey of a canal to convey water to the site. Within one year the canal, three miles in length, had been completed at a cost of three thousand dollars. On the 1st day of the year 1887, Apostles Snow and Thatcher, with others, drove on to the new townsite and dedicated it to be a gathering place for the Saints down the river. The same name that had been given to the colony, soon to be deserted, was bestowed upon the one soon to be established. Erastus Snow in the afternoon meeting referred to the conniving which resulted in the loss of their lands below as a betrayal analagous to betrayals of General Benito Juarez. Further he stated: "No man will hold an individual title to real estate, for when he apostatizes we do not want him to dwell in our land."

Immediately following the dedication, Sixtus Johnson moved to "New" Colonia Juarez. Soon thereafter came Helaman Pratt, Franklin Spencer, Ira B. Elmer, A. F. Macdonald, Miles P. Romney, and Isaac Turley. Before the close of 1887, many things had been done to change the face of things. Water had been brought to the townsite and a movement towards its beautification had set in. A good substantial building known as a Tithing office had been completed and for the present was to serve as a "Community Center." A road had been built from the colony to the Corrales Basin in the tops of the Sierra Madre Range to tap an extensive timber belt. The road, which passed up the picturesque and rugged San Diego Canyon, was built at great expense. With its completion a saw mill was installed in the Corrales Basin on a cooperative plan, costing $2400. Work on the mill was evaluated at the rate of $2.00 per day, Mexican money. This was the beginning of saw mill construction in the Sierra Madres that extended over a broad area and resulted in the manufacture of millions of feet of lumber and great quantities of shingles, used not only in the construction of the Mexican colonies, but also shipped in vast quantities to different parts of the United States.

Shortly after the removal to the new townsite a bishopric was appointed to preside over the colony, consisting of George W. Sevey as Bishop and Miles P. Romney and Ernest L. Taylor as his counsellors. Apostles of the Church in charge of all the Mormon Colonies in Mexico at this time were Erastus Snow, assisted by Moses Thatcher and George Teasdale. Later, with the death of Erastus Snow, which occurred while on a visit to Utah, and the return of Moses Thatcher to his home in Logan, Utah, Elder Teasdale became president of the Mexican Mission, which comprised not only the Mormon Colonies in northern Mexico, but in a general way over all the branches of the Church in and about the City of Mexico.

The missionary work in central Mexico at this stage was making considerable headway. Many converts had become affiliated with the Church, a large percentage of whom were of the poorer class. With the thought of bettering their financial condition the Church authorized the colonization of a group of the native converts in northern Chihuahua among the colonists from the States. It was felt that if they had the example of industry and thrift of a more industrious people constantly before them they would, at least in a measure, imbibe economic principles and social standards far in advance of anything they had before known. A company of these people, therefore, left Mexico City and its environs under the leadership of Elder Helaman Pratt, acting mission president, arriving in Colonia Juarez, May 10th, 1887. They were distributed among several of the colonies but the conditions among which they had come were so different from what they were accustomed to or had anticipated that the majority of the 41 who had come became discouraged and left soon for their former habitat. No further attempts were made by the Church to remove the people from their original homes.

Early in its history, Colonia Juarez, far more than any other of the Mormon colonies in Mexico, caught the spirit of industrialism. This resulted from the fact that her irrigable land was very limited, making it necessary for her residents to look to other channels than farming for a livelihood. The year following the removal to the new townsite, Bishop George W. Sevey established a tannery which very soon became a cooperative institution. The leather produced was of good quality though lacking the finish of the high-grade leathers produced in the United States. The colony was fortunate in having men skilled in the art of making shoes who could transform the raw material into footwear that would meet the needs and desires of all save the most fastidious. This industry was a great boon to the colonists since it kept thousands of dollars at home that would have otherwise gone to foreign countries, and furnished footwear much cheaper than could be imported, because of the exorbitant duties imposed on foreign made shoes. In 1889 a roller flour mill was installed and operated under the direction of its owner, W. R. R. Stowell. The machinery, which was of very high grade, had been selected with care in the city of Indianapolis, Indiana.

In 1890, a cooperative mercantile establishment was installed with Henry Eyring as general manager and Miles P. Romney, president. A small store had been set up in 1886, by E. L. Taylor and George Sevey, but they disposed of their stock of goods to the Cooperative Mercantile Company. The new store entered upon a period of prosperity.

A canning factory was built in 1892, and placed under the management of Joseph C. Bentley. The year following its establishment, 5,000 cans of fruit and an equal number of cans of tomatoes were put up and shipped to the city of Chihuahua and other parts of Mexico. The cans were manufactured in Colonia Juarez. The fruits that found ready market were peaches, plums, pears, grapes and berries, all of which were produced in great abundance at Colonia Juarez. Andrew Jensen, assistant Church historian, gives his impressions of Colonia Juarez as he saw it in 1894; "Juarez sustains a well-deserved reputation for possessing fine brick residences, thrifty orchards and beautiful flower gardens. It is said to be the best built town in the State of Chihuahua. * * * There are perhaps no better fruit lands in Northern Chihuahua, but the facilities for farming are very limited as the water is scarce. The stock range is fairly good." He reported that there were in the colony "one grist mill, a cannery, a tannery and harness shop, two shoeshops, a saw mill, a planing mill, a cheese factory, a cooperative store, and other institutions, most of them on a cooperative plan."

Reporting the social and moral condition he stated that the inhabitants were generally good and industrious, and that all were members of the Mormon Church. "Not an oath," he declared, "or expression of profanity has been heard on the streets by even some of the oldest inhabitants, and there are only three young men in town who are known to use tobacco in any shape or form. Neither has ever anybody been drunk on the streets of Juarez."

A correspondent under the title "Sierra Madre" addressed a letter to the Deseret News, December 3, 1893, in which he reported that $6,000 worth of cheese had been produced for export and that the "barns are full and stacks are plentiful on the outside." He reported also the organization of a Board of Trade, August 26, 1893, whose officers were nominated for three months. Joseph C. Bentley was made business manager, George W. Sevey, president of the Board and Helaman Pratt, vice-president. Referring to the social conditions, he says, "No profanity exists here within our gates, nor saloons for drinking, nor Sabbath breaking. Socially our young people are a credit to their parents and an honor to the Church."

CHAPTER VIII

THE FOUNDING OF COLONIA DUBLAN

Colonia Dublan, the largest of the Mormon colonies in Mexico, could be said to have had its beginnings in the latter part of the year 1888. It was then that George M. Brown, whose home was at Provo, Utah, negotiated with a German-Mexican by the name of Lewis Huller for a 73,000 acre tract of land in the Casas Grandes Valley about five or six miles down the river from the settlement of Casas Grandes.

Mr. Huller had promised to let Mr. Brown have the property on easy terms provided he could induce five hundred colonists of good repute to come in and settle on the land. Mr. Brown succeeded in stirring up considerable enthusiasm in the deal, resulting in several hundred people investing their money in the purchase. The first man to locate on the tract was George Lake, a Mormon colonist, who had some time before established himself at Casas Grandes. He came in the latter part of 1888 and the next spring others followed. Imagine the disappointment of the home seekers, however, when they discovered that, due to the insolvency of Mr. Huller and his agents, titles to the land could not be furnished them. Already they had made a payment on the property with the understanding that the balance due would be payed on easy intsallments. But since they could not secure the land they were most fortunate in having their money refunded. Nothing was left now for them to do but to rent from the native population or make individual purchases of Mexican lands. The planting season was now on and if they were to realize a harvest that year no time was to be lost. Accordingly those who were financially able purchased lands, while others had to content themselves with temporary leases, the use of the land to be paid for chiefly from the products of the soil.

The lands purchased were mainly "terrenos" that had been cultivated by the Mexicans for many years and extended outward from the east bank of the Casas Grandes River to an established line drawn through the valley. The "terrenos" were uniform in width but varied in length from one-half mile to two miles, the distance being determined by the bends in the river. Practically all of this land was irrigable and the water supply was raised from the river by means of dams that forced the water into canals which, in turn, conveyed the water to the thirsty land. The prices paid for these river bottom lands were determined not so much from the nature of the soil as from the value placed upon them by the several owners. They were worth usually just what the owners asked for them and what the purchasers were willing to pay. Prices ranged from about fifty dollars per acre to one hundred and fifty dollars, including the water right, these prices to be met in terms of Mexican Currency. When the fertility of the soil is taken into account these prices seem not at all exorbitant for there is perhaps not to be found more productive soil anywhere in Mexico than the land lying along the banks of the Casas Grandes River. Referring to the fertility of the soil in this valley an informed writer says: "We have seen many fields of corn where the stocks would average, the whole field through, twelve feet in height and a person on foot could reach but few of the ears without bending down the stocks." And he might, with due regard for the truth, have added that the ears of corn were almost as long as a man's arm from the points of the fingers to the elbow.

The Huller tract lay to the east of these lands individually purchased and, generally speaking, was of lighter soil, much of it being of a sandy loam. Eventually this property fell into the hands of the Mormons as I have indicated in a previous chapter. The water for the land was taken from the Casas Grandes River and conveyed by a huge canal into a couple of lakes or reservoirs which had likely been used for irrigation purposes by prehistoric peoples centuries before. I can scarcely conceive of a more splendid system of irrigation anywhere to be found, in the interests of efficiency and economy. The water that is poured into the reservoir represents a surplus which rushes down from the mountains above during the time of the rainy season. Here it is conserved to be utilized only at a time and under conditions when it will be most helpful to the crops.

Colonia Dublan is located approximately one hundred and fifty miles south from Deming, New Mexico, and nearly a hundred and seventy miles from El Paso, Texas. At the time of its founding, the nearest railroad point was Gallego, a small station on the Mexican Central railroad, one hundred and ten miles away. To make the trip there and return by team and wagon required about eight days of tedious travel and since a large percentage of the merchandise consumed must be imported from the United States, the task of supplying the demands of the colonists was not an easy one.

But a city so ideally located was not long to remain in isolation. In 1897, a railroad was built from Cuidad Juarez, opposite El Paso, to a point twelve miles beyond Dublan to a ranch belonging to Don Luis Terrazas, called "San Diego." Here sprang up a little town known as Pearson, later to become the site of a huge saw mill owned by the Pearson Company. Later the track was completed into the mountains, the idea being to tap one of the finest timber belts on the North American Continent. But the Revolution blasted the fond hopes of the company. The mill and other properties of the company were damaged or destroyed and the promoters were forced to abandon the project.

The railroad proved to be of immeasurable value to Dublan for now goods could be transported with speed from the United States to the Colony and, in addition, it offered greater facilities for the marketing of dairy and agricultural products supplied by the settlers.

7

The growth of Dublan was healthy but not phenomenal, and yet, had it not been interrupted in its development
it seems probable that it would have become one of the
most prosperous and influential cities of the State. At the
time of the Exodus, it had a population of more than twelve
hundred, but its size gives but little hint of its material
prosperity as expressed in its beautiful brick homes and
pleasant surroundings. These would have done credit to
a city of much greater proportions.

Dublan was fundamentally an agricultural settlement,
having but few facilities upon which to found an industrial
prosperity. Yet, her merchandising activity was such as
to justify a word of explanation and even of commenda-
tion.

The first store to be built was owned and operated
by John McFarland and was opened in August, 1891. It
flourished but a brief period when, for some good reason,
it closed its doors to be followed by another store, established by Anson B. Call and Joseph C. Bentley, in 1893.
Later the Union Mercantile, a co-operative department
store of large dimensions, came into being under the business
management of Henry E. Bowman, a man of considerable
experience and of no mean ability. Its trade was not confined to local people but extended far into the interior of
the country, resulting in returns, enriching not only its
many stock holders, but placing the prices of goods within
the reach of the masses. The Franklin D. Haymore Mercantile establishment, likewise of big proportions, proved
to be another fine asset to the community as did also the
Romney-Farnsworth store, established some time later.

In the early days of the colonies the Mormon people
were under the necessity of eating chiefly corn bread since
the price of flour rendered "white" bread almost prohibitive. Flour from the "States" was exorbitant in price owing
to the excessive freight rates and the outrageous duty on
foreign importations. Cheaper flour manufactured by the
Mexicans was obtainable but its quality generally was such

as to render it undesirable.   It was dark and sticky and frequently full of grit.

The advent of a first class flour mill installed by Colonist W. R. Stowell at Colonia Juarez was therefore, a great boon, not only to the residents of the colony in which it was built, but to the colonists throughout Chihuahua generally.   Of prime importance to the people of Dublan was the flour mill, a little later constructed by Joseph Jackson, a citizen of Colonia Dublan.   Jackson's mill was conceded to be the finest institution of its kind in the state of Chihuahua.   Thanks to these two men, flour could now be purchased right at home equal to any to be procured in the United States and, in addition, the farmers were given increased market for their grain.   Other sources of considerable gain to the people of Dublan were their dairy products, such as butter and cheese.   These could be produced in large quantities owing to the splendid grazing facilities and to the adaptability of both soil and climate to the production of alfalfa and other kinds of feed.

But the material interests of the people did not take precedence over the cultural and spiritual things.   Even in the very early stages of community living, the colonists of Dublan sensed the importance of the spiritual life.   Before an ecclesiastical organization had been effected the group would meet together to sing and pray and listen to the elders expound the scriptures and extol the mercies of God in their behalf.   These early gatherings would convene at the home a fellow churchman, Mr. Lake, and usually were under the supervision of Charles A. Foster, their spiritual leader by common consent.

It is important to know at this point that in its very early history, this settlement was known as "Colonia Huller" and by that designation it was known until it was given an ecclesiastical organization on April 14th, 1889, when its name was changed to the "San Francisco Branch" and became attached to the Juarez ward.   Frederick W. Jones was appointed by Bishop George W. Sevey of Colonia

Juarez to preside, to be assisted by James H. Carlton and Charles A. Foster. The organization persisted but a short time when the community was evolved into a ward with Winslow Farr as the Bishop and Frederick G. Williams and Phillip H. Hurst as his counsellors. Harry M. Payne was sustained as Ward Clerk. At the time of this organization, the name of the colony was changed to "Colonia Dublan" in honor of the secretary of the Federal Treasury.

It is pleasing to note that all of the auxiliaries common to a ward were set in motion at this time with able men and women placed to preside over them. The Relief Society was given as its presidency, Julia M. Jones, President, with Lydia K. Young and Ella Hurst as her counsellors. Samuel J. Robinson was chosen Superintendent of the Sunday School and was given as assistants, Harry M. Payne and Joseph S. Cardon. Those chosen to take the leadership in the Young Men's Mutual Improvement Association were M. C. Sorensen as Preisdent, to be assisted by Joseph H. Wright and Nathan C. Robinson. Minnie Robinson, assisted by Dora Pratt and Elizabeth Farr, were entrusted with the care of the Young Ladies organization, while Lydia K. Young, assisted by Josepha Wright and Julia M. Jones, were called to preside over the primary association.

The first Church house to be built was rather meager and was merely a temporary abode to be used until something better could be substituted. In the following year (1891) another building was planned and three years later was completed. This edifice served the needs of the community well until the time of the exodus, when it was burned to the ground by the Rebels. With the return of some of the Mormons to the colony after the exodus, a beautiful chapel was constructed at a cost of $25,000, nearly one-half of which was contributed by the Church from its tithing.

The educational and recreational needs of the community were likewise well provided for as was the case in the other colonies of Mexico. Competent teachers were employed whose training had been received in some of the best schools of the United States. Their salaries were low but they refused to allow that fact to influence them in the quality of service rendered, unless it served as a stimulus to greater effort.

Things were looking rosy for the colony and the people were planning for a greater city, when the Revolution raised its head and, like a fiery serpent, drove them from their homes.

CHAPTER IX

THE FOUNDING OF THE MOUNTAIN COLONIES

Geographically and topographically the colonies of Mexico could appropriately be listed under the following divisions; mountain, plateau and Sonoran. The plateau group comprised the colonies of Juarez, Dublan and Diaz all of which nestled in the valley of the Casas Grandes and its tributary. The sources of this stream are the towering peaks and jagged canyons of the Sierra Madres. From these mountain fastnesses the river, by a circuitous route makes its way to the plateau below whose elevation varies between 4,000 and 6,000 feet. This region constitutes a portion of a great area to be found in Mexico and is known as the Tierra Templada (temperate lands). In the main it is a treeless region except along the water courses where cottonwood and willows thrive luxuriously. These streams with their timber decorations furnish the only variety to an otherwise monotonous expanse of boundless grass-covered plains and rolling hills.

The mountain colonies consisted of Cave Valley, Pacheco, Garcia and Chuichupa, whose altitudes varied between 6,000 and 8,000 feet. Without exception these settlements were situated in timber areas consisting largely of pine and oak from which the inhabitants wrested a large portion of their living. The Sonoran colonies of which there were two, were situated on the Bavispe, a tributary of the well known Yaqui River, whose waters pour into the Pacific Ocean. The flora of this region is in marked contrast to that of the other two divisions, being semi-tropical in character.

With this general characterization I now pass to a brief consideration of each of the mountain colonies.

Cave Valley

This name is appropriately given to the settlement due to its close proximity to a series of caves that had been used by a prehistoric people as places in which to live. The caves were walled up at the mouth, having openings through which to enter and exit and two or three port holes. Within, the caves were partitioned off into rooms, the number being largely determined by the size of the cave. The outstanding one is the "Olla Cave," situated half way up a gigantic cliff, the entrance to it being about 200 feet above the bed of the creek below. The entrance is reached by climbing over the face of a sloping ledge for a considerable distance. The mouth of the cave is about 18 by 50 feet and the cave itself is about 200 feet in length. It contains a number of dwellings, some of them being two stories high. One of the buildings was evidently used for public worship and immediately in front of it stood what appears to have been an altar. An Olla—a great earthen vessel, whose circumference is 35 ft. and reaching from the floor to the ceiling, was built within the cave and was likely used for the storing of grain, though some have conjectured that it was used for the storing of water in times of a siege.

Cave Valley was located in a tract of territory purchased by Moses Thatcher, who felt that it would be a splendid range for cattle and would produce large revenues from its timber. The town was begun in 1887, and was built on a small stream which empties into the Piedras Verdes River from the north. The tributary furnished water for culinary purposees and for the gardens while the water of the Piedras Verdes was used to irrigate the farm lands. The town was laid off into blocks 16 by 24 rods with three lots in a block. The two principal streets were four rods wide while the cross streets were one rod narrower. The farming land was limited to few acres but was very fertile and was especially adapted to the raising of small grain, potatoes, and other vegetables. The first colonists to locate here came from Colonia Juarez to settle the Corrales Basin about eight miles away, but in a few days some of the group left and came to Cave Valley to establish homes. Among the number were George C. Williams, John Kartchner, John Rencher, Peter Dillman, Price Nelson, Price Nelson, Jr., Hyrum Nelson, and Joseph Moffatt, most of whom brought their families. In the early summer of 1887, Apostle Erastus Snow visited the infant colony and organized it into a branch of the Juarez ward and appointed Price Nelson, Jr., to be the presiding elder. A Sunday school was organized soon thereafter with John Rencher as superintendent. The sacrament meetings, Sunday school and day school, all of which were in operation immediately after the founding of the settlement, met, of necessity, in the shade of the pines. In 1889, the Relief Society, Primary and Young Men's Mutual Improvement Association were organized. The Young Women's Mutual Improvement Association was not set up until three years later, due to the limited number of young ladies in the community. During those three years the young women were to meet jointly with the young men. Dora W. Pratt was the first president of the Relief Society at Cave Valley and was assisted by Lydia Nelson and Annie Williams. John T. Whetton, assisted by James M. Nelson and Gaskell Romney, constituted the first presidency of the Young Men's organization, while Christina Heaton served as president of the Young Women's Association and was assisted by Charlotte Carroll and Mary R. Jensen. Olive Moffatt was the first president of the Primary Association at Cave Valley, her counsellor being Martha Dillman.

Industrially there was but little development in the colony due, chiefly, to its limited population. However, a saw mill was set up in 1889, but a few years later it was removed to Pacheco. A pair of burrs were brought in by the first group of settlers and were attached to the saw mill, but in 1891, a grist mill was built and these burrs became a part of its equipment. The following year a shingle mill was attached to the grist mill.

Discouragements came to the colony and many of its residents moved to other parts so that by 1894 there were only ten families left or a total population of eighty-one.

An interesting feature of Cave Valley history was the attempt made to live the "United Order" sometimes referred to as "Community ownership of property." The United Order was revealed to the Church during the first years of its existence. As early as February, 1831, the founder of Mormonism received a revelation commanding him to provide for the financial support of the needy of the Church by introducing an order of community life to be known as the "Law of Consecration" or the "United Order." It was designated that all of the membership of the Church having properties should turn them over to the Church and then receive back a portion thereof as a stewardship to be used wisely for the support of themselves and families. In the event of an accumulated surplus it was turned over to the Presiding Bishop of the Church to be used for the benefit of the poor and for such other purposes as the Lord might designate. "Inasmuch as they receive more than is needful for their necessities and their wants, it shall be given into my storehouse, and the benefits shall be consecrated unto the inhabitants of Zion; and unto their generations, inasmuch as they become heirs according to the laws of the kingdom."

The nature of each man's stewardship would be determined by his ability to administer it. Under this order of community life there would be need for all of the varying grades of occupation—the engineers, mechanics, farmers, artists, artisans, authors, professors, doctors and even the common laborers. Every man as far as possible would be expected to fit into the particular niche which nature and training had best fitted him to fill. The important thing was that there should be no drones in "Zion." The edict of the Almighty was: "Thou shalt not be idle, for he that is idle shall not eat the bread nor wear the garment of the laborer. The idler shall not have a place in the Church, except he repents and mends his ways."

This law was to apply to all having a Church membership as indicated by the following: "And behold none shall be exempt from this law who belong to the Church of the living God * * * for acording to the law every man that cometh up to Zion must lay all things before the bishop in Zion. Yea, neither the bishop, neither the agent who keepeth the Lord's storehouse, neither he who is appointed in a stewardship over temporal things" was to be exempt.

The purpose of this "order" was not only to provide for the needs of the poor but it was also to establish and maintain a standard of economic and spiritual equality among the membership of the Church. In the language of the revelation it was revealed "That you may be equal in the bands of heavenly things; yea, and earthly things also, * * * for if ye are not equal in earthly things, ye cannot be equal in obtaining heavenly things."

But the observance of this law was cut short by the weaknesses of man. As early as 1834, the Lord declared through revelation that some were not faithful in their stewardships and as a result He had cursed them with a "very sore and grievous curse." He furthermore declared that "The covenants being broken through transgression, by covetousness and feigned words; therefore, you are dissolved as a United Order with your brethren * * * only by loan as shall be agreed by this order in Council, as your circumstances will admit and the voice of the council direct."

It was no easy matter for them to turn over all their properties to the Church, receive the whole or a portion thereof back as a "stewardship" and then turn back the surplus accumulations from the stewardship into the coffers of the Church. Years later another attempt was made by certain communities of Latter-day Saints in Utah and Arizona to live the "Order" but after a few years the

principle was again abandoned but was reestablished at
Cave Valley by a group of people who had lived in it at
Orderville in Southern Utah.

For the enlightenment of the reader I submit in detail
the articles of agreement drawn up and entered into by
those who accepted this "communal order" at Cave Valley.

Articles of Agreement

January 9, 1893.

1. We, the undersigned, covenant to unite our temporal interests for the common benefit.

2. We will be known as the Cave Valley Commonwealth. Our organization can only be dissolved by the
Council of the Presidency of this Mexican Mission of the
Church of Jesus Christ of Latter-day Saints and a majority
vote of the organization.

3. We shall adopt for our guidance the rules known
as rules that should be observed by members of the United
Order.

4. This shall be a stewardship system. Its officers shall
be, President, two counsellors, a secretary and treasurer
and a board of directors.

5. Property shall be appraised and credited to those
contributing, the same as capital stock, which capital stock
shall not be added to by dividend, nor diminished by assessment during the time of our continuing in an organized
capacity.

6. Members desiring to withdraw shall not have power
to compel the company to deliver up their capital stock
till the end of three years, but the company may do so if
the board so decides, which decision must be presented
and sustained by a ¾ vote of the majority.

7. There shall be no shares of capital stock, but each
shall receive credit in dollars and cents for the amount
turned in.

8. We shall have a scrip or circulation medium, good

only to members of our commonwealth, and members will be paid in this scrip pro-rata for their support.

9. Membership in the Church and Commonwealth constitute eligibility to vote for the election of officers, which voting shall be done by uplifted hands.

10. Only authorized agents shall have power to do business in the company's name or with company property.

11. Offenders shall be handled for the offense within one month of the time of the offense becoming known, or [charges] shall not thereafter be brought against them. We do not assume authority to handle Church cases in a company capacity.

12. Members shall be received by the common consent and vote of the commonwealth, and membership withdrawn in the same way.

13. Members shall not receive any advantage one above another by any system of credits.

Andrew Jensen, Assistant Church Historian, who visited Cave Valley in 1894, stated that "all share alike of everything produced according to the number in each family. Facilities are limited for a large settlement but there is room for a few more."

Colonia Pacheco

Colonia Pacheco, named in honor of a famous Mexican General, was established in the tops of the Sierra Madre nearly seven thousand feet above the sea. It occupied a picturesque spot in a little valley known as the Corrales Basin.

This tract was purchased by agents of the Church after it had been carefully explored in 1885. The irrigable land was not extensive though the timber was abundant and the prospects looked fairly inviting to the cattle man, but the project was not one of such magnitude that the most sanguine could hope for a large population to migrate thither.

The first prospective settlers came in the spring of 1887, the vanguard being the "preaching parson," George C. Williams, who came on horseback, accompanied by his son-in-law, Peter Dillman, driving the wagon. Immediate preparations were made to plant potatoes and other vegetables adapted to a mountain climate. Seven days later, April 27th, others entered the valley, among whom were Jesse N. Smith, Jr., John Kartchner, Price Nelson, and sons, John Rencher, and Ira L. Wilson. Accompanying these men, in most instances, were their families. The day following their arrival the irrigable land was being surveyed into smal units 3½ and 5 acres in extent with the thought of having all share equally in choice land. One month later the water had been conveyed from the river on to the land and to all appearances the group had come to stay, but beneath the surface there were forces at work that resulted in temporarily uprooting the colony. Parson Williams had purchased land in the lower end of Cave Valley some eight miles distant and was using his influence to have the colonists settle there. Representatives were sent to inspect conditions and returned with such glowing reports that in the course of a few days the newly formed colony was deserted. This action greatly displeased Apostle Erastus Snow and through his influence a number of the families returned to the Corrales Basin and took up their labors where they had left them off. Others came in and ere long there was developed a thriving settlement that persisted until the time of the Exodus. Following the custom of the other colonies a school house was built in the spring of 1890, and in the latter part of the year, Pacheco was organized into a branch of the Juarez ward, with Jesse N. Smith as presiding elder. In the meantime a small settlement had been established at Corrales a short distance from Pacheco and the six families there had built a small gathering place of logs. In 1891, Pacheco was organized into a ward by Elder Moses Thatcher and Jesse N. Smith, Jr., was appointed to be the Bishop. Called to assist him as counsellors were James Sellers and Christopher B. Heaton. In 1895, Jesse N. Smith, Jr., moved from the colony and his position was filled by George Hardy. In 1908, a new meeting house was built, costing in the neighborhood of $12,000, truly a splendid monument to the industry of a handful of people.

The prosperity of Pacheco is referred to in a letter adddressed to the Deseret News in October, 1897. Says the correspondent: "In Pacheco apple trees for the first time are coming into bearing. Strawberries and blackberries produce wonderfully in quantity and quality." He states that the largest cabbages he has ever seen were growing at Corrales and that "sorghum cane, vegetables, corn and oats do well in the valley."

Garcia or Round Valley

The founders of Garcia were Alonzo L. Farnsworth and wife and children who arrived in what is known as Round Valley on March 1, 1894.

The Valley, as the name implies, forms almost a complete circle and when the first colonists arrived it was a veritable paradise of waving grass and beautiful flowers. Surrounding the valley was a forest of pines, whose trappings of green formed a beautiful background to the variegated colors of the encircled meadow. The valley contains about 1300 acres of the choicest land imaginable, but its altitude of more than seven thousand feet brings early and late frosts that frequently threaten and occasionally cut down the harvest before it has reached maturity.

By December of 1895, a sufficient number of settlers had arrived in the valley to justify the organizing of a branch of the Church. This was attended to by Elder Francis M. Lyman of the Council of the Twelve, with the assistance of President Ivins. Present also was Edward Stevenson of the First Council of Seventy, whose home was in Salt Lake City. John T. Whetten was selected as presiding elder and Alonzo L. Farnsworth and Brigham H. Bingham were to act as counsellors. On January 5, the following year the Sunday School was organized with Orson Cluff as superintendent, and the Relief Society with Agnes Macdonald as president, while Hyrum Cluff was called to the leadership of the Mutual Improvement Association.

The houses were built chiefly of logs and adobes, both of which were cheap and very serviceable.

On February 7, 1898, President Anthony W. Ivins and A. F. Macdonald visited Telesforo Garcia in Mexico City and negotiated for the transfer of the Garcia lands to the Mexican Colonization and Agricultural Company. Garcia allowed the forty-three colonists a small bounty on their colonization papers amounting to $124.23. The balance due on the land at this time amounted to $1,987.50, which was paid to Mr. Garcia by President Ivins, representing the Mexican Colonization and Agricultural Company.

On March 9, 1898, Apostles John Henry Smith and John W. Taylor visited Garcia and organized it into a ward. John T. Whetten was sustained as the Bishop and the counsellors selected were Vance Shaffer and James A. Macdonald.   In addition to farming the people engaged in the cattle, lumber, and shingle business. The lumber and shingles not used for home consumption were freighted in wagons to the colonies below the mountains or were delivered at Pearson, a railroad station near Colonia Juarez, to be shipped out of the country. This was a hard life owing to the mountainous character of the road and the exposure to all kinds of weather. The distance from Garcia to Colonia Juarez was thirty-five miles while Dublan lay sixteen miles beyond. In the event of the lumber being taken to Diaz a further haul of about fifty or sixty miles must be made.

Another distressing and expensive feature of the life lived in these mountain colonies was the freighting of all the flour and other merchandise consumed by the settlers, from the valley below up the steep winding canyon road to the top of the Sierras and thence on to its destination over a road that today would seem impassable. The women shared with the men many of the hardships of the mountain life, in most instances with a patience and fortitude seldom witnessed in men. As I contemplate their life of toil and struggle and their deprivation of even the bare necessities in the home I am led to glorify the name of woman.

Chuichupa

The name "Chuichupa" means in the Indian tongue, "The place of the mist." The title is not inappropriately applied to this little Mormon colony situated on the great back bone of the Sierra Madre Range which divides the waters that flow into the Pacific from the streams that find their way into the Gulf of Mexico far to the east. Eight thousand feet above the sea level, she nestles among the forests grown hoary with age and receives to her bosom the crystal streams as they pass from their haunts above on their way to join the mighty ocean. The streams teem with mountain trout[1] and the forests are alive with wild game of all varieties to tempt the hunter from nearly every land. Here feeds the deer while the turkey cock gobbles and struts about. Not far away are the bear and the cougar seeking their pray while myriads of birds with their variegated plumages flit from bough to bough undisturbed by the cracking of timber and other noises from below.

Chuichupa lies near the western border of Chihuahua, eighty-five miles southwest of Casas Grandes, thirty-five miles south of Garcia, and in the same direction, from Pacheco, forty-five miles. It is typically a dairy country though oats, potatoes and many other varieties of vegetables are profitably raised and that, too, in many instances without irrigation.

---

[1]Some idea of these mountain colonies as a fisherman's paradise may be gained from a report given me by an old friend, Theodore Martineau, a one time resident of this region. Mr. Martineau affirms that upon one occasion he pulled from a stream 300 beautiful trout in four hours' time.

The founding of the colony occurred in April, 1894, when Benjamin Johnson, Edwin H. Austin, James H. Carlton and son, Ben L. Johnson and Wallace Edwin Staley of Colonia Dublan pitched camp here in search of a new home and a few days later were joined by Sixtus Johnson, David E. Johnson and John McNeil.

The name first applied to the new colony was Mariano but soon it was changed to Chuichupa by which designation it has been known to the present. As in the case of the Garcia tract, the Chuichupa purchase was made from Mr. Garcia of Mexico City. And as the titles to the Garcia lands were transferred to the Mexican Colonization and Agricultural Company through the instrumentality of President Ivins in order to save the property to the colonists who had fallen behind in their payments—so was a transfer of title to the Chuichupa tract secured by the same company through President Ivins for the same purpose. The acreage under the Chuichupa purchase totaled 6,250 and cost the settler 40 cents per acre in gold.

The ecclesiastical organization of Chuichupa evolved in the same order as was characteristic of the other colonies —from the simple to the complex. Sixtus Johnson presided over the group from the time of his arrival in the spring of 1894, until June 9, 1895, when he was succeeded by Benjamin J. Johnson who bore the title of presiding elder. As a branch of the Church, Chuichupa was attached to the Pacheco ward until Garcia was advanced to the status of a ward in 1898, when it was transferred to the Garcia ward. Such was its status until it became a ward in November, 1900. The ward organization was effected under the direction of Apostle Abraham O. Woodruff and members of the Stake Presidency, Anthony W. Ivins and Helaman Pratt. George M. Haws was honored with the poistion of bishop while his counsellors were Benjamin J. Johnson and Samuel J. Brown. The auxiliaries were completely organized with the following men and women in charge.

8

Isabel M. Johnson was called to preside over the Relief Society with Lena Brown and Sara Martineau to serve as counsellors. The Sunday School was placed under the leadership of Henry A. Martineau, superintendent, and John W. Brown and Francis L. Johnson as his assistants. The Young Men's organization had as its president Joel H. Martineau, who was assisted by Samuel Brown and George A. Martineau, while the Young Women's Association had as its presiding officers Sarah E. Russell, president, and Sarah E. Brown and Mary E. Christiansen as her assistants. Arletta Cox was called to act as president of the Primary Association and was to be assisted by Nora Carlton and Alice Judd.

CHAPTER X

THE FOUNDING OF THE SONORA COLONIES

Oaxaca

Had it not been for the perpetual Indian troubles in Sonora it seems probable that this state, rather than Chihuahua, would have been the seat of the first Mormon settlements. It will be remembered that very early in the period of Mormon exploration in Mexico several expeditions were sent into the state to locate suitable lands for settlement, but in each case, untoward circumstances arose that influenced the general authorities of the Church to pass unfavorably upon the proposal to establish colonies in that region for the time being.

The purchase of about 200 square miles of territory along the banks of the Bavispe River by George C. Williams and John C. Naegle in 1892, marked the serious beginning of colonization in Sonora. Resulting from this purchase, was the establishment thereon of a colony named in honor of President Diaz's natal state, "Oaxaca". At the time of the purchase, this locality was known as "Los Horcones" (the forks) so called because of there being in the vicinity a certain large mesquite tree with unusual forks. Following the purchase the new town site was called "Fenochio" to honor General Fenochio, a party to the sale, but this name persisted only for a few months when it was displaced by the designation of "Oaxaca".

The founders of Oaxaca may be said to be a company recruited from several of the Chihuahua colonies, notably from the mountain districts. Leader of the group was "Parson Williams", chief purchaser of the land and accompanying him were Peter Dillman, Robert E. Vance, W. B. Millet, Martin Mortenson, Sixtus E. Johnson, Oscar Gruell, William B. Maxwell, James H. Carlton, John McNeil, Alvin D. Nelson, Harlem Johnson, John Nichols, James H.

Martineau and his daughter Anna and sons Moroni, and
Theodore, John Bloomfield and two sons, David Johnson
and a son and a daughter, D. Biglow and Mrs. J. M. Nelson
and J. W. Ray. Fourteen of the number had their families,
the whole company numbering 100 souls. The first part
of the group left William's Ranch on February 20, 1892,
and at intervals along the way their numbers were augmented until, by the time they had reached the Beresford
ranch beyond the Janos River, the company was complete.
There were fourteen wagons in all and twenty-two men
and boys to do the work. The distance to be traveled to
reach their destination was in the neighborhood of one
hundred and fifty miles from the point of beginning. With
a good road this distance could have soon been covered,
but the journey proved to be a tedious one, since a big part
of the way was through a mountainous country never before traversed by lumber wagons or vehicles of any sort.
Dugways must be built and rocks and brush had to be
cleared away before the caravan could proceed. In some
instances the wagons were prevented from overturning
only by having men heave on ropes that had been fastened
to the upper side of the wagon boxes. At other times trees
were fastened to the backs of the wagons to ease them down
the steep declivities where brakes were entirely inadequate.
Finally the herculean task was completed. On the 14th
of March the vanguard of the expedition, consisting of two
wagons driven by William B. Maxwell and Robert E.
Vance, emerged from the winding canyon of the foothills
into the picturesque valley of the Bavispe and the journey
was practically at an end. The day following the balance
of the party likewise emerged and that night around the
camp fire they planned for the future. The valley into
which these pioneers had come had for centuries been the
scene of thriving native villages. There was Baserac with
its 2,000 souls not more than 50 miles away and twelve
miles nearer was Bavispe, only one half as large, and still
closer was San Miguel with its 500 inhabitants. These

people through their officials extended the hand of fellowship to this band of weary pilgrims. The Presidente and other leading officials of Bavispe came out to meet them and with expressions of good will presented them with three beeves as tangible evidence of their sincerity. Colonel Kosterlitzky, who later visited their camp, complimented the colonists by remarking that the 3,800 men in the Bavispe district would have failed to accomplish as much in three months as this handful of men had done in a few weeks.

A most difficult problem confronting the band of home seekers was the question of a suitable spot on which to build their city. The area purchased consisted largely of grazing land, and the little land suitable for cultivation (approximately 1800 acres) was cut into 13 fragments by the winding course of the Bavispe. Its tortuous route can, in a measure, be realized by the reader when informed that the waters of the Bavispe travel the distance of 400 miles from Oaxaca to reach the Yaqui river while the direct distance is not more than 80 miles. Not only did the small parcels of suitable land make the choice a difficult one, but members of the group were not immune to selfishness and it, in a measure, influenced them in their judgment. The result was that two or three temporary camps were pitched before the final selection was made. It was not until December 25, 1893, that the choice was made and on the following day the survey was begun by John Rencher. The blocks as surveyed contained five acres cut into four lots each, while the streets were also laid out on a broad scale, being five rods wide throughout.

The Oaxaca ward was organized March 11, 1894, two years following the coming of the first pioneers. The organization was effected under the direction of the members of the Council of the Twelve, Brigham Young, Jr., John Henry Smith and George Teasdale, the President of the Mission. Franklin Scott was selected to be bishop with George C. Williams and James H. Langford as his counsellors.   Peter Dillman was chosen to be the clerk of the ward.   In addition to this responsibility he was given the direction of the Sunday School.   The Relief Society was organized with Pauline Naegle as its President.   James W. Ray was asked to head the Young Men's organization and to Lily Langford was committed the responsibility of directing the Young Women's Association, while to Sarah Naegle, came the honor of presiding over the Primary organization.

The material interests of the people must not be neglected.   The land was therefore classified according to quality and location into three classes and a fixed price set on each.   The first class farming land was to be sold for $16.00 per acre, the second class for $15.00, and the third class for $5.00 per acre.   These prices were to be paid in Mexican currency, whose purchasing value at that time was about one-half that of the American money.   Range land was quoted at 12½ cents per acre.

Liberal concessions were made the colonists by the government in the matter of taxes, duties and military services.   Furniture, food and other commodities were to be admitted free of duty for a period of ten years, in harmony with the provisions of the colonization law of the time. Exemption from taxation and from military duty for an equal number of years was another concession granted. To enjoy these exemptions it was obligatory that 25 men sign a contract to become permanent members of the proposed colony.   In due time there were 64 who signed the contract.

I have, in a previous chapter, pointed out that the Oaxaca tract cost the purchasers $35,000 which was to be paid in three equal installments.   Due to money stringency, Williams and Naegle could not meet the terms of the contract and it seemed probable that the deal must fall through, in which event the colonists would lose their all.   At this juncture President Anthony W. Ivins representing the Mexican Colonization and Agricultural Company, came to their rescue.   Williams and Naegle had paid approximately

one-half of the $35,000 leaving a balance due of $17,933.
The new contract called for $10,000 to be paid at once and
the balance to be paid in three installments; $2,000 the first
year; $2,000 the second year and the remainder, $3,933 at
the end of the third year.   The company hoped to get its
compensation from the sale of the lands.

In January, 1897, President Ivins made a trip to Colonia Oaxaca to make arrangement for the sale of property.
He placed on sale 40 lots on the townsite at $25.00 per
lot and a number of others, somewhat inferior, at $15.00
each.   He also listed for sale 500 acres of first class farming
land at $10.00 per acre and 700 acres of second class at
$3.00.   In addition, he offered 98,000 acres of range land
at 25 cents per acre.   One fourth of the purchase price
was to be paid down and the balance in one, two and three
years with interest at the rate being paid by the company
for its loan from the Church.   A committee, consisting of
F. D. Haymore, John Rencher and J. C. Naegle were to
look after the details relative to the land sales.   Parties having no land of their own were asked to pay pasturage at
the rate of 50 cents per animal for the year.

A fair measure of prosperity attended the efforts of
the colony for a number of years.   What land could be
cultivated was extremely fertile, producing abundantly
such crops as peanuts, sweet potatoes, melons, corn and
grapes for which there was usually a splendid market at
the mines.   Thousands of cattle belonging to the colonists
fed on a thousand hills the year round, supplying their
owners with their milk and butter and meat and a nice
sum of money at least once a year, from the sale of steers
that usually were disposed of to buyers from the United
States.   Splendid brick homes were built and other comforts were increasing rapidly to reward an honest, frugal
and industrious people when without warning a terrific
flood, caused by the heavy summer rains in the mountains
above, rushed savagely down the Bavispe, overflowed its
banks and swept the houses, barns and crops of the thrifty

colony into the onrushing stream, madly pushing on to join the waters of the Pacific. Almost nothing was left. The beautiful village which a few hours before had been alive with the music of little children and the mirthful laughter of youth and maid was no more. Much of the very soil itself—an accumulation of the ages—was carried away. Little was left but the gravel and stones to bear silent witness to the fury of the merciless storm. And where were the people? Clinging to the hill sides or wandering about in search of a kindly spot where they could be safe from the ravages of the flood. As the somber shades of the night fell over the scene the afrighted villagers gathered in groups about the crackling fires of mesquite, unable to shut out the roar of the waters below. Like Tyre of old, Oaxaca was bare as a rock. From the chaotic waste never again would the voices of little children be heard or the smoke from the hearth fire be seen.

Colonia Morelos

The second and last Mormon colony established in Sonora was distant from Colonia Oaxaca twenty-five miles, at a point on the Bavispe River where the Batepito empties its brackish water into the larger stream. Prior to the founding of the colony, the valley between the two rivers and lying along the banks of the Batepito for several miles, was known as the "Batepito Ranch." This region was in the main covered with forests of mesquite and catclaws, the notable exceptions being on the broad stretch of lowland where the tall sacaton with its roots firmly anchored in the soil bade defiance to other forms of vegetation. Here was the paradise of the deer where it wandered undisturbed except for an occasional intrusion of a prospector or cowboy enroute to a country farther on. Geographically it was on the border of civilization, being but fifty miles south of Douglas, Arizona, but topographically it was far removed. Hemmed in on all sides by nature's bulwarks, save for the outlet from the north up the rather narrow valley of the Batepito, this region was almost inaccessible. Except for a rancho here and there, primeval nature reigned supreme for many miles around. But such a fertile tract was not to remain forever idle. It must do its part toward the feeding of the needy multitudes. The soil, yards deep, needed but the hand of toil to make it yield an hundred fold of grain and other produce good for man.

The view of this country impressed President Ivins with its importance, as seen in a letter addressed to the Deseret News in the spring of 1898, in which he referred to it as offering "fine opportunities for colonization." Fully one-half of the 9,000 acres comprising the "Batepito Ranch," he felt could be brought under cultivation and the balance was unexcelled for grazing. "The land was rich and fertile and within one day's travel of the United States." The tract, he said, had been offered for $15,000 American money. A few months later he had made the purchase and soon thereafter, the land was dedicated as a future home for the Saints. Present at the dedication were thirty-two in all, chief of whom were Apostle Abraham O. Woodruff, who gave the dedicatory prayer, and President Ivins. Soon settlers came pushing in. Among the first to come were the Huish family, Lorenzo L., Edward H., William C., and Alfred. With them came the Snarrs, Daniel and Daniel, Jr., and the Hubers, John J. and Ernest. All having families were accompanied by them.

Although it was mid-winter when the first companies arrived, they began at once to make preparations for irrigating their land, since it seemed improbable that crops could be produced without water. At a mass meeting held on January 28th, 1899, it was agreed that a canal would be constructed on the south side of the Bavispe, and that single handed men should be allowed 25 cents per hour for their work while a man with a team should receive double that amount. It was most fortunate for the colonists that the climate was warm enabling them to work the year round, for in the main they were destitute of even the necessities, and were dependent upon a daily wage for their living.

The townsite was located in the winter of 1900 and the survey was made by President Ivins and James H. Martineau. The farm lands were surveyed into units to meet the needs and financial conditions of the people. Land on the south side of the Bavispe was cut into ten acre pieces, the squares being separated by streets two rods wide. In other localities larger units were set apart. The prices placed on lots and other lands seem unusually low when their intrinsic worth is taken into account, and still it was difficult for the purchasers in most instances to meet the payments. The town lots were placed in three classes, those on main street being valued at $15.00 each. The second class of which there were 76, were appraised at $12.50, while the value of the third class was placed at $10.00 each; of the latter class there were 100 in all. The farm land was also put in three classes. Under what was known as the lower canal, for instance, the best land sold for $6.25 per acre, the second class for $5.00 and the third class for $3.00. Ten per cent interest was assessed on all unpaid for land, and the land was held for security.

On September 24, 1900, the new colony was christened "Morelos" after one of the most distinguished Mexican patriots of the Wars of Independence.

The town was organized into a branch of the Church under a general supervision of the Oaxaca ward. Lorenzo S. Huish was appointed the presiding elder, and his brother Edward the branch clerk. Later, in 1901, a ward organization was effected with O. P. Brown, Bishop and Alexander Jameson and L. S. Huish, counsellors. John J. Huber was sustained as clerk.

The educational interests of the people were not overlooked, but the financial distress of the people was a retarding factor in the way of supplying the children with suitable quarters and equipment necessary for the best results. A combined church and school house was soon erected following the selection of the townsite, but it was nothing but a stockade building, having a dirt floor and a mud roof. There was no equipment within, except of the rudest sort. The benches were split logs with no backs and the few other articles of furniture fitted well into the primitive environment.   The work of the teachers, however, was in a class far above the quality of their surroundings.   Their patience under those trying conditions was sublime and their efforts to improve the educational standing of the pupils was most praiseworthy.   The fact that the salary was a mere pittance did not deter them from giving the best they had.   Their chief compensation came in the satisfaction experienced in seeing the children unfold normally, resulting in proper character development and in healthy mental growth. The revenue used for running the school was supplied by means of local taxes and tithing contributed by the Church.

The work of clearing the land was anything but an easy task in the absence of stump pullers and other machinery to lighten the burden of the farmer.   The grubbing hoe, crowbar and axe, swung by a strong pair of arms must do the work of ridding the land of its forests of mesquite, catclaw and other varieties of trees and brush.   I use the term "forests" advisedly for in this part of the State of Sonora where the climate is warm and the soil fertile, it is not unusual to see mesquite and catclaw twelve and even eighteen inches through the trunk, and as tall as ordinary oaks.   In addition to these giant growths there was mesquite brush and other varieties of vegetation that gave much of the territory the appearance of a jungle.   I recall that my own town lot and the one adjacent were so densely wooded that my wife attached a sheep bell to the neck of our eldest child so that in the event of his wandering off, the noise of the bell would give her a clue to his whereabouts.   The clearing of the land solved the question of fuel as it furnished the settlers with all the wood they could desire.   The soil was well adapted to the raising of wheat

and oats of the small grains, and corn did exceptionally
well.

In places corn grew to be fourteen and sixteen feet
tall with the ears so high on the stock that an ordinary man
had difficulty in reaching them. I have known watermel-
ons to grow as large as forty pounds and peanuts and sweet
potatoes were unexcelled both for quantity and quality.
After the first crops were harvested the food problem was
fairly well solved except for sugar and other such items
as could not be produced at home. The surrounding country was adapted to stock raising making it possible for nearly every farmer to have a few of his own stock from which
he obtained his milk and occasionally, at least, his beef.
Meat was difficult to keep on hand, however, since the
weather was warm the year round and few people were
blessed with refrigeration facilities. The clothing, as a
usual thing, would have been out of place on Fifth Avenue,
New York, but was well adapted to frontier conditions
where style was not the first and last thing thought of in
dress. It was customary to see children and even youths
going about the streets barefoot, the males garbed in over-
alls and Mexican sombrero and the girls in gingham or
calico dresses made in most instances by their mothers. The
homes of the people were frequently of adobe but a few
brick houses of comfort and with some ornamentation
added variety to an otherwise drab and rather monotonous
architectural prospect. I recall a striking contrast between
the plain and unpretentious appearance of Colonia Morelos
and the picturesque and almost metropolitan appearance of
Colonia Juarez. The answer to the question why this striking contrast is difficult to give. Perhaps the climate and
comparative isolation of Morelos tended toward conserva-
tism in the nature of its homes, but be that as it may, the
homes genreally were cool and comfortable and fitted well
into the scheme of things.

Little business outside of that pertaining directly to
the farm was engaged in. Two small stores and a grist mill

furnished the only other enterprises of which the village could boast. Yet the people generally were happy in the cultivation of their farms and in watching their cattle grow and increase in value, for they were thus insured against economic distress.

They were happy, too, in their social life. All were of one social class, so what did it matter if their conditions were lowly? They were all alike in their lowliness. The same customs in social affairs obtained in Morelos as in the other colonies and the same forms of amusement were engaged in. Oft, I relive in memory the social parties held in the old stockade building; the Cinco de Mayo festivities down at the grove, and the moonlight boat rides on the placid bosom of the Bavispe. Happy days indeed! and rendered doubly happy in the freedom that comes with isolation from the outside world. There were no jails nor penal institutions of any sort, no police courts, nor blind stills; no drunken revelries nor ribald intimacies. Like one big happy family devoid of deceit and hypocrisy, this unsophisticated group of Christian folk on the frontiers of northern Mexico innocently sought relief from their arduous toil in harmless if somewhat primitive forms of recreation. But this condition of isolation did not preclude entirely a knowledge of the outside world. Periodicals and magazines, bearing news of the world, found a welcome in the homes of many of the Saints whose love for reading and culture was not dulled by a frontier environment.

Occasionally, too, the quiet of this peaceful society was broken by the intrusion of a foreign element antagonistic to the puritanical spirit and ethics of the community. Vividly I recall a striking example of this. Two Mexican officers rode into the colony and reported that they had been on the trail of two noted outlaws for a period of twenty days. One of these outlaws was the notorious Narcross of Texas, who with his companion, had murdered a man in the state of Chihuahua to obtain his money. The officers had followed their trail to a point where it led down the mountain into the rugged Pulpito Canyon, a few miles east of Colonia Oaxaca. Fearful of their lives should they continue the pursuit into such a wilderness of trees and ledges, the officers, by taking a circuitous route and by travelling day and night, came in ahead of the outlaws to Colonia Morelos and demanded the services of three of the colonists in a search for the fleeing convicts. The lot fell upon David Winn, Benjamin Eccles and myself. We were instructed to attempt no arrest of the bandits but to locate them merely and return and report. About five or six miles up the highway leading from Morleos to Colonia Oaxaca, we met a couple of mounted men with a pack animal, making their way leisurely in the direction of Morelos. These, we suspected of being the men we were looking for. To avoid having them suspect our errand, Dave Winn asked them if they had seen any mules up the road, to which they responded in the negative. We continued following the highway until well out of sight when we halted to consider the next step to be taken. It was decided that Winn should return to the colony to make a report and the other two were to ascend a high point commanding a view of the country for miles around to follow the movements of the strangers.

On the brow of the hill overlooking Morelos they halted, put their horses out to pasture and then Narcross, leaving his companion to watch the horses, walked into town for some provisions. At the Huish store he was making his purchases when the two Mexican officers, having been apprized of his presence, entered at one end of the store and at the same time two of the colonists entered from the opposite end. Simultaneously the four men drew their guns on Narcross and ordered him to put up his hands. Hurriedly he raised his arms in the air, but only for a moment, when he shot them downward and seizing two of the guns, he forced them to one side and lunged for the door. As he did so he attempted to pull from beneath his clothes a revolver but was hindered by the trigger getting caught in his raiment. As he passed out of the door and was about to turn the corner of the building, he was shot from behind and fell to the ground, at the same time crying for mercy. He was disarmed and lodged in the tithing office building for the night, in the absence of a jail. The other convict made his escape amidst a fusillade of bullets that fell short of their mark. Narcross was to stand trial in the state of Chihuahua and a large part of the distance he must be taken in a light rig. The jolting of the vehicle, together with the intense heat, produced intolerable suffering for the wounded man. Infection set in and before he could be brought to trial for the murder, he had passed to a higher tribunal.

CHAPTER XI

COLONIA JUAREZ—THE SEAT OF CULTURE

Colonia Juarez by virtue of its geographical position, if for no other reason, was destined from its founding to become the educational and religious center of the Mormon colonies in Mexico. It was centrally located with reference to the rest of the colonies, thus making it the logical place for the transaction of the business relating to the colonies as a whole. In consequence of this, the five or six apostles who came to Mexico to make their homes during the first decade of colonization selected this beautiful spot as their abode. It was the home also of the President of the Mexican Mission. And, later, when an organized stake of the Church was affected, Colonia Juarez continued to be the center of ecclesiastical and educational activity.

George Teasdale, of the Council of the Twelve was the distinguished head of the Mexican Mission for a period of years. He was a man of culture and refinement whose early life and training were had in the busy marts of England, yet he adapted himself to the new pioneer conditions of the colonies with remarkable skill. At the same time he was not content to have his people remain in a state of quiescent non-progression, but urged the importance of seeking after all that is noble and beautiful in life. He placed great emphasis upon a fundamental doctrine of the Church that "A man cannot be saved in ignorance." This doctrine he preached constantly from the pulpit and in a still more tangible way he urged the importance of improved facilities for the education of the young. The old stockade building with its meager equipment had served a useful purpose in the days of dire poverty and hardship. Now that a fair degree of national and local prosperity was at hand, a community need was felt for better school buildings and more adequate facilities for religious instruction and social development.

With these ends in view an all-purpose adobe building was constructed at Colonia Juarez in 1888-1889, whose dimensions were 24 ft. by 40 ft. To raise the funds required for its construction a free-will community tax was levied, requiring all heads of families to contribute fifty dollars, while all single men beyond the age of twenty-five were to donate the sum of twenty-five dollars. The total cost of the building when completed was fourteen hundred dollars. It was felt that such a structure would meet the needs of the colony for years to come, but with the natural increase of a fertile people and the comparatively rapid influx of immigrants from the north it was but a short time, indeed the following year, when more space was needed. Accordingly another building of equal dimensions, except that it had two stories, was added to the former building. The additional structure was built of stone to the top of the first story while the upper part of the structure was of concrete. With ample room it was now possible to group the children into classes according to their ability and with some respect to age, to which but little attention had been given in the past. Considerable dignity was added to the school by giving it the name of "The Juarez Academy." The school at Colonia Diaz received similar recognition but neither the Juarez nor the Diaz Academy was anything but an elementary school, giving no instruction above the eighth grade, and each was local in its function. A school of elementary grade had been established at Colonia Dublan and it was given the designation "The Dublan Seminary."

In November of 1892, the "father" of the Church School System, Carl G. Maeser, visited the colonies primarily for the purpose of inspecting the schools at Colonia Juarez, Colonia Diaz, and Colonia Dublan. Following his inspection of these three institutions, Superintendent Maeser adopted them into the General Church School system and had a Church Board of Education appointed to supervise the school system of the Mexican Mission. George

9

Teasdale was made the President of the Board, and William D. Johnson, Jr., was selected to fill the position of Superintendent of the school system. Local school boards were appointed to supervise the educational interests of the specific wards of the Mission.

The social conditions at this time were encouraging not only in Colonia Juarez, but in the other Colonies as well. President Teasdale reported to the Deseret News, 1895, that the colonists "are all workers. There are no saloons, gambling houses or other objectionable institutions to defile our settlements. Federal and state governments have befriended the colonists. The Mexican authorities are anxious to have this country settled with sober, industrious people and are giving encouragement to that class."

Not only were the Saints showing advancement in an economic and social way but progress was noted in the changing form of their Church government. It has been noted that during the first years of their existence the colonies belonged to what was known as the "Mexican Mission." But with the growth in population and an expansion of territory the General Authorities of the Church at Salt Lake City deemed it advisable to institute a more advanced form of ecclesiastical government. A regular stake of the Church was therefore organized on December 9, 1895, whose headquarters was to be at Colonia Juarez. The man called to direct the affairs of the stake as its first president had for years been a prominent figure in civic and church affairs in the state of Utah. At the time he was called by the Church to go to Mexico it seemed probable that he was on hi way to become governor of his state. The leaders of his party had offered him the nomination and since he was intensely popular with the general populace there is little doubt that he could have won the election. The man to whom I refer is Anthony W. Ivins to whom the people of Utah need no introduction since at the time of his recent death he was one of the most widely known and

certainly among the most beloved, by all classes, of all
the citizens of the state.

President Anthony W. Ivins, son of Israel and Anna L.
Ivins, was born in Tom's River, New Jersey, September 16,
1852. His parents were cousins and belonged to the good
old American stock of English and Dutch extraction. Re-
ligiously, his progenitors for generations back had belonged
to the Society of Quakers, in fact, had been identified with
that religious body almost from its inception in America.

He was but one year of age when his parents moved
from New Jersey to the Basin of the Great Salt Lake, to be
with the membership of the Church of Jesus Christ of Latter-day Saints with whom they had become identified years
before in the East. Salt Lake City was the home of young
Ivins for the following nine years of his life and during this
time he experienced many privations common to dwellers
on the frontiers. At the same time there was being woven
into the warp and woof of his character the influences and
qualities of his surroundings—the strength, the loftiness
and the sturdiness of the giant granite-peaks of the Wasatch
—guardians of the eastern gateway into the Great Basin;
the tenderness, beauty and purity of the varigated flowers
that bedecked vale, lake and stream, and the pensiveness and
solemnity of the great sage-brush deserts of his mountain
home.

The years passed all too soon when the Ivin's family
again "pulled up stakes" and began their journey to establish a new home in Utah's Dixie land. A call had come
from the prophet of the people, Brigham Young, to build
a city on the Virgin River three hundred miles toward the
south. Among the sturdy characters selected for the undertaking were the parents of Anthony W. Ivins, and they
felt they must heed the call.

Few settlements in the annals of Western colonization of America have required so much patience, persever-
ance, and faith as was required in the founding and the
building of Saint George. The little valley in which the

city stands borders a river whose waters are murky and whose channel is a veritable quagmire of treacherous quicksand. Hemmed in by red sandstone hills and black volcanic ridges and with a temperature in summer of torrid heat, there was little here to invite even the extreme optimist seeking other than the kingdom of work. Only the genuine could endure the burnishing process; they must be gold. It was amid such scenes that the future President of the Mexico Colonies was brought to manhood and it was here that he received his call. At the time of his passing he was the First Counselor to Heber J. Grant, President of the Church of Jesus Christ of Latter-day Saints. He was also President of the Board of Trustees of the Utah State Agricultural College and was prominent in the business world. Fortunate, indeed, were the colonists that a man of such extraordinary wisdom and matured judgment should have been called to preside over them. No happier selection could have been made. He was peculiarly adapted to fill that position both by nature and by training. In an earlier chapter, I pointed out that he filled two preaching missions to Mexico during which time he became intimately acquainted with the natives of Mexico and developed a love for them that was abiding. His thorough knowledge and skillful use of the Spanish language was to serve him well in his new responsibility. He could sympathetically appreciate the frontier problems confronting the Mormon colonists since he, himself, had been a frontiersman during much of his eventful life. Much of his education had been acquired in the stern, exacting school of experience on the frontiers of Western America. Had President Ivins never attended school a day in his life he still would have been a great man. Nature had endowed him with all the qualities of true leadership and Providence had seemingly ordained that his life should be lived in an environment conducive to the growth and development of his innate qualities of greatness. His personality was strikingly impressive, compelling others to follow not from a sense of fear but out of

respect for one whom they recognize to be a superior character. Some men command a following due to a powerful
physique coupled with an aggressively dare-devil attitude,
but neither of these qualities was common to the leadership
of Anthony W. Ivins. His physique was never rugged and
his method of discipline and direction was always characterized by a quiet gentleness and gentlemanliness usually
typical of the truly great. His was rather the Robert E.
Lee type of generalship than that of Frederick the Great.
The power of his influence was found in the mental and
spiritual realm rather than in the physical. By the gentle
warmth and sunshine of his personality rather than by the
cold and withering blast of pent-up emotions he influenced
men to do his bidding.

He was strongly religious yet free from dogmatism.
He was intensely loyal to his Church and its membership,
but at the same time he was most tolerant and sympathetic
of those of other churches. Even the Agnostic and Atheist
came in for a full measure of tolerance from President Ivins.
In all men he recognized a spark of the divine and he deemed
no sacrifice too great in the work of saving souls. He was
typically a friend of man. His versatility was proverbial.
He could adjust himself to a great variety of situations. He
was equally at home with the cultured and the unpolished
man of the wilderness. He was equally at ease about the
camp fire and in the most splendidly appointed apartment.
He had a sympathetic understanding of the problems of
the mining man, of the cattle man, the farmer and the business man, indeed there was scarcely a field in which he did
not in a measure feel at home. I have tramped the mountains and canyons of Sonora with this man in quest of the
precious metals; I have observed him in the orchard and on
the farm; I have fished with him in the crystal streams of
the Canadian Rockies; and always I found him the outstanding genius, the man of consummate judgment and the
most self-sacrificing of all. To know him was to honor
him, to love him and to become his devout follower.

A sketch of President Ivins would be most incomplete without a reference to a distinguished honor recently conferred on him. It came as a beautiful benediction in the evening of his life when the shadows were stretching far to the East, and when the sun of his life was soon to set in a blaze of eternal glory. He was in his 82nd year. Time had bleached his well-kept hair to a pure white; his clear cut and somewhat pointed features were marked by age and yet behind them was the spirit of youth and a freshness seldom seen in a man of his years.

The Utah State Agricultural College stadium was well filled on its eastern side with thousands of College students, the faculty and friends of the great institution. It was college commencement day and hundreds of graduate students decked out in their caps and gowns sat tense with emotion, expectant of the honors to be bestowed on them that day. In this vast throng were wives and sweethearts and fathers and mothers with countenances beaming and hearts swelling with pride over the achievements of loved ones. Most distinguished of these was the wife of Anthony W. Ivins who had been his life long companion, sharing with him his sorrows and joys—ever a source of strength and inspiration to him in the many vicissitudes of life. She is the daughter of a former Apostle of the Church, Erastus Snow, next to Brigham Young the greatest colonizer the Church has produced. The fine qualities of elder Snow have been transmitted to his illustrious daughter.

The sunlight played on gorgeous colors bedecking the improvised platform on which sat many of the dignitaries of the State and College as well as the nation's Secretary of Agriculture, Henry A. Wallace. Mr. Wallace was present as an apostle of the New Deal to honor the occasion by giving the Commencement address. Truly it was a fitting occasion to do honor to one of Utah's greatest sons.

The music ceased and amid the hush of the throng the President of the College, Dr. Elmer G. Peterson, arose and in solemn tones proclaimed: "I arise now to perform a func-

tion in which I am directed by the unanimous action of the
Board of Trustees and the faculty of the college to confer
the honorary Degree of Doctor of Laws upon one of the
distinguished and beloved leaders of our state and of the
West."

"Anthony Woodward Ivins—Pioneer, Humanitarian,
Scholar, Leader of Religious Thought * * * remembers his
father mowing with a scythe the grass which grew in the
meadow and threshing wheat with a cradle and flail. He
has worn clothing made by his mother from cotton and
wool which she had carded and spun and woven, and tail-
ored with her own hands. He has studied by the light of
a tallow dip or a pine knot. * * * His actual schooling consisted of three months each year of mediocre instruction.

"Among his reading was that of law which later admitted him to the bar of Utah. It is said of him he never lost
a case. His studies have included geology, chemistry, min-
erology and engineering of which he has a comprehensive
understanding. His studies have given him a comparable
mastery of biology, history, political science and sociology.

"He has always been a land owner, a land lover, and a
breeder of pure-bred stock. He has acted as town con-
stable, county assessor, councilman, mayor, city attorney
and deputy sheriff, a member of the state legislature and
a member of the Utah Constitutional Convention. He has
risen to high position in his Church and wields a strong influence in the religious thoughts of our region, an influence
not confined to any particular Church.

"For seventeen years he has been a member of the
Board of Trustees of the College and for fourteen years
Chairman of the Board. His friendship is for all true edu-
cation and all worthy educational institutions.

"I desire in conclusion to use the words of the Year
Book of the College of 1931 which in its dedication paid
tribute to the man who has honored the college and the
state these many years by his distinguished service and upon

whom we now bestow the highest honor within the gift of the institution.

"Friend equally of the Indian and of royalty, of the toiler and the captain of industry.

"A frontiersman become modern but unspoiled by modernism in thought or in living.

"With the heart of a child, yet hard as steel under the stress of worthy necessity.

"Without diplomas yet finely educated.

"Patriot, but loyal only to truth and thus exemplar of the greater Americanism."

Less than four months after the conferring of the doctor's degree on President Ivins, he was called from this sphere of action, his demise occurring on the 23rd of September, 1934. He had barely passed the 82nd milestone of his life and it seemed probable, until a few hours before his death, that he was destined to live another decade, at least. From all outward appearances he was in excellent health and when I visited him a few days before his death he outlined to me a pretentious plan for the future. He had just completed the writing of a book on Masonry, from which he read me excerpts, and he was contemplating writing a history of the founding and development of Saint George and other settlements in Southern Utah.

The cause of his death was a heart attack which occurred on Friday the 22nd, but from which he temporarily rallied. He insisted that he felt well enough to be up and around, but the doctor, realizing the seriousness of his ailment, left orders that he was to spend the day in bed. Saturday night the family retired at his request, but very early next morning they were called to his bedside, and at 4:30 he breathed his last. Up until the last, his mind was perfectly rational, and with no visible sign of suffering, he bade farewell to mortal life.

The news of his death was announced through special issues of the Salt Lake Tribune and the Deseret News which were delivered free of charge to the many subscribers resident in Salt Lake City. Seldom, if ever in the history of the State of Utah, has the announcement of a death caused such intense sorrow among all classes of people. Scores of messages came pouring in to the grief stricken family of the deceased and to President Grant, a life long companion of his departed cousin. Men from the various walks of life gave expressions of their esteem for the great pioneer, and a goodly number of these messages were copied by the leading newspapers of the State. From a long list of such I submit a few as evidence of the high regard in which President Ivins was held by men in the varied walks of life.

J. Reuben Clark, former Ambassador to Mexico and now a counselor in the First Presidency of the Church of Jesus Christ of Latter-day Saints said of him:

"President Ivins was the most remarkable all around man I ever knew. * * * He was the typical, great pioneer. He stood for everything that was strong, courageous and righteous in our lives."

Governor Henry H. Blood of Utah declared that: "The state and nation have lost a man of loyalty and vast influence; the Church a man of faith, devotion and high leadership. * * * No man was more truly loved than he or held in higher esteem."

Senator William H. King was overwhelmed and bowed with grief with a sense of personal loss. "* * * The Church loses one of its greatest leaders and ablest defenders; the State one of its outstanding figures and the nation one of its noblest and most patriotic citizens."

George Albert Smith, a member of the Council of the Twelve, said of him: "He was a mighty man, humble as a child, fearless as a lion and friendly to all people," while John A. Widtsoe of the same Council declared that: "President Ivins was one of a generation. Highly endowed in body and mind, he used his kingly faculties for the good of his fellow men and the advancement of God's truth in the

world. * * * His death is a severe loss to the state, the nation
and the Church."

Elder Charles A. Callis of the Twelve and an attorney
said: "If President Ivins had not been the great Churchman
that he was, he would have adorned the bench of the Supreme Court of the United States."

Bishop James E. Kearney of the Salt Lake Diocese of
the Catholic Church expressed himself thus:

"I am very much shocked at Anthony W. Ivins' death.
He was a great religious leader. I am sure he goes to his God
with his hands full of good works. Salt Lake has lost a
great citizen and the Mormon Church a great leader."

The mayor of Salt Lake City, Mr. Marcus, paid President Ivins the following worthy tribute:

"He was a true friend of all humanity and a man of
amazing understanding and sympathy toward all. It is an
honor to have known him and to feel the influence of his
remarkable personality. I feel that a close personal friend
and colleague has gone from my circle of acquaintances,
leaving a vacancy that will not be filled."

Reverend W. R. Sloman of the Immanuel Baptist
Church of Salt Lake City stated that: "All the city mourns
the passing of President Anthony W. Ivins. His interests
were wide. There was no movement for progress and good
that did not receive his attention."

Reverend Rollin H. Ayres of the Presbyterian Church
and Vice President of the Salt Lake Ministerial Association
declared President Ivins to be a personal friend and a
"brother" in every sense of the word. "Creedal differences
did not modify our feelings of good will and love, each for
the other."

The funeral was one of the most largely attended in the
history of the State of Utah. Ten thousand mourners
crowded the great Mormon Tabernacle to listen to the high
tributes paid the venerable leader. The floral tributes were

oustanding both in quality and quantity and at the close of
the services, at the request of the family, many of the sprays
and wreathes were distributed among the hospitals of the
city to add cheer to unfortunate sufferers.   The principal
address of the occasion was delivered by elder David O.
McKay of the Council of the Twelve who eloquently por-
trayed the Christ-like qualities of the dead leader and narrated in some detail his noteworthy achievements.   Other
speakers who paid well deserved eulogies to the dead were
President J. Reuben Clark who conducted the services, John
G. McQuarrie, a life long friend of President Ivins, Mr.
Fitzpatrick, publisher of the Salt Lake Tribune and the
Telegram, President Franklin S. Harris of the Brigham
Young University and President Elmer G. Peterson of the
Utah State Agricultural College.

President Heber J. Grant was bowed with grief to a
degree that he refused to take an active part in the proceedings, preferring rather to occupy a place among the
mourners.

Those whom President Ivins honored in his selection
of Counsellors were Henry Eyring and Helaman Pratt. The
former he had known intimately for many years in Utah's
Dixie, and the latter had been his close companion upon
more than one mission when together they traversed the
plateaus and arid deserts of the Great Southwest and the
mountains and plains of Mexico as witnesses of the Master
to benighted races.

Others honored with ecclesiastical appointments and
constituting the high officials of the new stake were the
members of the High Council, next to the Stake Presidency
in authority.   Their names were as follows: William C.
McClellan, Philip Hurst, Isaac Hurley, Frederick W. Jones,
John J. Walser, Alma P. Spillsbury, Joseph Cardon, George
M. Haws, Joseph H. Wright, Orson P. Brown, Miles A.
Romney, and Harry M. Payne.   Alternate members of the
High Council were: Pearson Ballanger, Joseph C. Davis,

Daniel Skousen, Nathan Clayson, Thomas Hawkins and Brigham Stowell, Joseph C. Bentley was stake clerk.

The Patriarchs of the Stake were Henry Lunt, W. R. R. Stowell, John C. Naegle, and A. F. Macdonald.

The Presidency of the High Priests Quorum were A. F. Macdonald, President, and W. R. R. Stowell and Joseph Cardon, Counsellors.

Those selected to constitute the Stake Board of Education were the Presidency of the Stake, Miles P. Romney, Wm. D. Johnson, James A. Little, Isaac W. Pierce, and D. E. Harris.

The Auxiliaries of the Stake were also well officered by men and women generally of vast experience.

Over the Relief Society organization Mary B. Eyring, Ellen W. Lunt and Cynthia J. Stowell were called to preside. D. E. Harris was called to act as Superintendent of the Sunday Schools and was assisted by John C. Harper and Sullivan C. Richardson. The Young Men's Mutual Improvement Association was placed under the supervision of D. E. Harris as Superintendent, with Joseph Cardon and Joseph C. Bentley as his counsellors. As officers of the Young Women's Mutual Improvement Association, Dora W. Pratt was president, and was assisted by Mary L. Teasdale and Mary E. Durfee. The Primary Associations were presided over by Mary L. Teasdale as President and Victoria Pratt and Mary Farnsworth as counsellors.

The Board of Trade, whose duties were largely civic, were appointees of the Church and were selected from its membership. Those appointed to positions on the Board at the time of the organization of the stake were, Henry Eyring, Helaman Pratt, E. L. Taylor, Wm. D. Johnson, Jr., Philip Hurst, Jesse N. Smith, Jr., Ira N. Wilson, D. E. Harris, John Whetton and Joseph C. Bentley who held the office of Secretary and Treasurer.

Under the new regime the colonies awoke to a newness of life and the spirit of optimism spread. The business interests of the people were greatly advanced by the services of an efficient Board of Trade. While the industrial and agricultural output of the colonies was never phenomenal still there was need of markets for what surplus they did produce and the Board of Trade did yeoman service in dis-covering new and better markets as well as in helping the people see new avenues for economic expansion.

Particularly noticeable was the added enthusiasm in the field of education. Good schools had been provided for the younger pupils but more must be done to provide for the educational needs of the young men and women of maturer years and higher scholastic capabilities. With this object in view a town meeting was called at Colonia Juarez for the 27th of March, 1896, just a few months subsequent to the organization of the Stake. At this gathering the colonists voted to construct a building suitable for a Stake Academy and pledged themselves to contribute of their means to the extent of 8% of their income toward this worthy cause.

The building was pushed with such vigor that in a year from the laying of the foundation stone it was ready for occupancy. It was not an ornate building but was neat and substantially built and added much to the two units previously constructed of which this latter struc-ture was a part. Some idea of the impression made by this public building upon the aesthetic and utilitarian sense of the community may be gleaned from the exultant state-ment made by a student in 1898: "One can hardly contem-plate the convenience and grandeur of this building with-out contrasting it with the little adobe (stockake) room and split logs for benches which was occupied by the first school of Juarez thirteen years ago." He reports the build-ing as having six large class rooms, a large auditorium, a library, an office and a prayer room and two halls.

The Stake Academy opened on the 20th of September, 1897, with an enrollment of 291 students. Professor Guy C. Wilson, a former professor of the Brigham Young Acad-emy, Provo, Utah, was the Principal, being assisted by the following teachers: Sarah Clayson, Theodore Martineau, Samantha Brimhall, and William A. Clayson. The curriculum taught was practically the same as taught in other schools of elementary and 9th grade subjects with the addition of Theology and Spanish which were compulsory in all of the departments. The following year witnessed a slight growth in the teaching staff. In addition to Principal Wilson were D. E. Harris, father of President Franklin S. Harris of the Brigham Young University, S. C. Richardson, Ella Larsen, Pearl Thurber, and Sarah Clayson.

The school was supported by contributions from the Church fund. An income tax was levied on all mature male residents of Colonia Juarez and a small tuition fee of from five to fifteen dollars was required of non-residents. The rate of taxation on incomes for the maintenance of the Academy varied from year to year, but in 1900, it amounted to 4% per each family income. During the next decade other commodious brick buildings were added to the school plant and the curriculum was expanded to include household science, woodwork, agriculture and other subjects of highly utilitarian value. The tenth grade was added in 1900 and two years later all of the four year high school subjects were being taught. The influence of the Academy spread to all of the Mormon colonies in Chihuahua and Sonora and to many other parts of the Republic with the result that a considerable number of the Mexican youth enrolled along with the youth of Mormondom.

The Academy continued to function without interruption until the exodus in 1912, when it was closed for a short season. With the return of several hundred of the Colonists to their former homes it was reopened and has continued to operate up to the present time. Incidentally it is worthy of note that the present President of the Brigham Young University is a product of the Juarez Stake Academy as also are a number of his teaching staff. Many others are prominent teachers in other schools and in the seminaries of the Church.

The material and social prosperity of Colonia Juarez at this period of its history is clearly expressed in a letter addressed to the Deseret News by a prominent citizen. "It is a pleasure to be able to report that the people of this place are enjoying a time of general prosperity. Every one seems busy and a visitor will see no loafers lounging about street corners or saloons—by the way there is not a saloon in town nor would one be tolerated—and everything betokens peace and prosperity."

He reports the near approach of a railroad being built from El Paso to the Mormon colonies and expressed joy that the people will soon go by way of train to Salt Lake City. "This beautiful little village," he added, "has many and tasteful brick dwellings, some of which would be a credit to Salt Lake City. * * * There will be a considerable quantity of apples, pears, plums, prunes, cherries, grapes and peaches. The Mexicans say that if you want to buy good horses and cows, go to the Mormon settlements. They have them." He reports a cash market for "all the butter, cheese, eggs and poultry as well as cattle and horses produced."

At the conference held in Juarez February 19 and 20, 1897, President Ivins referred to the recent visit of the "government Colony inspector" in which he stated that "the inspector was greatly pleased with the progress made and went away with good wishes for the continued prosperity of our people." President Ivins felt that there was less profanity and closer observance of the "law of tithing" and the "word of wisdom" than in any stake of Zion that he had ever visited. He reported that during conference time he and the visiting Apostles, John Henry Smith and Heber J. Grant, on Saturday evening, attended the local theatre and witnessed the presentation of Othello by Miles P. Romney and his local dramatic company.

CHAPTER XII

EVENTS BEFORE THE EXODUS

The Latter-day Saints had barely placed their feet
upon Mexican soil when, as previously pointed out, an attempt was made by local Mexicans and officials of the state
of Chihuahua to have the colonists driven from the country, and but for the strong arm of the federal government,
the story of Mormon colonization in Mexico would have
ended with its first chapter. But this hoped-for drastic
measure was not a result of indivdiual or even group contacts of the native population and the new colonists, but
rather from inflamed minds superinduced by the malignant
tales circulated against the Mormons by certain enemies
from the United States, who sought their discomfiture.

During the decades that were to follow, the relationships between these diverse classes of people were fairly
congenial if surface indications mean anything; indeed,
I marvel as I attempt to reconstruct the history of those
years that greater open friction is not discernable. There
was likely no more friction between them than can usually
be found in any country where there is an intermingling
of races whose ideals, traditions and habits are so radically
different as were theirs.

Intermittently, down through the years, difficulties
arose resulting at times in tragedy, but these instances reveal
no widespread movement indicative of a race hatred but
were the work usually of an individual or a very limited
number of individuals bent on robbery. In a former chapter
I cited the case of Wesley Norton, a resident of Colonia
Diaz, who was murdered at Barrancas by Mexicans, ostensibly for his money.

This occurred in March, 1894, he being the first Mormon to be assassinated in Mexico. Other notable cases
were those of Mrs. Agnes Macdonald, wife of A. F. Mac-

donald whose home was at Colonia Garcia, and Christopher Heaton. Mrs. Macdonald had her sleeping apartment adjacent to a small country store of which she was manager. A morning came when the store seemed to be closed. Neighbors became apprehensive and upon investigation, to their horror, they discovered that sometime during the night a fiend had entered the room where Mrs. Macdonald lay asleep and smothered her to death and, after looting the store, made his escape.

Christopher Heaton was a man of surpassing qualities who had been instrumental in establishing the "United Order" at Cave Valley. At the time of his death he was living temporarily at San Jose, engaged in making molasses for certain farmers at Colonia Dublan who were furnishing him with the cane. San Jose was situated across the Casas Grandes River from Dublan, a few miles to the west. From the evidence gathered it appeared that two barrels of molasses, as well as some other things, had been stolen from the mill and while in the act of apprehending the thieves, Heaton was clubbed over the head and shot to death.

Many instances of thieving are recorded in the various Mormon colonies, evidently perpetrated by natives, but most of them did not end tragically, and in all of these cases of infractions against the law, I find no evidence that there was any concerted movement on the part of the Mexican people against the welfare and peace of the Mormons or other foreign population prior to the Madero Revolution. But to the contrary, frequent expressions of good will for our people were heard from the lips of representative Mexicans, and it was not uncommon for men of prominence to commend both privately and in public the Latter-day Saints for their industry, sobriety and good citizenship. At a fair held at Colonia Diaz, a decade following the advent of the Mormons into Mexico, one of the local Mexican officials said: "We acknowledge your superiority and we appreciate the example of thrift, prosperity and progress you have set us and we hope to improve

12

by it. We open our arms to you and receive you as brothers."

A report of Consul Buford which appeared in the
"Deming Headlight" in 1896, relative to the Mormon colonists in Mexico, declared: "Their holdings are in the finest
portions of Northern Mexico; the soil is very rich and productive and with the advent of railroads these lands will
greatly enhance in value. * * * The Mormons are exceedingly prosperous *and highly regarded.*"

Such quotations could be multiplied ad infinitum.
What then was the reason for a general exodus of the
colonists from the land of their adoption back to the land
from whence they had fled? The general verdict seems to
be that it was because the rebel forces demanded their
firearms, and being compelled to give them up, it was felt
unsafe to remain longer in the land. But may that not be
only a partial answer to the question? Is it not likely
that the demand to give up the firearms represents merely
the match that touched off the powder, and may not the
powder have been in the process of accumulation over a
period of years, silently and unobserved? Genetically the
two peoples differed. The Mexicans were predominantly
Latin, by nature temperamental and given to intense emo-
tionalism; inclined more to be theoretical than practical.
On the other hand, the colonists were largely of Nordic
extraction, less emotional than their neighbors and strongly
inclined toward the practical, having a tendency to be cool
and calculating and having a bent toward thrift.

By training they were even farther apart. The great
rank and file of natives had lived a life of serfdom and even
now were subject in the main to the dictates of overlords.
Under these conditions they were to experience little else
in life than grinding toil and hard-earned penury. The
colonists, while knowing not luxury, had lived a life of
independence, and having come from the thriving towns
and hamlets of the United States were not strangers to the
better things in life. Their methods of farming, of business

and of travel were on a higher plain than those of their neighbors. The steady but substantial growth of modern towns and villages from the once barren wastelands of Mexico; the thriving farms and well-kept orchards and vineyards; the many herds of well-bred cattle and blooded horses to be seen on every hand, and the well-established industries—all were fruitful sources of envy for a people who had known nothing but grinding poverty all their days and for whom the future held out no hope for better things.

Socially, the colonists were exclusive and seclusive, having few if any contacts with their neighbors. Occasionally, as a matter of diplomacy or as an expression of good will, government officials would be invited to participate in a national festivity or perchance some other form of entertainment, otherwise these social functions were entirely restrictive. Such was the avowed policy of the Church in the establishment of colonies in Mexico from the beginning and this policy was ever kept in mind. I note that on August 1, 1895, an Apostle of the Church, Elder Francis M. Lyman, advises the people of the importance of the Saints keeping to themselves socially. This policy inaugurated by the Church was not born of a "race superiority" complex, but resulted from a feeling that groups of people having different social standards, resulting from radically different environments, will have more enduring friendships for one another if they do not become too intimate.

In harmony with this general policy of the Church the colonists built up settlements of their own. It is true that occasionally natives would filter in among them to secure labor but the homes and farm lands were almost wholly in the hands of the Mormons, as well as the mercantile and industrial institutions. Even the educational system of the colonists was entirely separate and apart, as previously indicated, from the public school system of Mexico and was therefore supported entirely by local taxes, self-imposed, and by contributions from the general Church fund.

The colonies were not wholly independent politically, being subject as they were to the several municipalities in which they were located. In turn there was a general tie-up of these municipalities to the larger political division above them known as Cantons. But notwithstanding their nominal subordination to higher political divisions, the colonies were practically self-governing, usually having a president, town council and other town officials of their own choosing.

It is historically true that the immediate cause for the wholesale migration of the Mormons from Mexican soil was the demand made by the rebel forces for their firearms. But the ultimate, therefore more fundamental causes, were to be found in the contrasting natures, traditions, habits and ideals of the colonists and their neighbors; in the envy and covetousness of the natives developed over a long period of years and resulting from the material and social progress of the colonists as expressed in thriving settlements, well-cultivated orchards and farms, and convenient and comfortable homes and in their up-to-date educational system maintained by the colonists for the education of their children.

If it be maintained by those of opposing views that the local Mexicans had nothing to do with the decision of the colonists to abandon their homes; that culpability alone rested with the rebel forces, I would cite them the fact that many of the rebels themselves, including a large percentage of their leaders, were of local origin, as I shall point out in a later chapter. Furthermore, several of these local Mexicans in the ranks of the military, were there early selecting the Mormon homes they expected to occupy following the departure of their owners from the country. In any event, a large measure of blame must be attached to the natives living adjacent to the Mormon colonies for the leading part they took in driving the colonists from Mexican territory.

President A. W. Ivins

Mill Built by W. R. R. Stowell, Colonia Juarez, Mexico. House Where Brigham Stowell and Family Lived.

Old Church and School House at Colonia Juarez

COLONIA JUAREZ PARK AND BAND STAND

STREET IN COLONIA JUAREZ, SHOWING PART OF CO-OP STORE

OLLA CAVE

THE CLAWSON HOUSE, COLONIA, DUBLAN

RESIDENCE OF ELDER HENRY BOWMAN

DUBLAN RESERVOIR

HEADQUARTERS OF THE UNION MERCANTILE, COLONIA, DUBLAN

WILD TURKEYS OF THE SIERRA MADRES

GENERAL VIEW OF COLONIA DUBLAN

A VIEW OF COLONIA JUAREZ

THE RESIDENCE OF BISHOP W. DERBY JOHNSON, COLONIA DIAZ

RESIDENCE OF PRESIDENT A. W. IVINS
VISIT OF GOVERNOR AHUMADA OF CHIHUAHUA

THE JUAREZ ACADEMY

Junius Romney

ANOTHER PICTURE OF THE REBELS LEAVING
JUAREZ. THEY ARE RIDING MORMON'S HORSES

THIS IS WHAT WAS LEFT OF A BEEF THE REBELS
KILLED BY THE MEETING HOUSE. THEY WERE
CAMPED IN THE MEETING HOUSE.

MIGUEL A. CASTILLO, GENERAL OF
A GROUP OF REBELS WHO PREYED
ON COLONISTS

FLEEING MORMON COLONISTS AT TAPACITA

Chapter XIII

STRAINED RELATIONS

The Revolution initiated by Francisco I. Madero against the Diaz regime was the signal for uprisings, and in the course of a few months bands of rebels were terrorizing the inhabitants and ravaging the country far and near. The strong arm of Diaz had been successful in times past in terminating speedily any political disturbances that had arisen and the feeling was current among those familiar with Mexican affairs that the "grand old man" would likely be successful in riding any political storm that might gather and in striking a death blow to any counter movement against his authority at its first appearance.

But the unexpected thing happened. The strong hand that had ruled the Southern Republic for so many years had become palsied, letting fall the saber which had held in check fifteen millions of people for well nigh a third of a century.

The success of Madero in the overthrow of the Diaz regime cannot be attributed to a strong personality nor to unusual ability in the field of military strategy, for Madero possessed neither. Rather must his success be attributed largely to the conditions of the times. The masses were ready for revolt against a power which had kept them in thralldom to a privileged class until life to them had become intolerable.

Leadership was the thing needed and that leadership was supplied by Francisco I. Madero, a born aristocrat whose family was counted among the small group of multi-millionaires of Mexico. Fortunately, however, much of his educational training had been received in the colleges of the United States, where he imbibed a large measure of sympathy for the masses. It is idle to assume, however, that the blow struck by Madero was motivated entirely by a spirit of altruism, for he had a private grievance to settle and he had a strong desire to rule.

The Revolutionary leader had little difficulty in securing a following. All it needed was to insure his men a substantial living and the promise of a few acres of land at the close of the war. The followers of Madero could scarcely be called an army. They were little more than a mob. Many were without uniform and some of the Indians from the mountains were a spectacle to behold with their straight, black hair streaming wildly down their backs and with not a stitch of clothing on save a cloth girdle about the loins.

The Commander-in-Chief of the army was Madero himself, but a large measure of the responsibility of conducting the war was shifted to the shoulders of General Garibaldi, a grandson of the "red-shirted knight" of Italy, a soldier of fortune, and later a distinguished general in the World War. Others associated prominently with Madero were his brothers, Raul and Ernesto. The place selected for the opening shot was the town of Casas Grandes, long known in history as being the birthplace of more revolutions than almost any other place in the republic of Mexico. Very little resistance was here offered the forces of Madero, but a few casualties were reported, among them being the rebel chief himself, who received a bullet wound in the hand. From Casas Grandes the army pushed on to Cuidad Juarez, a distance of 175 miles, where a stiffer battle was fought, but again the Revolutionists were victorious. Northern Chihuahua was now in their hands. With his army augmented by the thousands who had deserted the Federal cause, Madero was encouraged to strike at the City of Mexico more than eight hundred miles to the south. The journey thither was a triumphal march in which city after city capitulated to the forces of Madero and upon reaching Mexico City, the Revolutionists found a people ready to receive them with little opposition. The rule of Madero, covering a period of only a few months, proved disappointing to the masses. His promised reforms did not materialize as speedily as was expected and this gave rise to a general spirit of discontent that furnished opportunity for political aspirants to obtain a following. In the North many of the mal-contents rallied to the standard of revolt raised by Pascual Orosco and their movement became known as the "Orosco Revolution."

A detailed consideration of the rebellion is important because of its intimate relationship to the future status of the Mormon colonies in Mexico. At the time of this uprising there were six principal colonies in Chihuahua, Colonia Diaz, Juarez, Dublan and the "Mountain Colonies," Colonias Pacheco, Garcia, and Chuichupa. In Sonora, Colonia Morelos was the only settlement of much importance since Colonia Oaxaca had been almost completely washed away by a flood.

During the Madero Revolution certain demands were made on the colonists for leather goods and other materials needed by the revolutionary bands for which receipts would be issued, with the understanding that the colonists holding the receipts would be reimbursed in case the revolutionary cause succeeded. Naturally the colonists objected to parting with their goods on such terms, but their protestations were usually met with grim threats. The policy then was to give as little as possible, making sure to get a receipt in return. In a few instances these receipts were accepted in payment for taxes due from the colonists, but in most cases the Mormons still hold these papers from which they have never realized anything. In justice to the federal authorities it can be in truth said that they made no exactions upon the Chihuahua colonies during the Madero revolution.

Upon the initiation of the Orosco Revolution the rebels increased their demands upon the colonists. On February 5, 1912, Enrique Portillo, Presidente of Canton de Galeana, with headquarters at Casas Grandes, came into Colonia Juarez at the head of twenty-five men and

made unreasonable demands of the citizens. In the name
of his superior, General Jose Inez Salazar, he demanded
of the colonists twenty-five guns and an equal number
of horses and saddles, together with a quantity of food
supplies. Naturally enough the people refused on the
grounds that they were foreigners and as such had no right
to interfere in what they deemed a family quarrel. An
attempt to enforce the demands resulted in Benjamin L.
Croft, of Colonia Juarez, being placed under arrest, he
having refused to part with his gun, while Loren Taylor,
a fellow townsman of Croft's went into hiding to escape
having to turn over to the rebels his gun and pistol.

At this point in my narrative I pause to introduce to
my readers the ecclesiastical head of the Mormon colonies,
Junius Romney. Young Romney had succeeded to the
presidency of the Juarez Stake four years previously when
Anthony W. Ivins, who had presided over the Colonies for
thirteen years was advanced to the Apostleship. At the
time of his appointment to this position Romney had not
yet reached his thirtieth year but he was far beyond his
years in the rich experiences which had come to him in
the various responsibilities under which he had labored. He
was admirably fitted to guide the destinies of the colonies
ecclesiastically as well as in a material way. By nature he
was fundamentally spiritual and this natural bent was re-
inforced by a splendid training in the doctrines of his
church. His training in the business world was thorough
and his knowledge of men was unusual. Added to these
qualifications was a fluent speaking and writing knowledge of the Spanish tongue, intensely important in a land
where Spanish is the dominant language.

President Romney was born in Saint George, Washington County, Utah on the 12th of March, 1878. He is
the son of Miles P. Romney by a third wife, Catherine Jane
Cottam Romney. He is the second son of his mother and
the third child of a family of ten.

From his parents he inherited to a marked degree the

fundamental qualities of honesty, integrity and dependability which have characterized his every act of life and won for him the confidence and esteem of a great army of friends. From his mother he inherited a mind with a strong bent toward philosophy and from the paternal line he was richly endowed with the dramatic instinct. These qualities, coupled with a keen intellect and a magnetic personality have given him an unusual prestige in the business and social world.

When but a child of about four his parents left Saint George to make their home in Saint John, Apache County, Arizona. The father had been called by the President of the Church to assist in the building of Mormon settlements in that region, but persecution of polygamists became so severe that the family was advised by Church authorities to flee to Mexico. The mother of Junius and her family of children were taken to Saint George to remain with the maternal grandparents of young Romney until his father and other branches of the family could establish homes in Mexico. After a sojourn of two years in Saint George the last branch of the family in Utah entrained at Milford for the Republic of Mexico. Romney was at this time eight years of age.

The conditions which confronted the new arrivals in their adopted home were anything but inviting, but the inconvenience and even distress occasioned by the absence of even the bare necessities were in large measure balanced by the joy which resulted from a reunion of the entire family in a land free from persecution.

Without means and in a land where wages were but a pittance it required the help of every available member of the family to insure against want. In this struggle, Junius nobly did his part in herding the milch cows, working on the farm and in other menial labor required of him. Early in life he showed signs of business ability and at the age of fourteen he was given a position in the Juarez Cooperative mercantile establishment as a clerk. Fortunate, indeed, was it for the lad that thus early he was started on a business career under the supervision of an efficient and painstaking business manager such as was Henry Eyring, at the head of the largest business house in Colonia Juarez.

The climb of young Romney from clerk to chief book-keeper and finally to the position of assistant manager was little short of phenomenal. Since then, however, his business career furnishes other notable examples of similar achievements.

Following the exodus from Mexico he found himself penniless with a family to support. He sought and obtained a position with the Beneficial Life Insurance Company of Salt Lake City as a sales agent. His ability as a salesman was soon manifest and before long he was known as the leading producer of the company. As a gesture of appreciation for his services, the position of "Superintendent of Agents" was created for him. With distinction he filled this new appointment until he decided to go into business for himself. At the present time he is secretary and manager of the "State Building and Loan," one of the strong real estate companies of Salt Lake City to weather successfully the economic storm of the past few years. Ecclesiastically he has always been active and at present is a member of the High Council in the Liberty Stake.

His success in the marital relations has been just as pronounced as in other capacities. He was fortunate in his selection of a life companion. In his early twenties he married Gertrude Stowell, a daughter of Brigham and Olive Stowell, by whom he has had six children, three boys and three girls, all of whom reflect the splendid training of the ideal home in which they were nurtured.

President Romney made a fine choice in the selection of his two counsellors, Hyrum S. Harris and Charles E. McClellan, both of whom were men of striking qualities.

Hyrum S. Harris had been a resident of Mexico for several years, much of his time having been spent in Mexico City where he went at the request of the Presidency of his church to study Mexican law and to acquire the Spanish tongue. It was felt that he could be of great service to the colonists in the event of difficulties arising between them and the native population. For a number of years he had presided over the Mormon missionaries who were proselyting for the Church in and around Mexico City and even in distant parts of the Republic.

Charles E. McClellan had gone to Mexico in his early teens and here he had grown to manhood rich in the experiences common to a life of service devoted to the building of settlements and the redeeming of waste land areas and making them fruitful fields. At the time of his elevation to the Presidency of the Stake he was a professor of English at the Juarez Stake Academy and was second only to President Guy C. Wilson of that institution in administrative functions. For years his influence among the youth of his people as a leader had been potent.

Recognizing the injustice of Porillo's demand upon the colonists President Romney, accompanied by Messrs. Joseph C. Bentley and Guy C. Wilson, had an interview with the Presidente during which they notified him that the citizens of these colonies did not propose to give up a single gun, even if they "had to use them to retain them;" that they proposed to test whether an American citizen had a right to have in his possession a gun for the protection of himself and his family; that they regarded "a request to surrender arms at such a time as equivalent to a request to surrender all that makes life worth living; that the Revolutionists having obtained arms, their next demand would be for property, that if they ran their natural course, they would next burn and plunder, outrage our women and murder those who sought to protect them." Following this protestation Croft was released.

The day following the above interview, February 6, 1912, President Romney addressed a letter to the American Consul T. D. Edwards, stationed at Cuidad Juarez, in which he narrated in detail the grievances of the colonists,

most of whom were American citizens, and requesting that
he address a letter to Presidente Portillo informing him
that the United States would not tolerate a continuation of
such proceedings. In response to this communication Mr.
Edwards addressed a letter to Portillo as follows:

"Sir:
    "I have the honor to communicate to you, in keeping
with the instructions of my government, regarding the
protection of a large number of American citizens residing
permanently in the District over which you have the responsibility and honor to preside, and to notify you officially as such Presidente that you will be responsible for any
damage or injury to person or property of said American
citizens that might come by reason of political disturbances
or by failure to enforce the law.
    "I have been officially informed that your people have
demanded of the Americans that they deliver their fire
arms, which are their private property, and which they
need to defend their homes, etc., and which I am informed
was resisted by the Americans.
    "I cannot see any good reason for such demand, on
the part of your people; and that the government of the
United States will sustain said citizens in remaining entirely neutral and also in refusing to deliver their arms at
this critical time, I am positive."
    "I have the honor to be, Sir, Your attentive and sure
servitor

                    T. D. Edwards, Consul."

    On the same day that Romney wrote the letter to the
American Consul he, accompanied by seven other colonists from Juarez and Dublan, called on General Salazar
and Mr. Portillo, at Casas Grandes, relative to the rights of
the colonists during the civil strife. The committee received assurances from Salazar that the colonists would
be unmolested so long as they remained neutral. Speaking

for the committee, President Romney requested a written statement and order to that effect and sufficient copies thereof to supply each colony with a copy to present to any of the Rebels who might attempt to interfere with the colonists' rights.

Salazar granted the request by issuing the following order:

Casas Grandes,
February 6, 1912

"To the Chiefs and soldiers of the Liberal Party.
"To whom this statement may be presented.

"You will kindly respect in every way the neutrality of the members of the various Mormon Colonies and in no way molest them.

Liberty, Constitution and Justice
El General, I. Salazar."

On the day of the issuance of this order the Rebels in Casas Grandes were distributing beef by the wagon loads to those who came for it, the beef having been appropriated from the Mormons without any compensation. At this time there were fully 250 rebels camped at the Dublan lakes about five miles east of Dublan who made themselves free with colony beef cattle and also looted the "Ketelsen and Degetaus' " place of business at Neuva Casas Grandes, taking with them $500 cash and thousands of dollars in merchandise. At Colonia Diaz similar acts of robbery were being enacted. Merchandise in large quantities was seized as well as ten horses and eight saddles for which no compensation was tendered the colonists.

On February 16, Salazar ordered the heads of the Union Mercantile, Farnsworth and Romney, and Ketelsen and Degetaus, leading mercantile establishments in the colonies, to meet him at Casas Grandes. There they met him at the Public Square. In an address to his soldiers present Salazar declared that they intended to respect the rights of foreigners. Four days later the Union Mercantile Store at Dublan was looted to the amount of $1500 in merchandise; the Farnsworth & Romney store of about $800 in merchandise; and many horses and cattle of the people were driven off by the Rebels and a considerable number of beef cattle were slaughtered. Again the Rebels raided the mercantile establishments of Farnsworth and Romney and took $800 in merchandise and from the Union Mercantile, they helped themselves to $1000 worth.

Persistent rumors among the Mexican people of intervention by the United States roused the natives to such a pitch of anger that Americans, other than colonists, left the country in large numbers. It was felt by the leaders of the Mormon colonists, however, that conditions were not serious enough to justify a general migration to the United States.

Several reports appearing in the El Paso papers concerning various indignities which had been inflicted upon the colonists proved irritating to Presidente Portillo and resulted in his requesting an interview with the ecclesiastical head of the Mormon colonies. On March 5, Messrs. Romney, Harris, Thurber, and Call, visited Mr. Portillo at Casas Grandes and had a lengthy interview with him. Mr. Portillo said he expected the Mormons to deny that any outrages had been perpetrated against them, to which the Mormon committee replied that they had given no information to the press and that they would not deny the truth.

Confirming the newspaper reports, Mr. Romney called attention to several outrages suffered by his people at the hands of the Rebels and stressed particularly the case of one Toribio Lara who had been convicted of thievery three different times and each time was released without punishment; and at that very moment he was committing depredations against the people of Colonia Juarez; that only recently he had returned from Casas Grandes to Colonia Juarez under the influence of liquor and attempted to break in the door of the home of a widow and had threatened to kill her unless she gave him $100 and a gun and ammunition. These malicious threats would likely have been executed but for the intervention of neighbors who seized the criminal and turned him over to the Mexican Presidente of Colonia Juarez, an appointee of Mr. Portillo, who in turn, released the culprit at once with the statement that "he had no jail in which to confine him."

On March 14, Mr. Romney addressed a letter to Consul Edwards giving in detail an account of an attack upon a young Mormon boy of Colonia Juarez by three Mexicans. The account is so thrilling and sheds so much light upon the general state of affairs that I submit the letter in full.

"I feel that I should report to you an occurrence which took place in the streets of this (Juarez) colony this evening which will serve to show you the terrible conditions which surround us, and how absolutely destitute of protection we are with existing conditions.

"A group of our school boys, of perhaps fifteen years of age were passing along the streets to their homes when they met three Mexicans, one of them our only policeman, another a grown man and the son of our presidente here in the colony, and the other a man with a family. The first is named Juan Trebizo, the second Florencio Acosta and the third Jose Torres. All the Mexicans were mounted.

"When the Mexicans saw the boys coming down the street they rode over to the sidewalk and Acosta reaching over caught Eugene Taylor, a son of E. G. Taylor, an American citizen, by the throat and making threats he would kill the boy, he took from his pocket his pocket knife but in attempting to open it and hold the boy he dropped the knife to the ground.

"My brother, George S. Romney, happened to be passing along the street with his wife and rushed over to the rescue of the boy, and seeing that Acosta had dropped his knife, George picked it up and began an argument with the Mexicans to induce them to release the boy.

"Acosta said he had lost some horses and felt sure the boy knew where they were and was going to kill the boy unless he should tell where the horses were.

"When my brother picked up the knife Acosta demanded it to carry out the threat he had made, but George told him that he would return the knife only after the release of the boy. Torres then demanded that the knife be given to him. When my brother replied that he would give it up only on condition that the boy should first be released, Torres struck George in the face three times, inflicting a wound on the cheek. George carried in his hand a short single tree and could easily have defended himself even killing the man if necessary but he realized how far-reaching the results of attacking them would be and desisted, preferring to endure insult and even injury rather than to precipitate trouble by retaliating unless the matter should become even more serious.

"By this time the policeman, who was armed with a pistol, and had been a short distance away, rode up and demanded that George hand him the knife, at the same time ignoring the fact that the Mexican had the boy by the throat. Feeling that the policeman was in sympathy with the actions of the other Mexicans inasmuch as he had neither interfered in behalf of the boy, when he was attacked, nor in defense of George when he was struck in the face without provocation, he refused also to surrender the knife to the policeman except he should first order the release of the boy. The policeman was in the act of drawing his gun when another witness, an American, named William Walser, stepped up and George handed the knife to him. Finally the Mexican let the boy go and the three rode off with a threat that they would kill the boy.

"Acosta is one of the three witnesses to a lie in connection with the killing of Juan Sosa during the Madero Revolution, by which action a persecution was brought

against four of our number for the simple performance
of their duty under the direction of a Mexican Presidente.
One of these four was the father of the boy attacked to-
night and as a result of this persecution the father has had
to be in hiding for many months now.

"It now develops that the father of the boy had been
notified by one of the other boys, and from the window
of a neighboring house witnessed the performance with
his rifle levelled on the Mexican making the attack, prepared to make a corpse of him if the thing had been carried
just a notch farther.

"Now what are we to do? It seems that our only
move is to go and make an appeal to Enrique Portillo, who
belongs to the same party and was elected largely as a result of the effort of the Presidente here, who in turn is the
father of one of the participants in the outrage, and placed
the present policeman in the position which he occupies.

"I tell you if conditions continue long as they are
there will be a reign of terror here such as you can hardly
imagine.

"We have endured a great deal in the way of property
loss as you have been informed and now it is getting to be
a very common thing for threats and even attacks to be
made against the persons and lives of our people.

"I think I reported to you that a short time ago a
confirmed thief made an attack on the house of a widow
and her family and threatened to kill them if they did not
give him $100 and a gun and that though all this was done
in the name of the Revolutionists and this man was taken
into custody by our own men who came to the rescue of
the family, he was promptly turned loose to carry out his
threats against us by the political authorities to whom we
delivered him. So far as I know, nothing has been done
to him to date, so you may imagine with what assurance
I undertake the mission before me tomorrow, namely, to
report this affair to our political chief at Casas Grandes.

11

"There are plenty of witnesses to the outrage committed this evening but this makes no difference in Mexico at the present time.

"Only the other evening my attention was called to a group gathered on one of the street corners at night, drunk, with one of them declaiming loudly against our people and foreigners in general. With such things as this going on I regard it as absolutely dangerous to go to the home of the Presidente at night to make a report, and even if such an affair were reported there would be nothing done for our portection, judging from our past experience.

"Only a short time ago I had occasion to go to the home of the Presidente to report a matter to him at night, and on my arrival I found the Presidente about half intoxicated and the policeman and a number of other Mexicans who had congregated there entirely so.

"When I left the house and started home I was followed up the street by the policeman and two Mexicans engaging in loud conversation which revealed anything but a kindly spirit toward us. The Policeman kept firing his gun, I suppose into the air. He fired in all seven shots between his own home and the Presidente's a distance of five blocks, and that right through the middle of town.

"What are we to do under such circumstances? We have done everything possible to keep from provoking trouble which would bring on international complications."

Reference is made in President Romney's communication to Consul Edwards and the killing of Juan Sosa. This event had such far-reaching consequences as to justify, in some detail an explanation of the affair. For weeks prior to the killing of Sosa certain citizens of Colonia Juarez had complained that clothing and other articles about the home had been disappearing and that suspicion pointed at certain local Mexicans as being guilty of the thefts. An investigation was instituted with the result that several of the natives were apprehended and placed under arrest.

Among the number implicated in the theft was Juan Sosa
at whose home some of the stolen articles were found.

In the temporary absence of the Mexican Presidente
of Colonia Juarez, Charles E. McClellan, acting presidente,
issued a warrant for the arrest of Juan Sosa.

The chief responsibility for making the arrest fell to
Guy Taylor a peace officer who in turn deputized three or
four other citizens of Colonia Juarez to assist him. Sosa
lived near the outskirts of the colony and at the time the
officers went to serve the warrant he was irrigating his
field crop adjacent to his home. To reach him the officers
must climb through a barbed wire fence. A man by the
name of Frank Lewis was the first to reach the fence and
while in the act of squeezing between the wires he was
struck a terrific blow over the head by Juan Sosa with the
edge of his shovel blade, inflicting a horrible scalp wound
which, at the time, had the appearance of being very serious. In self defense the men were ordered by Taylor to
fire. Simultaneously several shots were fired and when
the smoke cleared away the Mexican was seen stretched
dead upon the ground.

Notwithstanding the men were in the strict line of
their duty and shot only in self defense, they were placed
under arrest by order from officials of Casas Grandes, to
be held in custody to await trial. Since the colony had
no jail, the men were taken to the tithing office and placed
in the same room with a half dozen Mexicans who had
been charged with stealing colonists' property. Mexicans
were deputized to guard the American prisoners while
Americans stood guard over the Mexican thieves to prevent their escape. The tenseness of the situation can be
appreciated fully only by those who were eye witnesses of
it and were cognizant of the pent-up feelings of the two
groups. An unwise move on the part of either and a bloody
battle would have ensued.

At this juncture, it was deemed expedient by the
ecclesiastical authority of Colonia Juarez to send a com-

mission to interview General Creighton in charge of the
Madero forces at Pearson, seven miles distant, relative to
what appeared to be an impending crisis, and to ask for
the liberation of Taylor and his men.   It fell to the lot of
Professor Guy C. Wilson to fulfill this delicate mission and
a happy selection it was.   Since it would be unwise for
him to make the journey alone I was asked to accompany
him.   We found Mr. Creighton domiciled in one of the
substantial adobe houses at Pearson.   As we came into the
presence of this young adventurer from Texas we were
impressed with his abundant nervous energy and the highly emotional state of his mind superinduced by the tenseness of the situation.   At any moment he might be attacked by opposing military forces and at the slightest suspicious sound from without, his hand instinctively grasped
the handle of a revolver of which he had two swinging
from his belt.

He politely and sympathetically listened to our message and when we had concluded, he addressed a note to the
presidente of Colonia Juarez demanding the release of the
American captives.   Constitutionally he had no right to
issue such an order since the colonies at this time were
under civil law, but should the Madero Revolution be successful even civil authorities who disregarded the mandate
of the invading army would be liable to summary punishment.   Pleased with our success we returned to the colony
to make our report.   Our exultation was, however, of
short duration for the order was not carried out.   A few
days thereafter, Professor Wilson and I were on our way
to Nueva Casas Grandes to intercede with General Francisco I. Madero for the release of Taylor and his companions.   The journey was made in a one seated, black
topped buggy belonging to the Professor.   While he drove
the team I kept an eye open for any unusual happenings
that might arise resulting from the whole country being
infested with roving bands of malcontents.   But nothing
of an unusual nature happened to hinder our progress.

Upon our arrival at Nueva Casas Grandes we immediately went to see General Madero to whom we were permitted to deliver our message. At this time the General had his arm in a sling, he having received a bullet wound in his wrist a few days earlier while storming the old town of Casas Grandes. We were impressed with the fine appearance of Mr. Madero. He was immaculately dressed and the affability of his manner made us feel at ease in his presence. He was short of stature and this would have detracted from his power but for the dignity of his bearing, which seemed native to him. He was most considerate in his attitude toward us and at the conclusion of our interview, he gave instructions to have the Mormon prisoners brought to Nueva Casas Grandes to have a hearing before him. We at once telephoned his message to Colonia Juarez with the result that on the following morning early, the prisoners arrived in Nueva Casas Grandes by team. The streets of the town were thronged with Mexicans, both local and rebel, and as the wagon bearing Taylor and his companions passed down the principal street, the occupants were recognized by some local natives who spread the news among the rabble. A crowd rushed for the wagon and with guns drawn threatened the lives of the prisoners. As I stood looking on I shuddered lest a bloody massacre should occur that I was powerless to avert. The seriousness of the situation impelled Professor Wilson to rush to the headquarters of General Madero for assistance. A brother of Madero was dispatched at once to the scene of the trouble who gave orders for the crowd to disperse and at the same time instructed the colonist prisoners to make their escape from the town as quickly and secretly as possible. No second invitation was needed and without delay Taylor and his party shook the dust of the little city from their feet and were on their way back to their homes by the mesquite and cactus route.

Such an order, coming as it did from the head of the Revolutionary forces, was tantamount to a final pardon.

But with the withdrawal of the Madero forces from the region of the colonies to make an attack on Cuidad Juarez nearly two hundred miles distant, agitation against Taylor and his colleagues again become rife. Threats against them impelled the men to go into hiding.

Finally, when it appeared that no permanent settlement of the case could be reached outside of the courts, Leslie Coombs, a member of Taylor's party, consented to give himself up for trial. It was felt that Coombs could easily be cleared of culpability for the killing of Sosa since he had not fired a shot. With a verdict of not guilty for Coombs the Attorney for the defense surmised that the remainder of the group would automatically be freed.

Coombs was placed in jail at Casas Grandes to await trial before the civil court of that city. There he sweltered for several weeks and there he would likely have remained indefinitely awaiting the slow movements of a Mexican judiciary had it not been for an attack on the city by a band of rebels. Fearing for their lives the officials of the municipality fled from the approaching enemy but not before they opened the door of the prison. Coombs with the other prisoners, made his escape and a short time thereafter he left Mexico to live in a more congenial clime. The other members of his group remained in hiding for a number of months and then finally fled from Mexico with the other Mormon colonists at the time of the general exodus.

These incidents and others of a similar nature induced the head of the Mormon colonies to call together leading colonists from Colonias Dublan and Juarez to consider the matter of importing from the U. S. arms and ammunition to be used by the colonists in self defense. Such an expedient was thought necessary by him because of the limited supply in the colonies and most of the guns owned by the colonists were of short range. The group of leading men who met in conference upon invitation of the President, to take this matter under advisement, after due deliberation, responded unanimously to Mr. Romney's suggestion, and accordingly Orson P. Brown a representative of the colonists in El Paso, Texas, was authorized to make the purchase and arrange for the importation of the arms into Mexico.

Mr. Brown referred the matter to the Mexican Consul at El Paso who, in turn, laid the case before the President of Mexico. The President ruled that the Mormons should not be permitted to import their arms, notwithstanding the Federal Government was powerless to protect the colonists against the depredations of marauding bands of rebels infesting the whole of the territory occupied by the colonists. About a month later, April 11, Mr. Brown wrote a personal letter to President Madero setting forth the precarious condition of the colonists and asking for the authority to import into Mexico 24 Mauser rifles; 20, 30-30 rifles; 10, 30-40 rifles; 4 shotguns, calibre 12 and 25,000 assorted cartridges.

Mr. Brown's letter was referred by the President to the Department of War and Marine for disposition, and Mr. Brown was informed by that department under date of April 30, 1912, that, "the President of the Republic has been obliged to decide that it is impossible to permit the importation of the arms and ammunition to which you refer."

"The situation was so tense and the danger so imminent," said Mr. Romney, "that I determined to import the guns without the authority of the Mexican government, and indeed, without waiting for their final refusal as set forth in the letter of the Minister of War and Marine of April 30." Accordingly an order was placed for a considerable amount of ammunition and largely the list of guns as previously made out by Mr. Brown and in a short time the shipment was brought safely over the international boundary line and distributed among the several Mormon colonies in Chihuahua. These guns were not distributed to individauls but were held as community property to be used only in cases of emergency under the direction of the military commandant of each colony.

An unfortunate incident occurred at Colonia Diaz May 2, which very nearly catapulted the colonists of Diaz and the Mexicans of La Ascension into a life and death struggle. It happened this way: Two Mexicans at night broke into a store of Colonia Diaz and in so doing awoke Frank Whiting who lived not far away. He turned in an alarm which resulted in several armed colonists appearing on the scene. The Mexicans, bearing about $500 in merchandise, were commanded to halt but instead mounted their horses and fled from the scene. As they did so one of the colonists fired a shot into the air thinking to frighten the thieves. By this time nearly the whole town was awake and presuming it to be the beginning of warfare, some of the colonists fired at the fleeing figures with the result that one of the Mexicans was slain. Pandemonium prevailed in La Ascension when the news reached there of the killing of the thief and immediately dire threats were made against the Mormons of Colonia Diaz. Apprehensive of the outcome of the trouble a courier was dispatched from Colonia Diaz to Colonia Juarez, a distance of 75 miles, to confer with President Romney as to what should be done in the matter. Immediately upon receipt of the message borne by the courier Mr. Romney in company with three Mexican officials, set out for the scene of the trouble.

In the meantime a brother of the slain thief set out for the Mormon colony to wreak vengeance for the death of his brother. It mattered little to him who paid the penalty so long as he was an American. On his errand of death as he was approaching the outskirts of Diaz he saw a colonist by the name of James D. Harvey. Approaching him the Mexican threatened his life and being unarmed Harvey sought to escape by running behind the house. He was finally overtaken, and shot down in cold blood. The situation grew still more tense and when

Romney and his party arrived on the night of the killing, war between the two communities seemed inevitable. It was only by bringing together officials of both settlements and getting them to agree to certain compromises that the threatened storm was averted. It was agreed that the four men implicated in the killing of the thief should in the course of two weeks surrender themselves to be tried at Casas Grandes, the seat of the District. The men were tried and acquitted but the murderer of Harvey was never brought to justice although well known in the vicinity and he continued to live openly. But this invasion of the law and escape from punishment by the offender was common in Mexico. Not one of the assassins guilty of shedding the blood of nine colonists over a period of years was ever brought to justice notwithstanding all were known and remained in the localities where the crimes were committed.

The assassination of another colonist on July 2, brought forth a letter from Romney and Harris addressed to the Municipal Presidente at Casas Grandes, Mr. Enrique Portillo. Attention is called to the "assassination of another American colonist, William Adams, in the door of his own home" at Colonia Diaz. Continuing, the gentlemen wrote: "During our residence in the colonies of the country, we have suffered a total of nine assassinations in cold blood and not in one single case has the criminal been chastised, although several times we have delivered the guilty parties to the authorities and in all cases we have appealed to the respective competent authorities * * * during the conflict which exists in this country we have maintained strict neutrality * * * leaving the solution of political questions to the natives of the country * * * but as before said we look with alarm that they injure us not only in material interests; but that they have been allowed to kill our colonists without restriction, which offense seems unnoticed." An appeal is thus made for protection against such abuses and a wish is expressed that criminals shall be brought to justice. Upon the advice of General Salazar this communication was never presented to Portillo since by this time the whole country was under military law thus making null and void the civil authority held by Portillo.

President Romney also wrote the following letter to Consul Edwards at Cuidad Juarez:

"We are just in receipt of news from Colonia Diaz to the effect that a Mexican yesterday shot down another of our American colonists in his own door yard.

"Last evening fifteen armed men went to Colonia Juarez and spent the night trying to capture E. G. Taylor.

"The Rebels yesterday forced fifteen sacks of flour from Farnsworth-Romney and Company of this place.

"A commission waited on Salazar yesterday and protested against such things, and today we go up again to present to him a written statement of which we enclose you a copy.

"Although we feel that our conditions are perhaps the most critical that they have been at any time since the beginning of hostilities and it is difficult to tell just what the end will be, we hope for the best. We hope you will keep in close touch with the situation and that the United States will be solicitous for our welfare.

"We have suffered much wrong and prefer to continue to do so rather than be the means of trouble of an international character, but if things do not change for the better soon we are unable to say how long we can endure it."

It is evident from this communication that conditions were growing worse for the colonists, and the events of the next few days were to confirm the fears expressed. On the date that the above letter was written Salazar and Emilio Campo were reported at Casas Grandes at the head of 700 men and others were expected soon.

Merchandise was taken from the establishment of Ket-

elsen and Degetaus by Rebels who also looted the Union
Mercantile.

Daniel Skousen, owner of a grist mill at Colonia
Juarez, was ordered by Salazar to grind no more wheat
belonging to Mexicans under penalty of having the flour
from such wheat confiscated.

Rebels wandered about the streets of Dublan begging
food and stealing fruit from the orchards of the colonists.
Joseph A. Moffett, a citizen of Dublan, rebuked them for
their thievery, whereupon one of the Mexicans aimed his
gun at Moffett and threatened his life.

General Hernandez made a requisition for 100 sacks
of flour to feed his men and gave receipts for the same.

D. V. Farnsworth interfered with some Mexicans who
were taking horses belonging to James A. Young. One of
the men drew a long dagger on Farnsworth and threatened
his life. Young, witnessing the incident from within his
house, was ready to use his gun in defense of his friend
should the exigencies of the case require it.

But most menacing of all was an order from Salazar
addressed to President Romney asking him to furnish a
list of all the arms and ammunition belonging to the colonists. Romney informed the General that the arms were
private property and did not belong to the colony as a
whole, therefore he could not secure the information. Salazar maintained that he did not intend taking the colonists'
arms but that the information asked for was necessary to
enable him to locate smuggled arms and ammunition.
Salazar was so insistent that Romney finally agreed to send
runners to the various colonies for the information.

The following day the President dispatched men to
the different colonies with instructions to get the information desired by the General but while Salazar had asked
for hurried information Romney instructed his men "not
to expedite their report." "I wished merely to be in the
position," said Romney, "to report to Salazar that I had

immediately sent men to secure, if possible, the information he desired."

On July 5, 1912, the Associated Press received the following report from Casas Grandes: "Rebels under General Salazar, commanding the van-guard of the insurrect army have begun to terrorize this region. Tension among the Americans and foreigners was increased today with the imprisonment of C. E. Hollingsworth, manager of the general store of Ketelsen and Degetaus here. When he refused to give the rebels supplies, they looted the store. Demands have been made upon Mormon colonists for horses and provisions. When the main portion of the rebel army overruns the region it is feared trouble will result. Five hundred cattle already have been confiscated by the rebels from residents along the entire Mexican Northwestern railroad. Where the rebels now are gathered, there is a conspicuous feeling of nervousness as it is not known to what extreme the hungry rebel army will go in its looting."

A most drastic step was taken by a rebel leader calling himself Colonel Arriola at Colonia Diaz on July 12, when he confiscated all of the flour from the grist mill and then demanded all the arms and ammunition belonging to the colonists to be delivered to him on the following morning at ten o'clock. A courier was immediately sent with a report of the affair to Mr. Romney at Colonia Juarez, 75 miles away, where he arrived about 9:30 p. m. of the same day. Without loss of time Romney and Harris left for Casas Grandes in a buckboard to interview Salazar. They reached Casas Grandes about 11:30 that night and drove immedaitely to the Cuartel. The Americans were escorted to a house some distance from there where Salazar was asleep and upon being awakened the General listened to the report of Romney. At the conclusion of the report Salazar uttered a tirade against the Rebel leader who had made such drastic demands of the Diaz colonists and added that written orders had been issued by him that no such demands were to be made upon the colonists—"todavia no" (not yet). Then he checked himself, according to Romney, "as if he had inadvertantly made a disclosure he had not intended to make and then went on discussing other matters." Later in referring to this incident Mr. Romney gave the following statement: "I may observe that up to this moment of time it had never crossed my mind that the colonists would have to leave Mexico, but from this moment I was perfectly convinced that unless Salazar changed his attitude toward the colonists there would be nothing for us to do but to evacuate the country, or in the alternative, actually fight the revolutionists. His manner and expression were such as to convince me that he had already formed a definite plan for the oppression, if not the extermination, of the colonists."

The conference ended with Salazar giving the Committee an order to the Rebel officer at Diaz to desist from further molestation of the colonists. From this interview Messrs. Romney and Harris went to Dublan where they arrived about 3:00 a. m. and dispatched a courier to Diaz with the order from General Salazar. A meeting was then held with leading citizens of Dublan, all of whom expressed themselves stoutly against the idea of giving over their arms and ammunition to the rebel forces.

At the close of the meeting a disclosure was made to Mr. Romney by Bishop Thurber of Dublan to the effect that a friendly Mexican (Toribio Galindo) had recently informed two reliable citizens of the colony that a plan had been well laid by the Rebels to loot the Mormon colonies of everything for which they could find use, including their arms and ammunition, and then flee from the territory upon the approach of the Federal forces. The informant said he obtained this information at Rebel conferences where he posed as a Rebel, while at heart he was sympathetic toward the Federal cause. The looting he declared was to take place within ten days.

The events of the past few days were so serious that the head of the colonies left for El Paso to consult church and government authorities relative to the impending crisis. Salazar was on the train that bore Romney to El Paso and they two spent the major part of the time in conversation. Salazar demanded that Romney make representations that would induce the United States to change its attitude toward the Rebel cause. He stated that the Rebels had given every kind of guarantee to foreigners and particularly Americans and in return the United States had taken sides with Madero through the laying of the embargo on firearms into Mexico. "If the Americans are determined to kill us," said the General, "we will force them to come out and take their chances by bringing on intervention." He then added, "La intervencion ya es un hecho." (Intervention is already an accomplished fact).

Upon arriving in El Paso, Mr. Romney consulted with Anthony W. Ivins, who had been sent there as a representative of the Church authorities on the border. A telegram was then sent to the Church authorities in Salt Lake City in which Romney set forth clearly the impending crisis which seemed inevitable within the next few days and with the further observation "that to attempt to retain our arms and ammunition, meant to engage in an armed conflict with the rebels with odds of twenty to one against us; and that to surrender our arms meant to have our families at the mercy of demons." An answer to this telegram came the following day bearing the information that Mr. Ivins, Mr. Romney and the other leading men of the colonies were to assume the responsibility of deciding what was best to be done in the matter. Immediately President Romney returned to the colonies and was followed five days later by Mr. Ivins.

On July 20, Ivins and Romney went into conference with the leading colonists of Dublan and at about the same time General Rojas and Colonel Jose de la Torre brought in a force of rebels from the north by train and unloaded them at the stockyards in the north end of the town. At once they proceeded to appropriate to themselves all the horses and saddles they could find as well as anything else they fancied. Discovering that they were powerless to stop the depredations being committed, Messrs. Ivins and Romney returned to Colonia Juarez intending to take up the matter with superior military officers. On their way they were overtaken by a messenger bearing an order from General Castillo, who was located at San Diego, with a force of 600 men, to the effect that Mr. Romney was to come to him the following day, at 10 o'clock, with "horses and saddles, guns and ammunition, cash, merchandise and anything else that might be of use to his forces."

The next morning, July 21, Messrs. Ivins and Romney were at San Diego at 10 a. m. in harmony with Mr. Castillo's orders, but without the things he had demanded.

Mr. Ivins interviewed the General while Mr. Romney remained with the buckboard to see that nothing was stolen. During the interview that ensued Castillo reluctantly acknowledged to Mr. Ivins that he was subordinate to Orosco who was the Generalisimo of the revolution. He also promised not to force his demands until Mr. Ivins had opportunity to get in touch with Orosco at Cuidad Juarez and obtain his orders. From San Diego they drove to Casas Grandes where they found things in an uproar. Salazar was just preparing to send a large body of troops against a Federal force at Ojitos under Generals Sanjinez and Blanco. As the two Americans entered the office of Salazar he turned on them and, in an irritated tone of voice demanded, "What do you want?" Mr. Ivins proceeded to explain the object of their mission but was rudely interrupted by the General who savagely ordered them to "Get out in the street; when I want you I will send for you." They obeyed, and later were granted a brief audience with the officer but got no satisfaction from the conference. The only thing left for them was for Mr. Ivins to interview Orosco upon his return to El Paso.

Following Mr. Ivins' return to El Paso, Mr. Romney received a letter from Orson P. Brown informing him that he and Mr. Ivins had been conferring over conditions in the colonies and he (Brown) had come to the conclusion that it would be well "for every man to hide in a good safe place, at least a majority of his better arms and ammunition, for it is just possible that an individual search of every home may be made for these materials * * * it appears to me * * * that the very last thing that we want to do is to precipitate an armed conflict with this overwhelming multitude of rebels."

"I have reported our condition to the Mexican Consul, and as in the case of the people in Sonora, he advises that if we are in danger, that there is only one thing for us to do, and that is to move out of the country until the danger is past and that the government will pay all damages. * * * I am sure that the present U. S. administration have no intentions whatever to interfere in the Mexican situation, if it is possible to avoid it, but still feel that the inevitable is coming regardless of their dilatory action."

On July 26, President Romney received an order from General Salazar through Colonist Henry E. Bowman to meet him at Casas Grandes for an interview. In company with Guy C. Wilson, J. C. Bentley, H. E. Bowman, Hyrum Harris, and A. D. Thurber, Mr. Romney appeared in Casas Grandes at the appointed time. It was decided by the group that only two of their number should be present at the interview with the General and that Romney and Bowman should have that responsibility.

Passing by the guards the two gentlemen were ushered into the presence of the Mexican officer whom they found to be in a turbulent mood. His opening shot was to the effect that he had determined to withdraw all guarantees heretofore given the Mormon people and that no longer would he give protection to their lives or property. Mr. Romney called his attention to the many guarantees both written and oral that the General had given him and that he had always believed them to be valid. Salazar retorted, "Those are mere words, and the wind blows words away."

He went on to explain that following his consultation with
General Orosco it had been decided to take from the colonists all their arms and ammunition. Mr. Romney pointed
out the grave dangers such an action would bring to the
colonists with 2000 rebels in the neighborhood and other
thousands coming this way, but it was all to no purpose.
The General was adamant. Romney then requested that
they be allowed to get their women and children out of
the country before giving the General their final answer
relative to their firearms. Salazar insisted that there was
but one thing to do and that was to deliver over their guns
and ammunition at once and threatened, if that were not
done, to "take his vengeance out upon our women and children by removing all restraint from his soldiers and turn
them loose upon them." The president of the colonies
then asked for time to see Orosco, to which the General
responded: "No, we have have been acting the fool by giving guarantees to you people as long as we have. These
orders have to be carried out right now. Furthermore, we
cannot permit Americans to have arms in our territory
because intervention is now an established fact."

"Well, I will go and consult with the people and see
what they say about giving up their guns," to which Salazar
immediately replied, "No, you cannot leave here until that
order is complied with. You remain right here until it
is complied with." "That means then," said Romney, "I
will be with you a long time, because it will never be complied with. I cannot give any order to the colonists to
bring in their guns and deliver them. We have no military
organization. What few guns there are belong to the individuals. They have bought and paid for them, themselves.
They are their own property. I have no authority to order
them to bring them in."

The suggestion was then made by Demetrio Ponce, a
lieutenant of Salazar, that all the General wanted was for
Romney to make a suggestion to the colonists that they
deliver up their arms and that would result in the colonists

12

turning them over to the Rebel army. Romney replied
that he would refuse to even suggest such a thing, explain-
ing that they would think him a traitor and in league with
the rebels "for," said he, "When you some time ago, demanded a list of the guns I told them that you had given
your word of honor that you would not interfere with
their guns. In these circumstances, I cannot issue the order,
and I do not intend to; I will stay with you and you can do
with me as you please."

In the course of the conversation, Romney told the
General that he was not afraid of him or what he would
do to him. This statement angered the General and aroused
his pride. Well, you can go home to the colonists, neither
am I afraid of you. I will come and get the guns no matter
where I have to go for them. If your guns and ammunition
are not delivered to us we will attack you in the same
manner that we would attack the Federals. * * * We will
consider you as our enemies and will declare war on you
immediately."

Mr. Bowman in reporting the above interview confirms Mr. Romney's narrative throughout. These are his
words: "On Saturday last, Salazar sent for the leaders of
our colony. He told our leaders that among others he
wanted to see Junius Romney, the ecclesiastical head of our
Mexican colonies. * * * He stated that Orosco and his
advisers had decided that the Americans had done everything they could to harm their cause. They demanded
our arms. President Romney refused to issue such an order.
He told Salazar that the Americans were not a military
organization; that he could not issue such an order. "Issue
an order at once for the men in the colonies to give up
their arms," was Salazar's edict. President Romney refused
to do so. "You can stand me up right now and begin to
shoot and kill me," was Romney's reply. "I will not issue
such an order."

Recognizing the imminent danger threatening the
wives and children of the colonists and the widespread de-

struction of property that would result unless some con-
ciliation were granted the rebel forces, President Romney
concluded it was best to make at least a show of complying
with their demands, for the thought uppermost in his mind
and that of his associates "was the safety and protection
of our women and children, the situation of whom was
becoming gravely and increasingly dangerous."

It was therefore arranged between Salazar and Romney that Demetrio Ponce with twenty men should accompany Romney to Dublan to receive the arms and ammunition of the colonists.

Upon arriving at Dublan it was discovered that the
town was wholly occupied by Rebels and that they were
actually looting the stores at the time that President Romney and his group arrived.

A meeting was arranged for at once, to be held at
the home of Bishop Thurber, to which the leading men of
the colony were invited. Ponce evidently intended being
at the session as he marched into the room with his gun
in hand, but at the request of Mr. Romney, he retired. He
immediately placed a guard about the house making it
impossible for any of those in attendance at the meeting
to escape without permission.

At the meeting certain colonists of Dublan pointed
out the impregnable position held by the Rebel forces in
and about the city. At the northeast of town a small
battery of cannon and machine guns were trained on the
town and was supported by cavalry; farther east was another detachment of cavalry; at the south and west sides
of town there were other cavalry forces, so that the place
was entirely surrounded by rebel troops. Against such
a force it would be useless for a handful of colonists to
contend in battle array. To make a show at giving up arms
was the only thing left to do. Those present at the meeting
were, therefore, instructed to go out among the residents
of the colony and explain to them the seriousness of the
situation and ask them to bring their old guns and short

ranged guns, (and nothing but these), to a central place, the school house, where they would be delivered over to Salazar's representatives, with Mr. Ponce at their head. Such an arrangement was thought by the colonists to be better than to have each house visited for the firearms by the rebels, and to this arrangement Ponce agreed. The colonists responded by bringing to the school house 81 guns, 15 pistols and a quantity of ammunition for which a receipt was issued by Salazar's representative.

From Dublan President Romney telephoned the people of Colonia Juarez the procedure at Dublan with reference to the giving over to the rebels the arms and ammunition of the colonists and informed us that he would be at Colonia Juarez in the evening to attend a meeting to discuss the policy that would be adopted by the citizens of that place. At the time we received his message, practically all of the mature male population of the colony were under arms at the tithing office and one or two other central points, prepared to meet in combat the Rebel forces whom we had occasion to believe might come at any time to demand our firearms. For a month or two past we had been organized into military companies and under this organization we had been drilled in military tactics to prepare for a crisis which seemed inevitable. In harmony with the accepted policy of the entire group of Mormon colonies we had agreed to turn the other cheek to the enemy in the event of them demanding our substance, such as grain and cattle, but we would resist their taking our arms and ammunition to the death, if necessary. Imagine our feelings, if you can, when we learned that Dublan had capitulated to the enemy and had given up their firearms. We felt that it would be suicidal to attempt to hold at bay the thousands of rebels who were invading the territory in which our colonies were situated especially since Dublan had decided not to fight. But on the other hand, to surrender our firearms to the Rebels meant that ourselves and wives and children would be at the mercy of those whose

debased natures would tempt them to prey upon the innocent and defenceless, meting out such outrages as they
would deem expedient to reach their nefarious ends. Truly
our predicament was appalling.

A meeting was appointed, to be held in the Church
in the evening, in harmony with instructions received from
President Romney. Practically every adult male member
of the colony was present, and a serious body of men it
was who met to discuss one of the most far-reaching problems of their lives. The meeting was in process when President Romney arrived rather late in the evening. Upon his
arrival he found all the male colonists in conference except
four or five men who stood guard on the outside to prevent
any surprise attack from unfriendly Mexicans. One Mexican who was found eavesdropping was forced into the
meeting house to hear first-hand what was said. There
was lack of unity in the audience at the outset relative
to the policy that should be adopted largely due to the
lack of knowledge of the details of the true situation.
When, however, they had been supplied by Mr. Romney
and others familiar with conditions it was unanimously
agreed that we would follow the example of our sister
colony in giving up our arms and ammunition to the
rebels with, of course, certain reservations. It was also
decided at the meeting that all of our women and children
would be sent to El Paso as soon as arrangements could be
made for their transportation. The gathering adjourned
at 2:00 o'clock in the morning and the balance of the
night was spent in making preparations for the move.

CHAPTER XIV

THE EXODUS OF THE CHIHUAHUA COLONISTS

The decision to send all of the women and children of the Mormon colonies out of Mexico to a place of safety within the boundaries of the United States was a wise one. The colonies were now in the possession of the rebel forces whose leaders were swearing vengeance against the colonists "because of the embargo levied against them by the United States." A strict neutrality had been maintained by the Mormons during the entire period of the revolution, in fact, it had been their policy from the founding of the settlements to keep themselves aloof from the quarrels and factional strife of their neighbors. Very few if any of the Mormon population in Mexico ever took a decided interest in Mexican politics. They were content to be left alone to look after their own affairs, their chief aim being to build up and beautify their homes and subdue the wilderness that their children and unborn generations might come into inheritances of which they could be proud. At the time of the exodus their aim had been well nigh achieved and the thought of being permanently uprooted and the earnings of a life time left to others had never entered the minds of these industrious and frugal people. Always, they had indulged the belief that Mexico was to be their permanent abode and with that thought in view they had builded well.

A brief summary of the conditions in the Mexican colonies at the time of the exodus appeared in an issue of a leading western newspaper of July, 1912, a portion of which I submit to my readers: "The Mormon settlers in Mexico number about 4,000 people. They are generally thought to be among the most well-to-do people in the Church, possessing large tracts of the finest agricultural land in the entire country. Their farms have been improved and stocked with cattle and machinery; residences have been built, and irrigation projects and canal systems have been completed, making the property value reach into the millions of dollars. The 4,000 settlers comprise between seven and eight hundred families and a conservative estimate places an average individual property of each family, including improvements, water rights and stocks at $10,000, or a total of between $7,000,000 and $8,000,000 for the entire number of settlers. It has been ascertained that the Church properties in the colonies amount to $145,000 including ward meeting houses and other buildings valued at $50,000, stake buildings and academies worth $75,000 and office buildings worth $20,000."

Although the decision had been made to send the women and children to El Paso it was felt by most of us at least that their absence from home would be of short duration. Now that Colonia Juarez had determined on an exodus, President Romney felt that the other Chihuahua colonies should likewise prepare to get their families out of danger. He accordingly, on July 28, sent a letter to each of the following colonies: Chuichupa, Garcia, Pacheco, Dublan, Guadalupe and Diaz, informing them of the demands made by Salazar for the surrender of our arms and ammunition and the decision of Dublan and Juarez to accede to his demand and also of the decision of Juarez to send their women and children to the United States. Upon receipt of these letters the several colonies prepared to carry out the instructions of the President. The people of Colonia Diaz were instructed not to go to El Paso, but to go by team to Dog Springs just over the boundary line into the United States.

July 28 was the date set for our firearms to be delivered to the Rebels. As was the case at Dublan, a central place was designated to which owners of arms and ammunition were to make their deposits. Many years have passed since then but I recall vividly the melancholy expression on the faces of scores of men as they made their way toward the public park with guns on their shoulders or in their hands to turn them over to men whom they felt could not be trusted, but who without just provocation would use these firearms against their lawful owners.

But as many dramatic scenes in life are accompanied by bits of humor, so this one, somber as was the picture, was enlivened with tints of humor that even now seem most refreshing. What a collection of firearms this was. Some of them hoary with age, others with hammers gone and still others whose barrels were rusty, indicative of long disuse. I remember with what reluctance I brought forth my own good rifle from its hiding place. It was all I had but it was a beauty and only recently I had made the purchase. As I was on my way to give it up, I met my brother who was on a similar errand but instead of a brand new gun, his was one whose years could not be numbered. Truly it was an antique. Addressing me, my brother said, "Where are you going with that new rifle?" "To the same place you are bound with that old flint lock," I replied. "Let's trade," said he, "mine will serve the purpose just as well as yours." We swapped, he to return my new rifle to his own home as a permanent possession, I to place his antique rifle in the hands of the Captain of the rebel troop. As I gave it to him, he eyed the gun rather quizically and then looking up at me asked, "How do you work the thing?" For my life I couldn't have explained, and as I stood there stammering, not knowing what to say, a native, to my great relief, stepped up and showed him the combination.

While the guns were being collected the rebels were looting the homes of the colonists and at least one of the stores. An old widow lady who was gathering together a few of her personal effects to take with her on a long journey from which she was never to return, was robbed of $40.00, all the money that she had. The rebel had forced his way into her home while she stood helplessly looking on. Teamsters on their way to Pearson with the trunks and bedding of the refugees, who were to entrain for El

Paso, were held up in some instances and robbed of their personal belongings and one old gentleman, a veteran of the Civil War, was poked in the ribs with the barrel of a gun and threatened with death by a demon incarnate. "They could call us the vilest of names," remarked an eye witness, and "they hurled calumny at our wives and children that I did not believe before that a man could possibly endure."

With the report of such outrages pouring in, Mr. Romney informed Mr. Ponce, the rebel leader, that if such things continued, the collecting of firearms would cease. In the meantime one of the teamsters came to me with the information that he had been held up and robbed and that others had shared the same fate. He led me down to the tithing yard where a band of the rebels were camped and pointed out one of the thieves. I reported the matter to the Colonel and he sent an armed posse to bring the culprit to him. The fellow stoutly denied the theft, but a search of his person revealed unmistakable evidence of his guilt. That night as the sun was about to sink from view beyond the Sierra Madre range, the thief was borne to the summit of an elevated plateau overlooking the colony from the east and was shot to death on the order of the rebel chief.

The collection of guns continued. It is well to observe, however, that none of the community arms imported from the United States fell into the hands of the rebels. All were safely hidden away.

The seriousness of the situation was reported to Salazar at Casas Grandes, resulting in his issuing the following order to Mr. Ponce:

"When you shall have terminated the work which I commissioned you to do, you will designate, from the troops under your command, a captain with ten men, in whom you have absolute confidence as to their discipline and honor, who will be left as a garrison in Colonia Juarez, with the most severe and careful instructions to conduct themselves properly, energetically opposing any attempted abuse against the residents of the colony referred to or against their property. You will also see that your own soldiers do not appropriate any of the property or supplies of the colony referred to without first presenting an order from this headquarters.

"The head of the colony will furnish to you quarters and supplies sufficient for the needs of the garrison during occupancy."

Reform, Liberty and Justice,
Casas Grandes, July 28, 1912,
The General in Chief of the First Revolutionary Zone,
                    (signed)   Inez Salazar.

July 28 and 29 were busy and exciting days at Colonia Juarez. As indicated above, while the firearms were being turned over to the rebels, the women and children were being rushed to the nearest point on the railroad (Pearson), seven miles distant from Colonia Juarez. There was little time or inclination to gather together many personal effects for the journey. Usually they consisted merely of a trunk or two for each family, containing a change of clothing for the different members of the family, a few heirlooms and a roll or two of bedding. In most instances rugs and carpets were left on the floors, pictures were left hanging on the walls and the furniture much in the same position as usual. In my own case, all I got out of the colony was one trunk full of clothing for a wife and five children and a role of bedding. We packed another trunk with some of my wife's choicest things and bound it with a rope but we could find no means for its conveyance to the Railroad station. It was therefore left in our house with our other things to be made use of by those who took a fancy to them. After the family left I gathered up some of our choicest dishes and hid them away in the attic and at the same time, dug a hole in our garden where I deposited a quantity of our bottled fruit and sugar. The sugar

I placed in five gallon tin cans to protect it from the dampness. Up to the present I have never brought forth from their hiding places either the dishes or the eatables—the rebels may have done so.

While the last group of colonists were waiting for the train at Pearson, which was four hours late, a band of about twenty armed rebels came dashing up to them and with profane and abusive language threatened them and stole articles of wearing apparel. It thus seemed evident that Salazar was either powerless to protect the colonists or he had no desire to do so.

Similtaneous with the departure of the women and children from colonies Juarez and Dublan, the families of the colonists living in the mountain settlements, Pacheco, Garcia and Chuichupa, were deserting their homes and fleeing for safety. It was a big day's travel by team from these colonies to Pearson where they were to entrain for El Paso. In all there were about 450 from these settlements and since railroad cars were not plentiful, these poor exiles were crowded together almost to the point of suffocation, and to add to their suffering, they were not provided with any water to drink, and when night came on they were left in total darkness for the remainder of their trip. A resident of Garcia writing of the affair July 30, 1912, had this to say: "On this memorable day a sad procession of about thirty-five wagons moved away from Garcia, including the women and children of the settlement and a few men to drive the teams. We left everything behind but a few trunks and rolls of bedding."

On July 28, at 4 a. m., Levi L. Tenney came from Dublan with a letter from President Romney addressed to Bishop Ernest Romney at Colonia Diaz advising the colonists to leave for the States. Bishop Romney called the men together and in consultation with them it was decided to take the women and children to Hachita, New Mexico. By 11 a. m. of the same day eighty-six wagons were loaded and ready to move. The company reached the United

States in the evening and on the following day pitched camp at Dog Springs where it remained until August 1, when the colonists moved on toward Hachita. This little settlement was reached on August 3, and was the abiding place of the refugees until November 1, 1912, when they split up and as small groups or individually sought new homes somewhere within the boundaries of the United States and Canada. To return to their homes in Diaz was impossible since the rebels, after looting the place, literally destroyed it with fire.

A telegram sent by Apostle Ivins from El Paso to the General Authorities of the Church at Salt Lake City and dated July 29, bore the following message: "350 refugees reached here at midnight from the colonies. Expect two trains today with probably 1,000 persons. There has been no personal violence but many threats have been made. It appears to be the policy of the rebels to bring on intervention."

Another special report of the same date referred to the driving of the colonists from western Chihuahua under threats of violence by the rebels under General Salazar. The report stated that "350 colonists reached El Paso early today. More than 400 more arrived this afternoon on special trains and all women and children will come during the next twenty-four hours if trains can be secured to bring them. Refugees from the colonies tell of the threatening conditions there. All colonists were yesterday deprived of all arms and ammunition by the rebels. Houses were searched and colonists warned that resistance would result in severe treatment. Stores in the colonies were relieved of all arms and ammunition, and supplies."

The care of all these penniless refugees was a matter of no small moment, but the government and the people of El Paso were solicitous of their welfare, and while the shelters provided them on the spur of the moment were anything but comfortable, they at least furnished a partial protection from the heavy rains that were not infrequent during this period of the year. A special dispatch of July 29, stated that "Preparations have been made in El Paso to care for the colonists. An effort has been made to secure tents from the war department to establish a tent colony near Fort Bliss but Colonel T. Z. Stevens, commanding forces here, is unable to give the tents without authority from the war department. Until that authority can be secured, the colonists will be cared for the best way possible in hotels, boarding houses and private homes in El Paso."

But the exiles were not to enjoy the luxury of hotels, boarding houses or even private houses, but rather were housed in sheds at a deserted lumber yard with no shelter from violent thunder storms save the roof overhead and a rough board floor beneath. Here the larger group was quartered while the balance were housed in the upper floor of an old building. This building had as its covering corrugated iron that became almost red hot under the burning rays of a southern sun. Imagine if you can the distress of the refugees crowded together as they were in such a sweat box. I confess that the sights which met my gaze both here and at the lumber yard were such as to cause me to stand aside and weep.

The shed at the lumber yard was just a big open space, and when I arrived in company with Professor Guy C. Wilson, with whom I had been sent from the colonies to look after the refugees, it was filled to capacity with human beings destitute of practically everything but a hope that such appalling conditions would soon end and they would be permitted to return to their comfortable homes in the colonies. There was no privacy, each family being apportioned a few square feet of space on which to eat and sleep and when the beds were laid, there was literally not one foot of space between them. But most distressing of all was the humiliation of our mothers and wives in being subjected to the gaze of the curious as they stood or reclined, gowned in calico, the balance of their ample wardrobes having been left behind in the hurried flight.

At this stage, Orin P. Miller's report of conditions in the refugee camp will be enlightening. Mr. Miller was a member of the presiding Bishopric of the Church and in this capacity was sent by the Church to give material aid to the colonists. The following were his observations: "I arrived at El Paso at 5:12 last evening and found Elder Anthony W. Ivins somewhat improved in health but very busy. * * * I visited the refugees late in the evening and found a condition that was most appalling. Quite a number of women and children were ill; several infants had been born en route and since the arrival at El Paso. The committee was successful in getting 150 moved last evening to the St. Joseph Stake." Other companies, he reported, would leave for other parts at once. "The government is purchasing some supplies and the people of El Paso have been very liberal with their means and have rendered very valuable assistance. * * * The sight presented to my view is one of the most heart-rending I have ever witnessed—to see over 2,000 people, mostly women and children, driven from their homes without time to gather even their personal effects and most of them without a dollar to assist themselves with. We shall have to draw upon the Church for relief. We are expecting 500 tents from the government today which will be sent to the different settlements where we expect the refuges to locate."

Elder Ivins, on August 15, reported that "All the colonies have been looted. Heavy rains make conditions at refugee camps distressing. Friends in the North are assisting with funds which are thankfully received."

It was thought by the leading men of the colonies that following the exodus of the women and children conditions would become more settled and in a short time the refugees could with safety return to their homes. All of the adult male members of the several colonies save a few of the older ones, therefore, remained behind to look after their property. However, conditions continued to become more turbulent. "Insults and epithets from the Rebels,"

said President Romney, "were the rule, and the whole attitude of the Rebel forces was rapidly becoming unbearable."
Accordingly, Mr. Romney called for representatives of the
different colonies to meet in a conference at Colonia Juarez
to determine a future course of action.   It was evident to
all present at the conference that the removal of the women
and children had not "solved the problem with the Rebels,
of whom there were between two and three thousand in the
neighborhood of the colonies, whereas there were only 250
available male colonists—hopeless odds in view of our la-
mentable shortness of arms and ammunition—and that,
therefore, further measures would in the more or less near
future have to be taken."

Even before the conference was held leading men of
the colonies had begun to feel that there would be no peace
or safety in the near future.   Men of the colonies would
be forced to fight the Rebels or desert their homes.   With
that thought in mind, a movement was on foot both in
Juarez and Dublan to concentrate at a central point, the
arms and ammunition of the colonists, as well as a supply
of provisions.   Considerable difficulty was encountered as
a result of the Rebels patrolling the streets, but eventually
substantial deposits of these materials were collected.

On August 1, a rebel leader claiming to be "Cavaro"
entered Colonia Juarez at the head of 75 men.   Their first
inquiry was if the Mormons had killed any more of their
men.   It developed that the Mexican thief executed at
the command of Ponce belonged to their band and these
men had come intending to take vengeance on the Americans for the deed.   They demanded quarters and were given
the Redd home at the north of town.   That night they
posted guards around the colony.   Things were taking on a
very serious aspect resulting in another "secret" conference.
At this meeting it was determined to evacuate the colony
immediately.   To that end it was decided that all the
men of Colonia Juarez should meet at the place where the
firearms and provisions had been deposited, and with that

accomplished the next step in the program would be considered.

The journey to the rendezvous must be made at night
and the greatest secrecy must be maintained. The town
was, therefore, divided into two territorial districts and
over each was placed a captain whose responsibility was
to see that all of the men in his district were notified and
then to lead them to the place appointed, in the cliffs north
of town. Through some misunderstanding there was a
hitch in the program resulting in a delay but finally the
first step in the plan was completed.

Meanwhile, President Romney "sat down under the
shadow of the mountain about midnight and by the light
of a lantern" he wrote orders to the leaders of the various
colonies in Chihuahua, giving careful directions as to the
manner of evacuation and the place of general rendezvous.
This was to be an almost inaccessible place in the mountains known as "the Stairs" and located about seven miles
from Colonia Juarez. These instructions were carried
to Dublan and the mountain colonies by two heroic couriers
who set out at once.

The flight of the colonists from Dublan proved to be
a thrilling affair. The Rebels, finding that they had gone,
went in hot pursuit and when within range opened fire
upon the fleeing men, assuming that they were unarmed.
One of the rebel bullets struck the leg of a young fellow,
William Smith. At this juncture the Captain of the
Colonist band, Bishop Thurber, ordered ten men to fall
back and open fire on the enemy with their long range guns.
The order was obeyed and the rebels were halted in their
pursuit. The company pushed on and in due time were
at the "Stairs" with the company from Colonia Juarez.
Here they remained until the arrival of the men from the
mountain colonies of Garcia and Pacheco. The men from
Chuichupa were somewhat delayed and sent word that
they would overtake the main company en route to the
United States. A military organization of the entire group

was effected while encamped at the "Stairs." Bishop A. D.
Thurber was given chief command, Gaskell Romney was
made Quartermaster General with S. E. McClellan and
Ernest Hatch as his aides and A. B. Call Chief Sanitary
Master. The whole body was then divided into companies
of tens over each of which a captain was chosen to preside.
In all there were 235 men and 500 horses.

The mental and physical strain was beginning to tell on
the men for, as yet, they had received no word from their
families who had been sent to El Paso. Some of the colonists wished to return and fight the Rebels but the calmer
heads felt it would be suicidal for a handful of men to
attack many times their number. One of the band, John
Allen, became mentally deranged, temporarily, and leaving
the camp under cover of darkness, he made his way back
to his home at Colonia Juarez where he was found the next
day by volunteers, who went in search of him. Arrangements were made to have him cared for by friendly Mexicans until he should recover from his misfortune.

On August 7, the march toward the border began.
The first night and the following day were spent at Tapa-
citas waiting for an attachment from Chuichupa. When
on the march, the caravan was protected against a surprise
attack by a strong rear guard and a vanguard thrown out
several miles in advance. On August 9 two Rebels were
seized by the rear guard and brought into camp. One of
the Mexicans was riding an animal belonging to a colonist
and both men were well armed. From these men information was received that a few miles back there were nine
other armed Mexicans and these, a few hours later, were
brought to camp. Their firearms were taken from them
and they were compelled to march under a heavy guard.
The Janos River was reached on the 9th of August, the
colonists having traveled about sixty miles during the day.

On August 10, they "passed through Colonia Seco
and watered at Palotada. Here the eleven Rebels were
released with the promise that if they met any Americans

they would not molest them. They were permitted to
leave on mounts and were given ample provisions to last
them until they could reach the forces of General Blanco
which they expected to join. "They had been very apprehensive that we would execute them," observed President
Romney, "and were much relieved when they learned that
such was not our intention." The international boundary
line was crossed about sundown on August 10, and soon
thereafter the men reached Dog Springs where fifteen
American soldiers had been stationed to protect the ranch
from the depredations of Mexican rebels. As the colonists entered a rock corral at Dog Springs they narrowly
escaped being fired upon by the American soldiers who
were crouched behind a hill awaiting the approach of the
rebels who were reported to be after a supply of horses.
Luckily the colonists were recognized in time to avert a
dreadful tragedy. From Dog Springs the column pushed
on to Alamo Hueco. By this time the men and horses
were greatly fatigued, for the journey had been a trying
one for both. Many of the animals had become too tired to
travel farther and their dead bodies were left by the wayside.
A number of colts were also killed, it being impossible for
them to keep up with the company. Soon the men were
with their families, many of whom were in El Paso, and a
happier meeting cannot well be imagined. I was present
in El Paso when the dust-covered, bedraggled column entered the city and I shall always remember the affectionate
welcome tendered them by their families and friends and
by the people of El Paso in general.

CHAPTER XV

THE EXODUS OF THE SONORA COLONISTS

The same forces at work against the peace of the colonists in Chihuahua were disturbing the colonists in Sonora.

An Associated Press dispatch of July 9, from Agua Prieta, across the international boundary line from Douglas, Arizona, announced that "The determination of the Mormon colonists of Colonia Morelos and Colonia Oaxaca, south of here, to resist the demands of prowling rebel bands, coupled with the Mormon appeals to Washington presented a menacing situation today. The Mormons declare they will no longer contribute food or horses to the forces of Orosco. Nine Mormons have been killed by rebels since the revolution began five months ago. Most of the Mormons are American citizens. They have armed themselves and declare they will fight to protect themselves against rebel devastation. A few of the Mormons are naturalized Mexicans and great fear has been expressed that this circumstance might impel the rebels to assume they were justified in attacking the colonists if they resist demands for supplies."

On the same date Joseph F. Smith, President of the Church of Jesus Christ of Latter-day Saints, received a telegram from Bishop Charles W. Lillywhite of Colonia Morelos, dated at Douglas, Arizona, July 9, 1912, stating that the conditions had grown serious in that colony and that Federal troops were committing depredations much graver at Morelos than those of the rebel marauders at Juarez and Dublan. One hundred federal soldiers had been camped in the colony, some in the Church, for over a week and had lived upon the provisions of the colonists. Food supply was almost diminished; teams had been demanded. Sanjinez, in control, refused protection to the colonists' property. President Smith answered the wire expressing sympathy and advising "prudence and calmness." He suggested the desirability of following the advice of Senator Reed Smoot to keep accurate accounts of all losses and depredations they might suffer and that they communicate with the federal officials at Mexico and protest their grievances.

On July 15, it was reported that against the protest of the colonists more than 1,000 soldiers camped in the streets and that repeatedly women of the town were offended. Chicken coops and gardens were devastated and mercantile establishments looted. Intoxicated soldiers rode wildly through the streets yelling and shooting and their officers made no attempt to stop them. Women and children were afraid to appear on the streets and the conduct of the soldiers was such as to threaten a rupture between well-armed Mormons and the federal troops. Bishop Lillywhite reported that several women followers of the army acted in a manner highly objectionable to the morals of the community.

J. J. Huber, a prominent citizen of Morelos, confirms the report of Bishop Lillywhite with reference to the lawlessness and immorality of the federal troops in the following language: "Sanjinez with 1500 men came to Morelos and quartered on the streets and in the school building. A few of the officers were quartered in private homes. * * * During the next three weeks the colonists were compelled daily to view the most shocking examples of immorality, the soldiers being everywhere about the houses of the town. No place was sacred from their intrusion. Nude soldiers bathed in the city canal within the limits of the town and in open view of the houses. Beef were slaughtered in the very doorways of the best homes and offal left to putrify in the hot summer sun. Prostitutes, camp followers, plied their trade openly with the soldiers in broad daylight and in full view of a portion of the colonists' houses. Hen roosts were robbed and gardens stripped of vegetables, and trees of fruit, horses were taken from the fields and made to do service under federal saddles and, in fact, nothing movable was saved." When complaint was made to General Sanjinez he replied, "I regret that such things occur but I can give you no guarantee of protection. But I suggest that you place night watchmen at your places of business."

Sanjinez demanded colony teams and wagons to transport goods and ammunition in pursuit of rebels. "Teams I must have and teams I will have. * * * I will take them whenever and wherever I want them," emphatically declared the general. The colonists secretly drove many of their horses into the mountains to escape the covetous eyes of the troops. A telegram setting forth the terrible state of affairs in Colonia Morelos was dispatched to President Joseph F. Smith and copies of the telegram were forwarded by President Smith to Washington D. C., and to the United States Consul at Nogales, Arizona.

Sanjinez commandeered a number of the teams and wagons of the colonists to haul his supplies, but a compromise was effected by which they were granted leave to haul the freight only as far as Colonia Oaxaca instead of the long distance haul first planned by the Mexican General.

Word was received in Morelos that Salazar, at the head of a large army was speeding toward the Sonora colonies with the avowed intention of wreaking vengeance on the American colonists. The news was alarming and resulted in a hurried exodus of the women and children from the colonies to the United States. The migration began on August 30, and in the company there were nearly 450 people all of whom must be conveyed to the border in lumber wagons, of which there were sixty. Heart rending must have been the scene as the wives and children bade adieu to the husbands and fathers not knowing if it would be their good fortune to ever meet again. "As the company left the colony," said Mr. Huber, "sobs were heard on every hand." To add to the distress of the refugees the rain fell in torrents drenching nearly everyone to the skin. The only protection afforded the little ones were the stooped forms of their mothers as they bent over their offspring to shield them from the pitiless storm.

The journey was not free from its tragedies but most pathetic of all was the death of a little fellow whose life was crushed out of him by the overturning of a wagon. The little body was taken back to Morelos to be laid by the side of its kinsmen overlooking the waters of the Bavispe, while the caravan moved on. At last the weary journey ended and the exiles passed under the protecting care of Uncle Sam and the good people of the city of Douglas. The men who had remained behind were hopeful that conditions would become settled but to their dismay, lawlessness increased and human life became exceedingly cheap. In the midst of these threatening dangers the only safety seemed to be in flight. Scarcely had the last of the colonists abandoned their houses when the rebels came pouring in by the hundreds. Salazar with his rebel force entered Morelos on September 12, and soon thereafter came Rojas leading a band of 500. The stores were looted, cattle were killed for beef and every available thing deemed serviceable was confiscated by these Mexican hordes. Several of the Colonists on their way to Douglas were held up by the Rebels and their belongings taken from them. Ed. Haymore, a merchant of Colonia Morelos, was on his way to the United States with $25,000 in merchandise with the thought of getting it to a place of safety when he was overtaken by Rojas and his men. The merchandise was seized and his team of six horses fell a prey to the rapacious greed of the Rebels and he himself was held a prisoner for three days. When at last he was given his freedom he was turned loose without food to make his way as best he could to a place of safety.

Three other colonists, Anderson, Jones and Nichols were driving a band of horses from the colony hoping to evade the Rebels who were infesting the country. Suddenly and unexpectedly they were overtaken by Salazar and his followers who seized all of their loose horses. These they

immediately saddled, including the colts. Then they robbed
the colonists of their arms and ammunition and ordered
them back to the colony. As they journed toward the
colony under guard Salazar talked freely with them and
accused President Romney of being responsible for the
removal of the colonists from Mexico and for the failure
of the colonists to deliver all their guns. He said he was
waiting for Romney's return to Mexico when he would
"fix" him. The Rebel band camped near San Jose a few
miles from Colonia Morelos and at once a foraging party
was ordered to Don Rust's place to bring back chickens
for the camp. At the same time fences were torn down
and the horses were turned into Mr. Rust's growing grain.

The kidnapping of Haymore and other indiginities
suffered by the colonists of Sonora induced President
Romney, now at Douglas, to dictate a letter to General
Sanjinez who was just across the Mexican boundary line
at Agua Prieta. The letter calls the attention of the
Mexican General to a petition made the day before by the
American Consul and the father of the kidnapped man
asking that troops be sent to the "Gallardo" Ranch to investigate the whereabouts of the missing man. The General is notified that C. W. Lillywhite and two brothers of
Edward Haymore had gone to the Ranch in search of him
and upon arriving there had found his two wagons abandoned with the majority of the harnesses strewn upon the
ground. The merchandise had been stolen and a part of
the clothing of Mr. Haymore was found hanging to the
furniture in the wagon. A feeling is expressed that the
rebels have assassinated him or that he is detained against
his will and the General is requested to send troops immediately to the Ranch to investigate, and to look for the
body of the colonist, Edward Haymore." In conclusion
Romney says: "The majority of the colonists including
all of the women and children, have had to flee from their
homes and are at the present time in this city without
funds. As all our crops are abandoned and are in urgent

need of cultivation and irrigation and as we have about two million dollars of property in the colonies of the State of Sonora without protection while our families are here suffering for want of the necessities of life, therefore, I petition you most earnestly that you will kindly take into consideration our conditions and send the necessary forces to our colonies to rid that region of Revolutionists and protect our properties and provide the necessary protection for our families who desire to return to their homes at the earliest possible date."

As indicated above Edward Haymore was released by his kidnappers and eventually joined his family in Douglas, but to his discredit, Sanjinez remained indifferent to the afflictions of the colonists.

On the last day of September, 1912, twelve male refugees returned to Colonia Morelos hoping to rescue a few of their hard-earned savings of a quarter of a century, but the sight they beheld where once a flourishing settlement had stood was indescribably painful. They found that every house in town had been looted; sewing machines and furniture in general had been smashed and musical instruments in numerous instances had been used for kindling wood. On one broken organ they beheld the inscription "Long live the Liberals and death to the Mormons." Carcasses of animals lay strewn about the streets and a few drunken Mexicans kept ribald watch over the dreadful scene. Like Goldsmith's Deserted Village, the colonies of Sonora had passed away perhaps never again to be inhabited save by an occasional ranchero or some wandering nomad.

CHAPTER XVI

EVENTS FOLLOWING THE EXODUS

A relief committee consisting of prominent Church offiicials and some of the leading men of the colonies had been organized in El Paso at the time the colonists arrived there from Mexico. The duty of this committee, as the name implies, was to seek financial relief for the exiled Saints and to give such advice and comfort as lay within their power. It seemed not to have entered the minds of the committeemen that it would be necessary for the exiles to long remain away from their homes. It was felt that a stable government would soon be established in Mexico and with its return, all who desired could be reinstated in their posessions with a guarantee of safety for the future. Born of this feeling the thought was expressed by the committee that, "all of the male refugees from the Chihuahua colonies who could leave their families and who desired to return to the colonies for the purpose of regaining possession of their properties and of protecting the same should do so at the earliest possible date that it could be done in safety, and that to this end the assistance and protection of the civil and military authorities of the Mexican Government would be requested, and that every possible effort would be made to work in harmony with such authorities, the colonists to return unarmed and to continue their policy of strict neutrality."

Accordingly President Romney called upon the Mexican Consul at El Paso and obtained from him the promise that the Mexican Government would establish garrisons in the country sufficient to guarantee peace and the protection of the colonists who would be privileged to return to their homes in the course of a few days. The Consul informed Mr. Romney, also, that he would take up the matter with the Governor of returning the colonists' horses from Hachita to the colonies, as well as the matter of the colonists being permitted to return with their firearms.

On August 21, the Relief Committee passed a resolution authorizing four men to go by special train to the colonies on the following morning to ascertain conditions there. The men selected to go were Miles A. Romney, Daniel Skousen, Alonzo S. Taylor, Hyrum S. Harris and D. V. Farnsworth.

On August 24, Mr. Romney had an interview with General Tellez at Cuidad Juarez. Tellez gave the same assurances as had been previously given by the Mexican Consul at El Paso, that the Mexican Government would maintain a strong garrison in the Casas Grandes Valley for the protection of the colonists and further, that it would be safe for the citizens of the Colonies of Juarez and Dublan to return to their homes in a few days. However, he advised against the speedy return of the colonists to the Mountain settlements and Colonia Diaz. The Rebels and other bandits must first be driven out, and for that purpose he had dispatched General Sanjinez with a force into the mountain settlements and upon his return he would send him to clean up things at Colonia Diaz. He expressed a feeling that it was the duty of his government to do all possible to protect the lives and property of the Americans and to that end he would dedicate his high office.

Three members of the committee sent to investigate conditions in the colonies, Messrs. Harris, Farnsworth and Taylor, returned to El Paso with their reports which were anything but encouraging. Mr. Harris and Mr. Farnsworth reported that at Colonia Dublan houses had been looted, and "clothes, dishes and bedding had been carried off." Much of this work had been done by local Mexicans. They met General Sanjinez who informed them that it would not be safe for the colonists to return in the immediate future as the country was still full of Rebels and, "We may be called away at a moment's notice."

Reports that reached the committeemen through

Mexicans, of conditions in the mountain settlements, were to the effect that many of the houses had been wantonly destroyed and that crops had been ruined through Rebels pasturing their animals in the fields. Taylor's report of conditions at Colonia Juarez were anything but reassuring.

The assurances given President Romney by General Tellez impelled him to leave El Paso for the colonies on August 25 accompanied by a few of the colonists from Dublan and Juarez. "I thought it proper," observed Mr. Romney, "that I should go down with the first who should return with a view to remaining in order that I might be in a position to make whatever arrangements should be made with the military authorities to the end of securing our horses which might have fallen into the hands of the Federals and of getting from them some official acknowledgement of the condition of our houses and property at the time of our return."

Upon arriving in the colony of Dublan, Mr. Romney learned that Generals Sanjinez and Blanco were in Pearson and accordingly set out to interview them, arriving at Pearson early in the afternoon of August 25. He found both Generals together and being acquainted with Blanco, Romney addressed himself to him, but Blanco deferred to Sanjinez and left the room. During the conversation that ensued Sanjinez stated that it would not be proper for the colonists to return at the present time as the country was still infested with Rebels. He admitted that nothing had been done to clear the mountain settlements and could give no assurance as to when that would be done. Mr. Romney urged upon him the necessity of our families being permitted to return to their homes at the very earliest possible moment as they were without food and they must depend upon their crops, now fast perishing, for their winter supply. An appeal was made to the General to have some one appointed to make a critical inspection of the Mormon settlements to ascertain the extent of the property damage before the return of the colonists. The

request was also made of the Mexican official that he issue
a written order demanding the return of all colony property within a given time, with the assurance that those
who complied would escape punishment, while those who
refused to comply with the demands of the order would
be dealt with according to law. It seems evident from
Romney's report of this and subsequent interviews with
Sanjinez that the General was determined to shoulder no
responsibility in any matters relating to the colonies. Invariably, he referred the representative of the Mormon
colonists to the civil authority of Casas Grandes for adjustment of all such difficulties.

Mr. Romney, in company with the local presidente of
Colonia Juarez, Felipe Chavez, visited Talamantes, Presidente of Casas Grandes, and asked for an official inspection
of the colony properties. The Presidente responded by ap-
pointing the acting judge of the District as inspector. The
work of inspection was begun at once in Colonia Dublan
and the results of the investigation revealed a sad state of
affairs. From the two principal mercantile establishments
of the colony at least one hundred thousand dollars in
merchandise had been stolen and in some of the private
homes not one piece of furniture remained. One of the
most pathetic examples of vandalism was the looting of
the large brick home belonging to Mrs. Mary Farnsworth.
The home had been well furnished throughout. A plentiful supply of provisions had been left there, as well as
several boxes of merchandise which the boys had brought
from the store to conceal from the Rebels. All had disappeared from the place or had been destroyed except a
China cupboard with glass front from which every dish
had been taken. A large portrait of Father Farnsworth
"hung on the wall but it had been utterly ruined by having
a two quart bottle of blackberries hurled at it. The carpets
had been torn from the floors and the window blinds and
curtains from the windows."

Reports of conditions in the other colonies were similarly disheartening. Edmund Richardson reported to the committee in El Paso that every house in Diaz except one had been looted of practically everything having any value.

The mountain settlements, particularly Pacheco and Garcia had a most desolate appearance declared eye witnesses. In Pacheco, according to the report, "There is absolutely nothing of worth left in the town except the homes and these have been considerably damaged by holes chopped in the ceilings and floors with axes by persons looking for anything that might have been hidden away and by the breaking of windows and doors."

"The organs, stoves, chairs, dressers, and in short, all kinds of furniture that they have not been able to haul off, have simply been broken into pieces and strewn from one end of the town to the other. Cattle have been shot down by dozens and skins never opened. A clean sweep has been made of all horses * * * fences had been cut and what cattle were about the town were in the crops."

At Garcia the potatoes were rotting in the field due to excessive moisture, while the gardens had been ruined by hogs turned loose to wander at will.

Following a collection of all the reports, President Romney addressed a summary of conditions in the colonies to General Blanco at Pearson. Among other things he said, "The envoys who now return from the colonies informed me that they found all of the houses there completely looted. Only the houses remain and these are terribly injured. The doors and windows are broken and the floors and ceilings have been destroyed with axes. Such furniture as they have not been able to take the looters have completely destroyed.

"So far as the crops are concerned the envoys found the fences torn down and that the revolutionists had destroyed much by turning their animals into the crops. They find, however, that there is still left in these two colonies approximately forty thousand dollars ($40,000) of unharvested oats, including the crop of Colonia Chuichupa.

* * * In addition to the oats mentioned there still remains a part of the corn and part of the potato crop. These represent many thousands of dollars and must be harvested at once or they will be lost.

"Of the many horses which were owned in the colonies none remain and the same may be said of the harnesses. The machinery has been destroyed by breaking it into pieces.

"The residents of these colonies are at the present time in El Paso, Texas, absolutely without resources and waiting only to learn if it will be possible for them to return to their homes and harvest their crops which yet remain." The letter closes with an earnest appeal in behalf of the exiled colonists.

But nothing came of the letter and noting the general indifference of both Blanco and Sanjinez, Romney made the following comment: "My best judgment after visiting the colonies and talking with those who visited the mountain colonies, and after consulting with Sanjinez and Blanco and preceiving their manifest indisposition to pursue the rebels and their apparent indifferences to the conditions in the colonies, was that it was not safe for the colonists to return with their families at this time."

Added to these discouragements were the vindictive threats still being uttered against the colonists by Inez Salazar, epitomized in a purported statement of his to the effect that the Mormons had escaped him once by deceit, but that he would get them yet.

On September 6, Romney and Brown had an interview with General Huerta and Consul Llorenta in Cuidad Juarez. Upon this occasion Huerta assured them that within four days he would have a strong garrison of cavalry troops stationed at Palomas, Janos, and Ascencion, thus making it perfectly safe for the Mormons to return within five days to the three valley Colonies, Juarez, Dublan and Diaz.

Fearing that he had not made sufficiently impressive

certain matters of importance while in conversation with General Huerta, Romney on the day following the interview, wrote the General a lengthy letter in which he outlined in detail the losses suffered by the Americans. He urged the importance of the military authorities, rather than those invested merely with civil authority, looking after the property interests of the colonists. He maintained that the major losses in property had been incurred at a time when civil authority had been superceded by the military, therefore upon the latter rested the chief responsibility of adequate adjustment. By this time it appears evident that the President had given up hopes of all the colonists ever returning to their homes in Mexico for in the letter above quoted he continues: "It must be apparent to you, that since 4,000 people have in the present instant, been driven from their homes penniless and without previous warning, into the United States for safety, they have become scattered from the Mexican to the Canadian borders, and in many instances will never return to their homes in Mexico, if ever so desirous." Based on this assumption, Romney feels that it would be only just and right that the General permit the appointment of a commission "from the colonies to receive any and all properites belonging to our people, and that this commission be permitted to take colony property wherever found upon presentation before the proper authorities of suitable witnesses." Mr. Romney asks that a garrison be placed in the colonies of Dublan and Juarez where there is not a "single policeman to give protection to the property that is left and almost nightly, crops and even furniture and other property is being hauled away from the unprotected fields and homes." A copy of this letter was forwarded by Mr. Romney to the Mexican Consul Mr. Llorente in El Paso.

About the middle of September, Charles E. McClellan, a counsellor to President Romney visited the colonies on a tour of inspection and returned with such a favorable report of conditions that the following resolution was addressed to the refugees from El Paso with the signature of the stake Presidency Romney, Harris and McClellan. "In view of the recent visit of President McClellan to the colonies in the Casas Grandes District, and his report, based upon the most thorough information he could obtain, we feel that now is an opportune time for men having cattle, farm products, or household goods that need caring for, to return to the colonies, if they care to, and look after their interests.

"The conditions that make the present time seem opportune for this work are that there are apparently few Rebels in that part of the country at present; and but little Rebel activity manifest; while Federal garrisons already occupy the towns of Pearson, Unero, Casas Grandes, La Ascencion, Sabinal, and Guzman, while a detachment of 135 Federals are now on their way from Guzman to Palomas. There are many cattle belonging to the colonists in the district and good offers have been made to buy most of these cattle. There is much lucerne, hay, corn and oats that might be harvested and perhaps sold."

It was felt unsafe by these gentlemen to counsel the return of the families to their homes since they felt the trouble in Mexico was far from being settled. Their fear was confirmed by a report from A. D. Thurber three days later announcing that the Rebels were in the neighborhood of Dublan and had recently disarmed men who were gathering cattle in the mountain settlements. Two days following the announcement by Bishop Thurber, Bowman's camp in the mountains was looted and Demar, a son of Henry Bowman, was held for a ransom of $1,000.

Just at this time Joseah Spencer came in from the colonies to El Paso and reported looting by Rebels and said that rumors were circulating among the local Mexicans to the effect that it had been the intention of the Liberals to drive out the Mormons or kill them. In the opinion of Spencer it would not be wise for many to return to the colonies. Panco Miranda had told him that personally he would be willing to protect American interests, but that he was unable to control the men under him.

Upon the return of Mr. Thurber from the colonies he confirmed his previously written report relative to the presence of Rebels in and about the colonies. He informed the Relief Committee of the kidnapping of Demar Bowman and Niels Larson who were being held for ransom and felt certain that their abductors were the ones who later took Billy Orr and Joe Place prisoners after completely looting their commissary. Orr was roughly handled, the report being that he was severely whipped and finally his prostrate body trampled upon until he delivered to his captors the demanded sum of $2,500. Thurber felt that the sentiment among the returning rebels was decidedly anti-foreign.

An attorney, Edmund Richardson, formerly of Colonia Diaz reported a thrilling experience with the Rebels an account of which I give in his own language.

"On October 1, I was travelling in company with my son Ray L. Richardson, a boy fifteen years of age, and a Mexican, a hired man, driving a herd of cows, forty in number, from the upper colonies toward Colonia Diaz, having in my pocket a safe conduct with permit to export forty head of stock signed by General Pascual Orosco and also by his father Colonel Pascual Orosco, in which all Revolutionaries were ordered to permit me to export in peace said forty head of cattle. At a point some four miles south of Ascencion, at which point the country is covered with a thick growth of mesquites, I was suddenly surrounded by some forty or fifty Red Flag Revolutionists, who, with their guns drawn, demanded me to halt and to turn around the wagon and herd of stock and travel in the opposite direction to which I had been going, that is, to retrace my steps, presumably with the object of getting me down into low ground out of the sight of field glasses from

14

Ascencion, at which place there was a force of Federal soldiers. While travelling back to said low ground, I was told by the officers in charge of the detachment that they had taken me prisoner, that my earthly career in that country was at an end, that I had done all the mischief that I should ever be able to do, that I was now going to pay the extreme penalty. I asked what mischief I had done, and they accused me of having aided in and in fact caused the execution of Marcelino Charrez, the man who murdered Will Adams; of being accessory to the death of the Red Flagger who was shot by the sheriff in Hachita some weeks previous; of being the person who engineered the exodus of the Mormon colonists with their horses, guns, and ammunition from Colonia Diaz, thus depriving them of the necessary war material for successfully carrying on their revolution, and many other like misdemeanors. I answered them all in a joking way, until they came to accuse me of belonging to a nation that had caused their defeat by withholding ammunition and war material intended for their use. I then replied that I did not belong to that nation, having been a Mexican citizen for more than twenty years, and that therefore my death would not be considered an offense against the American nation and would give no service to their cause to kill me. They were struck with this answer and admitted that it was well founded, and after some consultation ordered me to unhitch my team, after driving it off the road for a half mile into a lonely place, where they had intended the execution to take place, and mount one of my work horses and accompany them, sending my son and hired help on ahead, taking my typewriter, my valise, some blankets and clothing and many other articles with them from the wagon.

"After travelling some distance and consulting together as they travelled they decided to exact from me a ransom of $600, to be paid in the evening of the next day at a certain grist mill some ten miles west of Colonia Diaz and turn me loose, holding my boy as security for said ransom, but releasing my hired help and stock, but not allowing me to communicate with my boy. I returned to my wagon, gathered my stock as best I could and took it to Colonia Diaz the next day, borrowing the money for a ransom as I passed through Ascencion and taking it to the place agreed upon at the hour appointed. The Rebels, however, did not appear at the place at the time agreed upon because of an expedition into that locality that had been made by the Federal soldiers from Ascencion on the afternoon of the same day which had undoubtedly scared them away. I kept trying to communicate with them in order to get my boy, until I heard some days after that the boy had made his escape from them and gone to Dublan."

In view of the unsettled conditions in and adjacent to the colonies the Relief Committee and the leading colonists decided that it would be unsafe for the refugees to return to the colonies at the present time. The conclusion was that it would be best to establish themselves in the United States for the winter at least. This conclusion was supported by the judgment of men who had received first hand knowledge of the conditions in the colonies and reports left no room for doubt that should the Mormons return to their homes they would not receive a welcome from the local Mexicans. Already some of the best homes had been taken over by natives whose intention was to make them their permanent abodes. Another discouragement against a speedy return was the scarcity of foodstuffs and other commodities resulting from the frequent looting of the colonists' homes by Rebel bands. The prospects of even a scanty subsistance in a land of peace was preferable to economic uncertainty in a county infested with bandits.

With the hope of returning to their homes for the present blasted, the exiles were forced to look elsewhere for abodes for the coming winter. Since their hurried flight across the Rio Grande two months before, these wayfarers had been subjects of charity much against their will, and while they acknowledged a debt of gratitude for the favors bestowed by their Church, the United States and the people of El Paso, they longed to become self-sustaining.

Mindful of their feelings of independence the government of the United States offered to transport the refugees to any section of the country in which they might choose to locate, entirely without cost to them. This magnanimous offer on the part of the government was supplemented by generous offers of assistance from relatives and friends, some of whom invited these homeless ones to come and make their abode with them. Accordingly, before the winter had set in the colonists were scattered like wheat from the Rio Grande on the south to Canada on the north. Some preferred to remain in proximity to the international boundary line in anticipation of a relatively speedy return to their homes, while others, despairing of even a remote reinstatement therein, went wherever conditions seemed most inviting for the establishment of new homes. A very few of the more daring ones returned to the colonies but the activity of the Rebels proved too much for them and again they passed over the border line into the United States.

But the natural longing of man to return to his old haunts persisted even in the breasts of the most skeptical of the refugees, who felt that it would be impossible for them ever again to return to the land of their choice. The climate, the soil, the grandeur of the Sierras, the finny myriads in the crystal streams, the droves of deer, the flocks of wild turkey, the screaming parakeets, the romanticism of the people, the moon-lit sky, the soul-stirring yet dreamy music of the Mexican orchestra, the promenades at the plaza, the half playful and bewitching smile of the Spanish maiden, the fiesta, the bull fight—all these had a charm whose grip even the passing of a quarter of a century cannot efface.

No wonder, then, that the lure of the southland finally wove its magic spell about certain ones of the exiled band and gave them faith and courage to again return to the land of their adoption to rebuild and reinhabit a region war-torn and made desolate by the tramp of dusky feet. But this story will be told in a later chapter.

CHAPTER XVII

WAS THE EXODUS NECESSARY?

The question of the necessity for a wholesale exodus of the Mormons from Mexico would seem superfluous in the light of evidence already presented were it not that certain of the exiles, themselves, have questioned the wisdom of such a move. In the majority of these cases those taking this position have been conscientious, their conclusion having been arrived at after a rather careful consideration of the Mexican situation at the time of the exodus. On the other hand there are likely those who have been influenced in their judgment by motives that are not ethical, such, for instance, as an obsession for material things that would risk the lives of humanity to safeguard property interest.

As for myself I confess that I have no sympathy for and little patience with those who would unduly jeopardize life for property; but for those whose objections to the migration from Mexico were based on a sincere belief that the welfare of the colonists would best be subserved by remaining in the country, I have the greatest respect. As one who was a resident of Mexico for a quarter of a century and who was intimately bound up in the affairs of the colonies during the fitful days prior to the exodus I re-confess a confidence in the superlative wisdom that dictated a general movement into the United States. Any other course I feel would have resulted in ever-increasing tragedies in human life and in the destruction of property. Contemplate for a moment a situation in which a handful of Americans are surrounded by a multitudinous rabble, irresponsible, and subject to no strongly centralized power capable of holding them in check. To add to the horror of the picture, witness these Americans dispossessed of their firearms, in the main, with no means of protection against likely attacks superinduced by lust and rapacious greed.

The men responsible for the exodus had ever shown a

sublime physical and moral courage in defending their followers against the aggression of the enemy. But now a crisis had arisen. The issue involved challenged the highest courage and the profoundest wisdom of the greatest. Should the colonists in the face of imminent danger to the sanctity of their homes and an ever-increasing menace to life and property attempt to maintain themselves in their possession against tremendous odds or should they relinquish their hold on the earnings of a life time and become refugees in another land to which the younger generation were strangers? The leaders of the colonists courageously met the issue and after due deliberation chose the latter alternative. Such a choice called for an exercise of the highest moral courage. Easier would it have been to die fighting for the possessions of the Saints had wisdom so dictated, than to have risked the charge of cowardice that was likely to be hurled against them by the irresponsible and thoughtless.

Some have seemed to see in the flight of the Latter-day Saints from Mexico an analogy to the migrations of the same people from Missouri and Illinois. The analogy breaks down, however, when viewed in the light of the causes of the trouble in each case.

The expulsions from Missouri and Illionis resulted from a religious hatred on the part of the enemies of the Mormons while no such antipathy by the Mexicans was manifest against the colonists who fled from Mexico. The question of religion, if an issue at all was not a dominant factor in the trouble between the two races. Rather was it economic. In a letter written by Bishop Joseph C. Bentley under date of May 5, 1920, occurs the following: "The going out of our people from Mexico is often referred to and spoken of as our having been driven from our homes and out of Mexico, and is sometimes likened to the expulsion of the early Saints from Missouri and Kirtland. Such is not the case. The Latter-day Saints have never been driven from their homes in Mexico nor from the Country." He acknowledges, however, that many of the colonists

received harsh treatment, and were robbed but not because
they were Latter-day Saints. Other Americans, he maintained, were treated to the same harsh measures while a
number of the wealthy Mexicans received no measure of
consideration from the hands of the Revolutionists, their
property being confiscated wholly or in large part by
marauding bands. Mr. Bentley's statement that the "Saints
have never been driven from their homes in Mexico nor
from the Country" is however, misleading. While tech-
nically speaking armed bandits did not forcibly eject these
people from their homes, they did murder, rob, and plunder to a degree that living in the colonies became exceedingly hazardous. The Latter-day Saints fled from Mexico
not because they were driven at the point of the bayonet,
it is true, but they left because the Mexican bandits made
it uncomfortable and extremely dangerous for them to remain longer.

Confirmatory of this view I quote at length from an
address delivered by Joseph F. Smith, President of the
Church of Jesus Christ of Latter-day Saints, delivered at
the General Conference of the Church held in Salt Lake
City, October, 1912.

"They (Mormons) have been robbed, plundered and
driven from their homes, their rights have been denied
them, their property taken away from them, the safety
of their wives and daughters jeopardized and their lives
threatened, and at last they found it *necessary* to abandon
their homes and possessions, and come from that land of
riot and murder, brigandage and robbery, in order that they
might escape at least with their lives; and quite a few have
not been fortunate enough to get away with their lives,
but have fallen by the hands of marauders and assassins.
* * * Many of us, perhaps have not worried much about
the people in Mexico, but it has been a constant source of
anxiety to me and to my brethren of the Presidency and
the Twelve. * * * We have regretted exceedingly the
necessity they have seen to move away from their homes

(many of which are equal to some of the best homes that we possess in this land) and from their lands, their fields, their orchards, their flocks and herds to escape the indignities that were heaped upon them by brigands, renegades, marauders, and murderers. * * * I think it is fortunate that our people have escaped from the land with their families and we wish it understood that their mission there is at least for the time being, at an end, and that they may feel at liberty, not only to abandon the country if they choose to do so, but to go elsewhere, where conditions will favor their endeavors to make new homes and establish themselves in a civilized land, where life is protected and where the possession of property is safe and where they can dwell in peace and be happy.

"I could not advise our people to go back to Mexico under existing circumstances. Indeed, *I would advise them not to go back,* if I should give advice at all." He then compared the drivings from Mexico with those from the Eastern States and in all of these drivings he saw the hand of Providence. Continuing, he said: "In Mexico within a few miles, at the most, are some of the most progressive and beautiful settlements and towns that can be found in the land, which have grown up in a few years by the industry and perserverance of the Latter-day Saints, are old Spanish towns that have existed for hundreds of years that would be unfit for civilized people to dwell in. These contrasts have been pointed out to these degraded people and in reply one of the commanding officers said to the rebels; ' "See how these Americans prosper in your land! How they build colleges! and look at your little hovels that you and your fathers have lived in for ages! We want to get rid of these Americans."

"If our good people from Mexico will only maintain the spirit of the gospel they will see that the Lord Almighty has delivered them perhaps from death and perhaps from something that would be worse than death, if they had been permitted to remain. You have been patient and forbearing; when your brethren have been shot down in cold blood you have restrained your passion. * * * He (the Lord) has given us a chance to get up like gentlemen and come away from the scene of strife and hypocrisy to where we can find peace and freedom. That is far better than to have the stain of blood upon our hands. We do not want their blood on our hands, nor do we want our blood shed by them."

Judge Bartch testified before the Senate Sub-Committee to investigate Mexican affairs on May 24, 1920, as follows:

"It has been shown that about the time of the Madero Revolution the Mexicans conceived a plan to create an anti-foreign sentiment among the people which was especially directed against the citizens of the United States living there. There appeared to be a concerted plan both on the part of the military forces and the nationalists to drive Americans from Mexico. This move led to acts of violence toward Americans and depredations on her citizens which were hitherto without precedent.

"But few Americans can conceive of the unrelenting atrocities which were committed by federal and nationalist authorities since the Diaz regime. In some settlements the entire male population were killed and the women were ravaged. Innocent boys and girls were brutally beaten and killed. Officers of the Mexican government took part in the numerous ravages to terrorize the American people to leave the country, so that their property might be confiscated among the Mexicans. Generals of the Mexican army publicly proclaimed their intention to drive the "gringos" out of the country, and through speech and action encouraged their soldiers into still greater acts of violence."

President Ivins in an article written for the Young Woman's Journal near the time of the exodus stated that "since the beginning of the present revolution the rights of American Citizens have been ignored, their property confiscated and destroyed, and the most insulting and offensive epithets applied to the United States and the American people. In numbers of cases Americans have been killed and wounded and in no instance, so far as we are aware has there been restitution."

In another letter addressed to the Improvement Era under the heading, "Mexico After the War," President Ivins refers to the happy and prosperous conditions of the Mormon colonists before the Revolution. "Then came the war," said he, "without warning, with scarcely time to reach the waiting trains which were to bear them to the United States border to friends and safety, with only the few belongings which they could hastily collect and carry in their hands, not even stopping to exchange everyday clothes for the better suits which hung in the closets, the people fled. In November last (1917) the writer in company with elders Oscar Kirkham, visited Colonia Diaz and other points for the first time since the war which followed the Madero revolution, devastated the country and turned back the wheels of progress and civilization at least one generation. The devastation which war leaves in its wake, whereever it goes, was in evidence everywhere. The flocks and herds have disappeared from the ranges. The fields were uncultivated; the fruits and flowers gone! Where happy homes stood there remained only blackened walls."

The strain of those fearful days prior to and during the exodus stamped itself upon the faces of the exile band as was borne witness to by those present in El Paso at the time of their arrival. Referring to this matter President Joseph E. Robinson of the California Mission, present with President Anthony W. Ivins when a visit was made to the lumber yards in which the exiles found temporary lodgment, said: "The strained, frightened look in the eyes of the children, the haggard faces of the women and the gaunt-silent men, all called up with vivid memories the aftermath of the quake and fire at San Francisco. * * * Seldom if ever before has such an exodus been participated in twice by the same set of men and women, and yet their faith in God and their courage are undaunted. * * * It wrings my heart to see them in such a hapless condition, yet it thrills me with pride to note the devotion to God, their unbounded faith and good cheer." (In a letter written to President Joseph F. Smith.)

If further evidence is needed to convince the skeptical that the exodus was dictated by wisdom let them read the following incidents, the like of which could be multiplied many fold:

Two Mormon families remained behind in the colonies at the time of the exodus deeming the move from the country unnecessary. One of the families remained at Colonia Dublan and the other one at Colonia Pacheco. The family at Colonia Pacheco particularly felt secure under the shadow of the lofty peaks of the Sierras and hemmed in as they were by the denseness of the primeval forests. But in the midst of this feeling of security, death lurked in ambush and with one full swoop the husband and father was hurled into eternity.

This briefly is the story. Two maidens of the family were in the garden a short distance from the house when suddenly and without warning two Mexicans sprang at them from some bushes that had hidden them from view. Terrified, the girls fled from their assailants in the direction of their home, followed closely by their pursuers.

The cries of his daughters brought Mr. Stevens hurriedly to the door and peering out he saw the occasion of their flight. Seizing his gun he rushed from the house and in a determined tone of voice ordered the assailants from his premises. To make certain his orders would be obeyed the irrate man followed the intruders down the pathway leading toward the gate of his inclosure. Suddenly the Mexican, immediately in front of Mr. Stevens turned on him and thrust him with his dagger before the unsuspecting man could defend himself. With a courage born of desperation, the wounded man raised his gun to his shoulder and poured forth a deadly volley. One native fell dead and the other with a gaping wound fell prone, with his back upon the ground. With the spring of an enraged animal the bleeding American sprang upon his foe and in a deathly struggle the two men clinched.

Upon hearing the shots, one of the Stevens girls, who had witnessed the encounter from the window of an upper room, came running from the house to the scene of the trouble. Imagine if you can the feelings of the maid when she beheld her father astride a struggling form and grasping with his hands the two outstretched arms of the bandit. Seizing her father's gun which had fallen from his hand in the struggle, the girl stood ready to defend her father when to her horror she saw his body lunge forward upon the ground; his hands released their hold—the dagger had done its work; her father had breathed his last. In the face of death the native's anger was not abated. Struggling to his feet, he advanced toward the girl as if to do her harm but peering down the barrel of the threatening gun his ardor cooled and slowly he left the scene of his encounter and made his way up a wooded draw to die.

Some time later his body was found and it and that of his companion were buried side by side in a secluded spot not far from where they died. The body of Stevens was prepared for burial and in a rude coffin his earthly remains were buried beneath the leafy branches of a giant pine. Tears bedimmed the eyes of the little group as they stood with bared heads while the eldest son of the dead man consecrated the spot as a last resting place for the earthly body of his sire.

Scarcely had the whistle of the last train, bearing the refugees to safety died away, when some of them became obscessed with a desire to return to their homes. Like Israel of old in their flight from Egypt they longed for the "leeks and onions" of the home land. As the days came and went their hunger increased and in the course of a month or two a number of the colonists had returned to take up the routine of life where they had left off.

They found rebel bands still infesting the land but by peaceful and hospitable means the returning colonists hoped to conciliate the invading bandits and permanently establish themselves in their possessions. At Colonia Juarez peace and quietude seemed to hover over all. The colonists were busily engaged in the ordinary affairs of the domestic and public life of the community when detached members of a rebel band entered the home of a colonist and proceeded to help themselves to whatever appealed to their fancy.

Discovering that the husband and father was absent from home, one of the number made an attack on the mistress of the home and must have succeeded in his nefarious design but for the heroism of a child of the family. Witnessing the precarious condition of her mother she rushed to the window of an upstairs room, leaped to the ground to give the alarm and in so doing fractured her leg. The screams of the girl reached the ears of the bandit and in fear he fled from the house.

News of the incident was borne to the husband and madly he rushed to his home, seized his rifle, and set out in quest of the bandit upon whom he was determined to wreak vengeance. He had gone but a short distance however, when he was met by the bishop of the colony who pursuaded him to cease following the criminal and let the law take its course. Assurance was given him that on the morrow the bishop and others would accompany him to the rebel headquarters and report the matter to the commander in charge of the garrison. The next morning early, the group of Americans, headed by the bishop, made their way without incident to the rebel camp located a few miles north of the colony and reported to the Commander-in-Chief the purpose of their errand. The military chieftain in a tone of fiery indignation ordered his men to file past the visitors for inspection. Finally the guilty one was recognized by the woman who had been attacked and with but little ceremony he was condemned to die. The outraged husband was given the opportunity to carry out the execution, but declined in favor of a firing squad.

The condemned wretch was marched to a point a short distance from the camp where he was blindfolded and then as the rifles barked forth in unison he slumped to the ground in a heap, dead. Solemnly the little group of Americans made their way back to the colony convinced that there was still some honor to be found with the leaders of the revolutionists but not unmindful of the dangers that threatened their existence on every hand in a land of revolutions.

Equally thrilling was the experience of Anson B. Call, who for many years had been a prominent citizen of Colonia Dublan. With a few others he returned to his home soon after the exodus and was employed as a bookkeeper in the mercantile establishment of Romney and Farnsworth. Ecclesiastically he was prominent having been Bishop of Dublan for many years.

While seated at his table eating his dinner on November 14, 1914, a group of "Red Flaggers" consisting of eighteen men and one woman called on Bishop Call and asked for the use of a corral and sufficient feed for fifty head of horses. In addition, sleeping quarters were solicited for the men. Provision was made for the animals at the Tithing Yard and the band of rebels were given quarters for the night at the store of Romney and Farnsworth. The people of the colony felt no little uneasiness due to the presence of the "Red Flaggers" as evidenced in the fact that so important an event as a marriage festival was cancelled for the time being.

The next morning at the command of Tomas Perez, in charge of the rebels, Call appeared at the store where he was cordially greeted by the commander and a private conversation between the two ensued. Perez asked Call if he knew who had given the information leading to the arrest and execution of Jose Para, a "Red Flagger," by order of General Pancho Villa. An answer in the negative by Bishop Call was followed by a statement from the interrogator that he had reliable information implicating the Bishop in the plot. Furthermore, he said he had been ordered by his superior officer, General Castillo, to have those implicated executed or to bring them to him and he would have the matter attended to. The colonist stoutly affirmed his innocence but to no purpose. He was placed under arrest and three men were appointed to guard him. He was escorted to his home to secure a mount and other necessary things for a journey and not for one instant was he from under the surveillance of the guard. They followed him from room to room and were with him when he gave the farewell kiss to each member of his family. As he was borne away, he cast a backward glance and saw the "tears streaming down the faces" of his loved ones, who were fearful lest this parting should be the last one. The usually stout heart of the Bishop, also, was melted. Fearful he was of the outcome of it all.

Upon arriving at the camp of the rebels he discovered that his friend, William Young, had also been arrested because he refused to turn over to the rebels a gun he had borrowed from Josiah Spencer. The march began with Call and Young side by side in the midst of the rabble. Reaching Nueva Casas Grandes a few miles from Dublan the party halted for an hour and then proceeded on their way passing over the Casas Grandes River to the old town of Casas Grandes where they arrived early in the afternoon. It was decided to remain here for the night and the colonists were placed in a room by themselves in a house belonging to Manuel Hernandez, adjacent to the Plaza. This gave the Americans opportunity to converse with each other freely. Call urged Young to give up the gun coveted by the rebels and thus gain his freedom to return to his anxious family. Young finally agreed that it was likely the best thing to do and so notified Commander Perez. He was thereupon released to return home with a definite understanding that he would return with the gun the following day. Call described graphically the feeling of loneliness that came over him when his companion bade him goodbye in the gathering darkness, to return to his loved ones, while he was to be held a prisoner by an irresponsible mob who, at the time, were imbibing freely of liquor.

Darkness had scarcely fallen when the American prisoner prepared his bed for the night, consisting of a blanket, a saddle blanket and his overcoat, spread out upon a board floor. He tried to sleep but his slumber was frequently disturbed by the distracting conditions by which he was surrounded. A fitful light in the hall was kept burning the night through and a drunken guard made the night hideous with ribald jest and threats. To add to his discomfiture a change of guards was made at midnight. In a conversation distinctly heard by Call, one guard informed the other one that the prisoner was guilty of giving the information that resulted in the execution of Jose Para and should he make an awkward move he was to be shot like a dog. During the remainder of the night the Bishop scarcely moved, preferring to suffer from aching joints resulting from lying on a hard bed than to risk becoming a target for a drunken guard.

At breakfast time the following morning a Mexican by the name of Toribio Galindo, who was friendly to Call, asked him if he had brought with him anything to eat. Informed that the prisoner had no provisions, Galindo disappeared and shortly returned with food. While the Bishop was eating, his friend admonished him to be of good cheer and imparted the information that he and others were doing all they could to procure his release. An hour later Galindo appeared again and informed the Bishop that he had just come from having an interview with Perez and that his pleadings had been in vain. The rebel chief had informed Galindo that it was not within his power to release the prisoner and that he would be executed.

15

At this juncture William Young and Morley Black arrived from Colonia Dublan with the gun promised the rebel band and with provisions for the Bishop. Black went at once to intercede with Perez for his friend and at the conclusion of a lengthy conversation he was promised that Call would be released upon the payment of ten thousand pesos. The idea now occurred to the American that he was being held for ransom rather than on the charge preferred against him. He was still more confirmed in his belief when some time later in the day, President Joseph C. Bentley arrived from Colonia Juarez to sue for his release. He and Black jointly interviewed Perez and this time the rebel chief agreed to cut the price exaclty in two. With the money stringency among the colonists and with their crops destroyed by rebel bands the payment of even such a small sum as that was out of the question.

All efforts for his release having failed, Call was taken by the bandits as far as the ranch of Don Jacobo Anchondo, a short distance above Casas Grandes, where the party pitched camp for the night. The rain poured down all night long but the next day at nine o'clock the journey was resumed until San Diego was reached, when camp was made again. This ranch was one of the hundreds owned by Don Luis Terrazas, a former multi-millionaire of the State of Chihuahua. The rebels took possession of his groups of houses and helped themselves to what beef they needed.

Sometime in the afternoon of their arrival Bishop Call was given an interview with Perez and, upon this occasion he was promised a release from captivity upon the payment of a thousand dollars, but this amount, paltry as it seems, was beyond the reach of the captive.

Night fell and Call was ordered by Perez to make his bed by the side of his trusted lieutenant. His fears were greatly increased when he witnessed the rebel chief and his lieutenant conversing in an undertone. He surmised that they were planning to make away with him and his surmisings proved to be correct. At 3 a. m. the prisoner was ordered to arise. Startled, he obeyed the order at once and began to roll up his bedding to be ready to march. He was informed that such procedure was unnecessary as he would never need his bed again. He was told that his execution was near at hand and that he was to make ready at once to accompany the firing squad to the place of execution.

How prone man is, even in times of apparent doom, to look for a "ram in the thicket." Even a "drowning man will catch at a straw." At this critical moment when the life of the Bishop appeared to be hanging by a thread a flash of hope burst in upon his soul. He remembered a letter recently received from Brother Ivins, a member of the Council of Twelve, in which occurred the following: "They may rob you of all you possess and put you to every test that the enemy of righteousness can imagine, but they shall not have power to take your life."

Frightened, yet with a glimmer of hope in his breast, Call was led to a large cottonwood tree a short distance from where he had spent the night. Here he was asked if he preferred to be blindfolded or would he die with his eyes fixed on the firing squad? He replied that he had no choice and they could do as they pleased in the matter. He was placed with his back against the tree; the firing squad stepped off four paces, cocked their guns and pointed them at the Bishop. Fervently in the face of apparent death the trusting man prayed for a fulfilment of Ivins' promise.

The lieutenant counted "una, dos" and just as Call was expecting to hear "tres," the officer asked the condemned man what he was willing to do to save his life. He would gladly have given the world did he possess it, but this much he would pledge himself to do. He would go to Colonia Juarez and attempt to raise two hundred pesos. The Lieutenant agreed to place the proposition before Perez in the morning for his consideration, but was careful to inform Call that he could give him no assurance of its acceptance. It was not improbable that he would be executed at sunrise. For this brief respite, the colonist was grateful and his spirits arose. The hours between then and the time of his conference with the rebel chief dragged on and were tense but, finally, they were at an end and he was in the presence of the chief to whom he made his proposition. Perez was favorable to it and agreed that Call should be accompanied to Colonia Juarez by an escort and upon presenting them with two hundred pesos, he would be released.

Upon his arrival at the colony an interview was had with President Bentley, with the result that a committee was appointed to make a house to house canvass of the town, to raise the amount of ransom money demanded for the release of the Bishop. The people responded nobly; the price was paid the abductors and in the afternoon of the day of his arrival in Colonia Juarez, the kidnapped man was on his way to Colonia Dublan to join his family from whom he had been ruthlessly snatched a few days before.

Edward Lunt, a son of Bishop Henry Lunt, founder of Cedar City, Utah, had experiences with Mexican soldiers which were almost as thrilling as that of Anson B. Call.

On July 24, 1912, he was at the general mercantile store owned by George A. Johnson in Colonia Pacheco, when a force of soldiers under General Salazar, about 150 in number, rode up to the store, fully armed, dismounted and looted the store. Mr. Lunt returned to his home in Cave Valley 10 miles from Pacheco the same day where he met two officers of insurrectionary forces with about 35 men each. They had a signed order from General Salazar to seize all horses, guns and ammunition of the Americans residing at that place. One of the officers, Marrufo by name, overstepped his commission and took in addition to horses and ammunition, a girl's side saddle, Navajo blanket and clothes. Justifying himself for so doing, he said Mexico was for Mexicans and it would be a matter of only a few days when the "Gringos" would be driven from the country. Lunt told Marrufo that it looked like he was nothing but a woman for taking a side saddle, at which the officer became enraged. He jerked out his gun and was going to shoot Lunt when the other Mexican officer, Gonzalez, an acquaintance and friend of Lunt, quickly threw his own cocked gun in Marrufo's stomach. This act saved Lunt's life.

In November, 1912, Mr. Lunt returned to Mexico after the exodus for the purpose of trying to recover some of his livestock and to sell or otherwise dispose of his crops which he had instructed his Mexican employee to harvest. Upon arriving at his ranch in Cave Valley, in company with Williams Haws, another American, Lunt was informed by his Mexican employee that his life had been threatened by a Mexican, Benino Terene, and his followers. He urged Lunt to leave before violence was done him. Soon thereafter a force of 15 men under Terene rode into the ranch and took the two Americans prisoners. Lunt was placed immediately in the custody of four armed Mexicans. The prisoner overheard a conversation engaged in by his guard in which Terene stated he had definite orders to kill Lunt; that it was his custom to do his killing about sun-up or sun-down; that it was just after sun-down but that they could take no chances of the prisoner getting away and that they would proceed to hang him after drinking some whisky which a local Mexican said could be had a short distance away. All except the four left to guard Lunt went for the whiskey. When they were gone the Mexican employee invited the four guards into his room to drink. Secretly he then informed the two Americans that he had a saddle horse and mule awaiting them and urged them to flee for their lives while the four guards were drinking. The Americans mounted the anmials and went at top speed. In the meantime the first group of Mexicans who had gone for whiskey returned and, seeing the Americans fleeing, followed after them, but were outdistanced. Finally they gave up the chase, and upon their return to Lunts' ranch, they beat the Mexican employee and his wife nearly to death. This treatment was typical of that visited upon all Mexicans who in any way showed consideration for Americans.

About 1913, an American family by the name of Wright lived on a ranch in Hop Valley, not far from Lunts' ranch. Forces under Francisco Villa raided his premises, took Mr. Wright and his wife as hostages and started toward the American border. The soldiers divided into two groups, one group remaining in the rear with the husband and the other going on ahead with the wife. Mrs. Wright heard a shot and learned later that the troops had, without any apparent reason, shot her husband to death. Mrs. Wright was taken to the American border, but finally escaped, making her way under great hardship to Columbus, New Mexico, and thence to El Paso, where she came to the home of Lunt's mother and related her terrible experience.

In February, 1914, Maximo Castillo, formerly a bodyguard of Madero, captured a freight train on the Rio Grande Sierra Madre and Pacific Railroad, ran it into the south end of the Cumbre Tunnel, about 300 feet. The tunnel was about 3700 feet in length and was situated in the district of Guerrero, State of Chihuahua. He set fire to the cars and the woodwork of the tunnel, and thereby set a trap for a passenger train which ran into the fire from the north end of the tunnel. The trainmen, including a number of Americans were killed—maliciously smothered and burned.

In January, 1916, eighteen American citizens were deliberately shot and killed by a Mexican military force near Santa Ysabel, Chihuahua. They were riding on a train on the Mexican Northwestern Railroad under assurances of safety from a passport issued by Mexican Governmental authorities. It was sooon after this that Francisco Villa crossed over the American border and burned part of Columbus, New Mexico, and killed nine Americans and several soldiers of the United States.

In the year 1913, five armed Mexican soldiers broke into the home of Mr. Cooper, manager of the Pearson Syndicate at Pearson, near Colonia Juarez. They proceeded to rob him of his watch, diamond ring and several other items of value and then marched him, in his bare feet and night clothes, to the company's office about three-fourths of a mile away. They then stood him up in the corner, one Mexican holding a knife about fourteen inches long against Cooper's throat, and threatened to kill him if he made an outcry. They then ransacked the company's vault, taking about $750.00 cash and other valuables. The imprint of the knife held by the Mexican was left in about four places on the prisoners throat. Upon leaving, the Mexicans took Cooper with them. He suspected they were taking him out to kill him. One of his captors who had hold of his arm slipped on a railroad tie and fell, whereupon Cooper jerked loose from the other one who held him and in the darkness made his escape by crawling on his hands and knees for some distance.

CHAPTER XVIII

A REMNANT RETURNS TO THE COLONIES

The story is related with a fair degree of reliability
that a number of years ago a band of horses raised on one
of the islands of the Great Salt Lake, was sold to a rancher
living in southern Utah. The horses were taken by the
purchaser to his ranch which was covered with a luxuriant
growth of grass, much in contrast to the barren pasturage
conditions of their native habitat. Little had they been
used to except sage brush and scant patches of bunch grass
from which they munched a scant living.

At first they seemed to feel at home in their new environment but with the coming of autumn came a feeling
of loneliness that overcame them and they made their way
over a distance of several hundred miles back to the Great
Salt Lake. When they came to its shore and had a glimpse
of the homeland across a wide expanse of briny water they
heeded the "call of the wild" and swam the distance that
separated them from the place they loved.

Man himself is highly endowed with this same animal
instinctive tendency such that however inferior may have
been his native habitat to the new environment in which
he may later find himself, he is likely to tire of changed
conditions and long for the scenes of his childhood days.

In applying this fundamental principle to the exiles
from the Mormon colonies of Mexico and the return of
some of them to their former homes I trust I shall not be
misunderstood. I do not wish to infer that Mexico is
economically inferior to many of the places to which the
exiles migrated following their exodus from their homes,
but merely to point out that irrespective of economic conditions, there was a something which appeared to grip the
vast majority of the colonists and beckoned them back to
the land from whence they were driven. I confess I was no
exception to the rule. I recall even now, after a lapse of

something more than twenty years, the feeling of loneliness which almost overpowered me when I contemplated that never could I relive again the pleasant experiences of my life lived in the land of Manana. For years I struggled against the desire to return and perhaps my principal reason for not responding to the urge was the uncertainty connected with a government whose most certain quality was uninterrupted change. As I prognosticated the future in terms of the past I could see no sound reason for assuming that conditions would materially improve in the Southern Republic for years to come. As a student of Mexican history I recalled that for the greater part of a century revolution followed revolution throughout the length and breadth of the land. Foreigners had been driven out intermittently and the lives of Mexican citizens had almost continuously been sacrificed upon the altars of greed and political ambition reared by unprincipaled autocrats.

I remembered with a deep sense of gratitude to my father's memory that he refused to become citizenized lest revolution should again raise its head and his sons would be conscripted to fight side by side with the down-trodden peon. This was long before the outbreak of the series of revolutions which ultimately resulted in the movement of the Mormon colonists from Mexico. I was not ignorant of the fact, to be sure, that for a period of more than a quarter of a century Mexico was comparatively peaceful but this tranquillity was founded on the military prowess of one man. With his overthrow what hope could one have for the future stability of the country? When again would a genius arise like unto Porfirio Diaz who could quiet and hold in check the seething millions of darkskinned sons of Moctezuma whose equilibrium had been greatly disturbed.

Since the days of which I speak, a lengthy chapter of turmoil and carnage has been written into the national life of poor distressed Mexico, resulting in continued economic bondage for the masses of her people. Some measures of reform, it is true, have in recent years, been placed upon the statute books and at the present time there are signs of improvement in an economic and political way.

But to continue with the thread of my story: The more optimistically inclined toward Mexico and a few who felt they would prefer taking a risk in a land where life was unsafe than to begin to build anew a barrier against want, returned to the colonies soon after the exodus. The first to return were men who left their families behind, fearful that conditions would not justify them in exposing their wives and children to the unsettled state of affairs such as existed in the vicinity of the colonies. The thought with them was to return and care for the unharvested crops and to look after their livestock should any have escaped the ravages of warfare. They were also concerned lest their homes, uncared for, would fall into decay. Later when conditions seemed to warrant a return of the families they were sent for and all were hopeful that now they would be permitted to pursue a normal life undisturbed by the clanking of the sabre and the sound of the war drum.

The returning refugees for some time felt it unsafe to occupy the mountain colonies due to their isolation and there was no inducement to reoccupy Colonia Diaz since the torch of the ruthless had burned to the ground all the homes of the people, leaving nothing but their blackened ruins as evidence of the thrift and artistic qualities of those who built them. A few returned to the Sonora settlements but the threatening attitude of the natives made a second exodus imperative and that, too, without delay. The two colonies, Dublan and Juarez, are therefore the only ones that we shall have occasion to consider during the first few years of Mormon re-occupancy, following the return of the refugees to their Mexico possessions.

It will be remembered that the colonies were vacated by the Mormons in the mid-summer of 1912. Soon thereafter, brief visits were made to them by a number of the leading brethren to ascertain the extent of the damage done and as to the possibilities of an early return. The next step in the process of re-occupation, as already pointed out, was the return of the men singly and then finally a filtering in of the wives and children. The year following the evacuation of the colonies, three or four hundred had returned to repossess their homes. In a letter written by Apostle Anthony W. Ivins to the Deseret News under date of Dec. 8, 1913, he says: "There are still many refugees along the line. They are feeling as well as they can under the conditions and are still hoping to be able soon to return to their homes. Between 300 and 400 are now at their former places in Mexico. While there is undoubtedly some danger for them they consider it insufficient to their being in the country. The farms and homes there have not been greatly damaged except at Colonia Diaz. So far as Colonia Juarez, Colonia Dublan and Colonia Morelos are concerned, the farms have hardly been injured at all, but Colonia Diaz has materially suffered. Also some of the farms in the mountains have been damaged.

"It would be difficult even to endeavor to predict when the refugees may again be able to reoccupy their homes in Mexico. It would certainly not seem advisable for them to do so at present, and until the solution of the trouble it will continue to be dangerous."

In the early part of 1914, Joseph C. Bentley reports the conditions as follows:

"In Colonia Chiuchupa the homes and property of the colonists were not seriously molested until some time after the people had left, when finally Mexican people began coming in and occupying the vacant homes and farms and many household effects were carried away and other property stolen. There are no colonists living in the colony at present."

"In Colonia Diaz, the homes and property were not seriously molested until some time after the colonists left, when Mexican people began carrying away household goods and occupying some of the vacant homes, and finally, in February, 1913, a band of Red Flaggers came into the colony and burned about 40 of the principal homes, mainly along the main street, including the meeting house. There are no colonists living in Colonia Diaz.

"In Colonia Dublan a few Saints returned to their homes, and while some household effects, wagons and farming implements have been stolen, the homes and farms of the colonists have not otherwise been injured." He reported that there were about sixty people then residing in Dublan.

"In Colonia Garcia, soon after the colonists left their homes, native people and soldiers came into the colony and carried off and destroyed a great deal of property, and did much damage to the homes of the colony." He stated that there were no colonists living there at the time.

At Colonia Juarez he reported that there were about 200 residents. When the Saints fled from the colony in 1912 many of them left their orchards and farms in the care of natives and when they returned a "month or so later," said Bentley, "they found the homes and the entire colony in excellent condition."

The same correspondent reported that the Red Flaggers had greatly damaged the property at Colonia Pacheco. Some of the homes had been entirely destroyed.

The Mormon property in Sonora had likewise, by this time, been greatly damaged, indeed as early as February of 1913, conditions were appalling as can be seen by the following report from the Deseret News of February 28, 1913: "Maderista activities in Sonora are menacing the Mormon colonies in northern Sonora. Colonia Morelos and Colonia Oaxaca have been taken by the rebellious Maderistas. Today an exodus from the Mormon colonies is on. Many colonists are there, having returned to their homes after the Salazar revolution had failed in Sonora. Now it is feared the destruction wrought in the Chihuahua colonies will be visited upon the colonies in Sonora."

The situation in northern Mexico in the spring of 1914 was so serious that the General Authorities of the

Church at Salt Lake City were greatly exercised over the safety of the Saints in Mexico. Accordingly, President Joseph F. Smith under date of April 26, 1914, issued instructions for all of the Latter-day Saints to leave at once for the United States. That this counsel was heeded universally seems evident in the light of the fact that when later, June 21, 1919, advised to leave Mexico by a Mexican officer because of the disrupted state of affairs, officials of the Mormon colonies declared it to be their intention not to have the colonists "leave their homes at this time and considered it improbable that another exodus similar to the 1914 exodus will be repeated. It would mean the looting of the colonies." Absence from the colonies was only for a short time. With a measure of peace in sight the exiles returned to their homes.

The year 1915 was ushered in amidst great national and local confusion. The previous October elections had been a mere farce. Less than 10,000 votes had been cast for president. There should have been more than 2,000,000. Members of Congress had been arrested and put in jail some time before and Huerta had made himself dictator notwithstanding the citizens inhabiting two-thirds of the territory in northern Mexico refused to vote for him and were even in hostile opposition to him. Following the reprimand administered Huerta by the United States for insulting the American flag the Constitutionalists under General Villa and in the name of Venustiano Carranza took Cuidad Juarez defended by Federal troops. The capitulation occurred on November 14th following which Captain Jose Torres was executed by 25 of Villa's troops who fairly riddled his body with bullets. A little later the cities of Chihuahua and Ojinaga fell into the hands of the Constitutionalists. Fearful of an impending doom that awaited them should they remain in their homeland, Generals Orozco, Salazar, Rojas and some 1500 refugees fled across the border into the United States, the refugees being domiciled at Fort Bliss, adjacent to El Paso. It cost Uncle

Sam forty-one thousand dollars each month to care for them. It was during these turbulent times that William S. Bennet was murdered by Villa, which nearly resulted in intervention in Mexico by Great Britain.

This national upheaval was bound to have its effect upon the Mormon colonies in northern Chihuahua. In the early part of the year, following the split between Villa and Carranza, conditions in and about the colonies were especially precarious. In an article written by Mrs. A. B. Call of Colonia Dublan under the caption, "Why Did They Turn Back?", the author has this to say:

"Rumors that Villa was coming from the south to deal vengeance on Americans filled all with concern. Carranza's army began preparation to defend themselves and natives began moving from Dublan to Casas Grandes for protection." The report refers to the killing of an American by the name of Wright a short distance from Dublan and the holding of his wife as a prisoner, thus leaving her year old child to the care of friends. Naturally the tragedy doubled the anxiety of the colonists. Many would have taken the train to El Paso but there was no train running. In the absence of moving trains, wagons were packed and made ready for a prospective forced move but the colonists feared to stir lest they run into Villa's camp. Unarmed and unprotected, there was "utmost fear," said Mrs. Call, "when we learned of Villa's raid on Columbus."

A priesthood meeting was held in the morning at the home of Gaskell Romney at which a committee was appointed to go to Colonia Juarez to interview President Joseph C. Bentley regarding the trouble. Anson B. Call, John Whetton and Harvey Taylor constituted the committee and soon they left in a car to fill the appointment. In the evening a report reached Colonia Dublan that these men were captured by spies sent out by General Villa but the report proved to have no foundation in fact, much to the relief of the colonists. A correct report, also, came to the ears of the colonists of the killing of five Polanco brothers not far away, simply because they were in the employ of an American company. Commenting on the situation Mrs. Call says: "Oh the fear! And the husbands not at home. Men can fight and die, but as for women, who would prefer to die rather than to live disgraced and bear the stain of vile, wicked men for life—fear is utmost, and the terrified, crying children outside, each wrapped in a quilt, walking, watching and begging for papa! Aunt Theresa and the girls came and in the dim moonlight we saw the big camp fires (Villa's) at Corralites. * * * All the Americans and Mexicans had left the north end of town. Ours would be the first home approached." But, by a divine interposition of Providence, thought Mrs. Call, Villa's forces passed by without molesting the people of Dublan.

Referring to the same incident Elder Anthony W. Ivins reported that "After a successful raid on Columbus Villa returned over a road leading from Palomas to Boca Grande and on to Dublan via Diaz, Ascencion, and Corralites. At Boca Grande he killed the foreman of the Palomas Land and Cattle Company, an American, and at Corralites executed the Polanco family, father and sons, because they were in the employ of Americans. He was now within 15 miles of Dublan and declared it to be his intention to kill all Americans and Mexicans who were in American employ in the district. The following day he moved his army to within a few miles of Dublan. During the night he broke camp and as he neared the settlement and observed that lights were burning in many homes, and that a train was moving on the track near the station he judged that soldiers were there prepared to give him battle, so he turned east, passing within gun shot of the town and on into Galeana Valley. He would go to El Valle, 50 miles away, he said, leave his wounded there, and then return and settle accounts with the Mormons. * * * Colonists were greatly alarmed, fearing he would carry out his threat to return and attack them. What a relief when a long line of United States troops toward evening filed down the western slopes and established camp near the colony. So rapidly had they come that Mormons and Mexicans were not aware of their approach. Knees bent in gratitude."

In a letter written by Theodore Martineau, a resident of one of the colonies, he stated that it was Villa's intention to slaughter the people of Dublan as he had slaughtered people at Columbus a few days before. While camped east of Dublan he called his officers together to decide upon the best method of attack. Some of the officers wanted a repetition of the Columbus affair while others remembering the kind treatment of the colonists when they had some time before come into the colony hungry, wanted to pass them by. Villa was determined to make the attack, thereby hoping to bring on intervention. "He went for a walk at night," said Martineau, "and returned with a changed heart." His secretary later informed one of the colonists why he changed his mind. "He told me," said the secretary, "that while he had been away alone trying to decide as to the destruction of the colonies, some unseen power had impressed him with the conviction that any such act upon his part would bring upon himself the vengeance of a just God."

With the removal of the United States troops from Mexico in January, 1916, Martineau says that all but about 200 of the colonists followed them across the boundary line. Then followed a period of anarchy. General Castillo closed up the Cumbre tunnel with a freight train. Later a passenger train struck the freight train and caught fire, with the result that 50 lives were lost, 28 of whom were Americans. On Villa's return to this region a battle was fought between the Villa and Castillo forces, resulting in a victory for Villa.

Mr. Martineau relates the rather amusing incident of Fanny Harper ejecting from her beautiful home in Colonia Juarez a group of Villistas. These men had been using her home for some time as their headquarters and when their commander returned from a short trip and found that they had vacated and was given the details he remarked, "Well, it seems evident that you could not frighten the Senora and no real man would fight a lady, so there was nothing to do but let her have her way!"

About this time a group of colonists went to Garcia to see the condition of affairs. The company was made up of J. E. Whetton, C. W. Whetton, E. S. Cluff, Orin Farnsworth and Frank O'Donnel. In a drizzling rain they camped on the outskirts of Garcia and were about to eat prepared venison when they were startled with "Quien Vive!" Fifteen armed men lined the boys up under the dripping eaves and proceeded to make way with all the food in the house. Following the supper the Americans were marched a few miles up a box canyon where camp was made for the night.

A strong guard was placed over the captives with orders to shoot should they attempt to escape. All night they lay huddled together, drenched with rain. With the coming of morning each was taken aside and asked for his gun. Only one firearm was in their possession. The following night the men were stripped of everything but their underclothing and then tied to trees and left to their fate. In the darkness of the night "a dim form," said Martineau, "crept up to the men and cut the rawhides that bound them. Little was said but it meant much, 'I was hungry and you fed me.' "

Some months prior to these events narrated above, Villa had camped in Colonia Dublan enroute to the state of Sonora. He had under his command fifteen or twenty thousand soldiers. These together with ten thousand horses preyed upon the possessions of the two hundred residents of the little colony. Fences were broken down, crops were destroyed and supplies taken. Following their defeat in Sonora many of the soldiers came straggling back, discouraged, hungry and many of them wounded. Blaming the United States for their disastrous defeat they were in an

16

angry mood. Villa was not with them at this time, he having gone into Guerrero, and a number of his officers whom he had left in in command declared their intention of going over to the cause of Carranza. Confusion reigned and the soldiers assumed a threatening attitude toward the helpless colonists. Toward midnight the army broke up into small squads and passing from house to house threatened, robbed, looted and burned. Truly it was a night of terror for the defenseless people, but when morning came the rabble had disappeared. Many of the Saints had narrowly escaped with their lives, shots had been fired into houses where people were, and fires started in several of the homes. The house of Bishop Samuel J. Robinson had been looted and burned and his life was sought by the looters. Several years later while paying a visit to the colonies I was shown several bullet holes made by rebel bullets, fired into the walls and ceiling of Anson B. Call's beautiful home. Two or three of the rabble entered the home and beholding a number of colonist wives and daughters congregated in a room advanced menacingly toward them. The women fled up the stairway and were being followed by the soldiers when Mr. Call heroically took a stand at the foot of the stairway to beat them back, declaring that they would pass over his dead body if they went up the stairway. His plunder the homestead.

My brother, who likewise lived in Dublan related to me an experience with the rebels almost equally as thrilling in which several shots were fired by them into his house.

The home of P. S. Williams was broken into and robbed and a band of marauders visited the ranch of James Skousen situated a short distance from the old town of Casas Grandes. Mr. Skousen being away from home the women folks fled to a neighbor's leaving the bandits to plunder the homesteads.

Apostle Ivins in a report of December 27, 1915, notes that, "The colonists feel, however, that at present they are passing through the most critical situation of the war, as the Villa factions naturally resent the recognition of the Carranza forces by the United States Government and are still smarting under recent defeats. The settlers are doing no planting as they have no horses."

A few months earlier in the year he referred to the money stringency in the colonies. The supply was not only limited but the purchasing value of Mexican money especially in foreign markets was little above the zero point. In exchange for foreign currency it was worth only $3\frac{1}{2}$ cents on the dollar. Such devaluation of the native currency worked a great hardship on the colonists since most of their supplies were purchased in El Paso. Mr. Ivins cites an instance in which a father purchased a cap for his son for which he paid the fabulous sum of one hundred dollars in Mexican money.

I previously referred to the coming of the United States troops into Mexico and of their establishing a camp in the outskirts of Dublan. These troops were under the command of General John Pershing and had been sent by the Government of the United States to hunt down and punish General Villa for his raid on Columbus, New Mexico, in which a number of American lives were sacrificed. As will be recalled, the expedition failed to accomplish the mission for which it was sent due to no fault of the expeditionary force, but rather, to the inaccessability of the mountainous region into which Villa fled. But while the punitive expedition failed to achieve its major objective, it proved a godsend to the Americans living in proximity to its temporary headquarters established on Mexican soil. During the several months sojourn of the United States troops in Mexico the colonists were undisturbed by the native population and were permitted to come and go at will. The garrison of American troops furnished also a splendid market for colony produced goods such as lumber and shingles, leather and canned goods. The merchants of Dublan also reaped a rich harvest since the merchandise they handled was given preference by the American soldiers.

The prosperity of the farmer and stockman was limited only by the small quantities of foodstuffs they were able to furnish the garrison. The prices paid were all that could consistently be expected.

With the withdrawal of the troops, the colonists and other Americans and other foreigners in northern Chihuahua became almost panicky, if we accredit fully an El Paso report under date of January 29, 1917. "Like the flight of the children of Israel from Egypt," runs the report, "more than 1500 refugees are following in the wake of the American Expeditionary forces on the march out of Mexico. Mormons were riding in automobiles, covered wagons of the prairie schooner type, in farm wagons and on horses and mules, according to the cattlemen. They were driving their milch cows ahead of them, while behind tramped hundreds of natives, Chinese and others who had no means of transportation on the long trek to the border."

"Nothing that could be brought out was left behind, it was said, and many of the settlers in the beautiful valley of the Casas Grandes River carried all their worldly possessions with them. National guard encampments here which have been abandoned since the troops went home will be used to house the refugees until they can find homes."

Joseph Jackson and his two sons remained behind to care for their flour mill near Casas Grandes, but were tormented continuously by the Mexicans with the result that they decided to follow the family and the other refugees to El Paso. One fine morning early they hitched their horses to their buggy and began the journey toward the United States. They had not gone far when they were overtaken by a band of men who ordered Mr. Jackson and his sons to return to the mill to grind a quantity of wheat for them. One evening after their return, Mr. Jackson was at home reading by the light of a lantern when he was accosted by a masked man who had abruptly burst into the house. "Come out or die" was the command. Mr. Jackson hesitated a moment but, convinced that the intruder meant business, he stepped outside where he was confronted by several other men wearing masks. He was ordered to the mill to fill their sacks with flour. The order was obeyed and each man put a sack of flour on his shoulder and started for the door when to Mr. Jackson's surprise, the leader of the group dropped his flour to the floor and informed the miller that it was not flour they were after but that they had orders from Casas Grandes to take him there either dead or alive. "Let me see your order," said Jackson, whereupon they ordered him to hand over his money. Forty dollars in change was handed them which likely would not have satisfied their greed, but fortunately for the miller, at this juncture, one of his sons and a Mexican friend unexpectedly appeared on the scene and the thieves made their exit without further ceremony.

The Mormon colonists were not to remain long from their homes, a few months at most. So soon as conditions were such as to promise even a measure of security, families began to filter back into the Colonies of Juarez and Dublan. As early as June an expansion from these colonies was contemplated for we have Mr. Bentley reporting by letter to President Ivins "that a number of the colonists are considering going into the district of Garcia to put in crops in the fall if conditions are settled." However, he expressed the opinion that it would be unsafe for them to permit their families to accompany them. A number of families who had gone to the "border," Mr. Bentley reported as making preparations to return to the colonies. A diversity of opinion obtained relative to the conditions in Mexico. President Ivins expressing the view that "Villa had about come to the end of his rope" while a visitor in the colonies at the time expressed an assurance that the trouble in Mexico was by no means over.

By September of this year (1917) the outlook for peace was such as to elicit from Mr. Bentley a statement to the effect that Garcia, which had been deserted by the

Mormons for five years would now be re-established. He added, however, that none of the returning farmers for the present would take with them their families. A few of the natives had been living there until recently ordered out by the government officials. None of the property there had been destroyed except houses burned accidentally. The re-occupation of Garcia, Mr. Bentley explained, would be an experiment and if it proved successful the other mountain colonies, Chuichupa and Pacheco, in turn, would be reinhabited. The revolution, he felt was over.

But it proved to be but another lull before a storm. Near the close of 1918 we read from the pen of President Ivins the following: "Most people feel the pincers of the tax collector once a year but the Mormon colonists in Chihuahua, Mexico, not only pay the federal government the regular tax, but hand over any available surplus to Villa and his band of expert and lawless collectors now and then. When Villa needs more money he swoops down on the defenseless colonists and takes it. If the money is not forthcoming he kidnaps some wealthy and influential citizen and holds him for ransom. If the amount is not secured in time, he kills the citizen by way of warning for the future."

President Ivins then cites the case of A. M. Tenney, a wealthy Mormon rancher who was recently kidnapped with two more mining men. "Although unaccustomed to long hikes, the men were made to march with the army for hundreds of miles over rough roads. At length growing impatient at not receiving the ransom money, the bandits sent Tenney back to Chihuahua to get $20,000, threatening that if he did not return in a given time the mining men would be executed. Fortunately, he arrived in time to save them, but not before they had been tortured by the evident preparations for execution."

"Not only do the bandits take money but all property they happen to fancy. The colonists live in terror of the bandits who respect neither lives nor property. Carranza has promised to protect the colonists and for that reason the bandits delight in pillaging and murdering whenever they can.   Federal troops run from Villa troops."

In the following year conditions had become so chaotic that the Mexican government was forced to admit its inability to protect the colonists.   Commenting on the situation an editorial in the Deseret News June 23, 1919, declared that, "The most pitiful and humiliating feature of this Mexican business is the confession of the Mexican government that it cannot give protection to its colonists and settlers.   The best it feels able to do is to take them thus into its confidence and advise them that if they are not numerically strong themselves to beat off an attack from rebels and bandits they had better get out."

On June 21, 1919, a warning was issued by General Manuel Diegnez, commander of the Northwestern Military zone, through the American consul to the Mormon colonists, to the effect that to remain longer in the country was dangerous.   The Mormon officials replied by saying that it was "impracticable for the 630 Mormons living in the Casas Grandes district to leave their homes at this time." Another general exodus such as they had experienced in the past was declared to be improbable.   "It would mean the looting of the colonies."

In the following month Bishop Call reported to President Ivins that the colonies had again been looted by bandits.   I give his report *in extenso.*

"When the City of Juarez was threatened all the troops were withdrawn from here, leaving us at the mercy of any band of marauders that might come and make a demand on us, or the defenseless natives in our vicinity. Only a few days after the withdrawal of the troops a band of 21 men very poorly equipped came into the state and began pillaging.   Ten head of horses were taken from Dublan.   A committee was appointed to take up a collection of provisions and cash.   These were turned over to the bandits who went from whence they came.   Besides the horses which they stole they obtained something like

$900 in Mexican money. We thought it was better to do this than to have them loot."

Three weeks later they returned and looted, taking everything there was in a Chinaman's store. A pitched battle ensued but no one was hurt. The bandits forced five local men to haul off their loot.

The abandonment of the city of Juarez by Villa gave hopes that railroad communications would be resumed at once as far as Dublan.

CHAPTER XIX

GREATER PROSPERITY SEEN

By the fall of 1919 a marked change for the better seems to have taken place. Dr. Franklin Stewart Harris, then a member of the faculty of the Utah State Agricultural College, visited Colonias Juarez and Dublan to conduct a teachers' convention. Reporting on the conditions of the colonies, he refers to the excellent crops and the fine grazing facilities. He notes, however, that the codling moth is attacking the crops; that there is a blight on the apples and pears and that the army worm is preying on the crops at Dublan to an alarming extent. A committee is appointed at his suggestion to investigate different farm bureaus as to constitution and organization with the view of organizing one in the colonies. The function of such an organization would be to deal with the purchasing of seeds, insecticides, farm machinery, stock breeding and marketing of farm and orchard products.

Mormons had gone to re-settle Chuichupa, among whom were Thomas Sevey, Charles and Edward Martineau and families. The health conditions in the colonies were excellent and with prospects for abundant crops, the outlook for the colonies was brighter than ever before since the Revolution began. There had been peace in the colonies since June, when the Villa forces were defeated by the Federal troops at Cuidad Juarez.

In the latter part of 1920 President Ivins paid a visit to the colonies for the purpose of negotiating for the return of abandoned lands to the rightful owners. He found conditions in the colonies greatly improved. The next year a spirit of optimism prevailed. Many improvements were to be seen about the homes. Many shade and fruit trees were being planted. Chuichupa and Garcia were both prospering. At Chuichupa a saw-mill was leased from the Pearson Company by Bishop George Sevey and

others and was to be an asset in the matter of employment and in furnishing materials for building purposes.
Considerable land was prepared for the planting of crops.
At Garcia a water system was installed for culinary purposes. A number of new residents had arrived, chief of
whom was Alonzo L. Farnsworth, one of the founders of
the colony in 1894. He had returned to spend his last
days with his children.

Under the heading, "Colonies in Chihuahua Again
Enjoying a Healthy Growth," the Arizona Gazette, Phoenix, Arizona, dated August 22, 1921, gave out the following: "According to reports received by government officials
in this city many Mormons from the United States have
visited the colonies of their co-religionists in this country
and found them so well situated that they have decided to
remain. Prospects for crops are better than in years. Before the revolution began the total population of the five
colonies was approximately 6,000 (only about 4,000). It
was only 816 at the recent census."

A report of the population of each colony together
with other detailed information follows. Colonia Chuichupa had at the time of the report (1921) 101 people, all
American citizens. 6,000 acres of land belonged to the
colony, the crops produced the previous year being valued
at $15,000. Not all of the land was under cultivation.

Garcia had a population 121 most of whom were
American citziens. The products of the colony combined,
consisting of lumber, oats, corn, potatoes, hogs and other
livestock brought $26,000 the year before.

Colonia Pacheco with 64 inhabitants had produced
the preceding year $5,000 in oats, corn, potatoes and fruit.

Colonia Juarez having a population of 237, of whom
197 were American citizens produced $30,000 from its
land, shops and mills.

Colonia Dublan had a total population of 293, of
whom 269 were American citizens. The crops of the previous year were valued at $60,000.

From the above report there would seem to be but scant basis for the development of a spirit of optimism. Not more than one-fifth of the original inhabitants had returned to the colonies and the total annual income from all the colonies was rather meager. The optimism of the colonists, no doubt, largely resulted from an abiding faith in the future growth and prosperity of the colonies rather than from evidences visible to the naked eye.

In a strain of hopefulness Joel H. Martineau, writing from Colonia Pacheco in mid-summer of 1921 bears witness to a universal spirit of optimism among the colonists and other foreigners when he says: "There is a feeling of greater security in Mexico now than for several years and many Americans are entering this country in search of mines and business opportunities." He continues by saying that there is greater stability in government and greater strides toward the emancipation of the Republic. This is being accomplished by the government seizing the landed properties of big companies and wealthy individuals and dividing them among the poor and down-trodden. The Presidente of Casas Grandes expressed himself to Mr. Martineau in the following terms: "All lands that have been for years abandoned may be settled on by any American citizen. If the owner comes back later and pays all back taxes and expenses, we will let him have his property back. The time has now come for those who own farms to cultivate them or let others have them who will do so, that Mexico may become a more productive country."

The writer then expostulates on the opportunities for settlers in the state of Chihuahua and affirms that this one state alone has potential facilities for the support of one-third of the entire population of Mexico while at the present time only two and one-half per cent of the population live in Chihuahua. "There are many people who left Mexico during the revolution who would do well to return and settle down on their property and cultivate it or sell to some one else who will, for otherwise they may lose it."

"When the common people are land owners instead of servants of the rich there will be little cause for unrest and revolt and we may expect a development of the resources of this country."

While Mr. Martineau's eyes are open to the great possibilities for a livelihood in northern Mexico, they are not blinded to the obstacles in the way of progress. He refers to the great difficulties encountered by some of the colonists in ejecting natives from their homes and other possessions. "Our past experience in getting rid of those whom we put in our homes at the time of the exodus," avers Mr. Martineau, "does not impress us favorably. It took good sums of money to get some of them out again, besides we lost all of our house furnishings. The natives have already taken possession of many of the farms of Hop Valley, Cave Valley, Middleton, Dry Valley and other places so long abandoned, and it will be difficult for the owners to again get possession of these lands.

"Few people realize the present bankrupt condition of the country or the ruined condition of their once prosperous homes. Recently a young lady wrote to a friend in one of the colonies to get some article of clothing from a bureau in an upstairs room and send it to her. That house was burned five years ago. It is safe to say that a few months after the exodus scarcely an article of clothing remained in any house in the mountain colonies; every window was broken; most of the doors were carried off; floors were ripped up in every room, ceilings pried loose and furniture hauled away or smashed up. Since then nearly all fences have been destroyed and three-fourths of the houses burned. Plum bushes and black locust thickets fill the lots and we must begin almost from the wilderness. * * * All colony wagons disappeared and all farming implements were either destroyed or carried off soon after the exodus. We feel that the day is not far distant when we shall not only have an abundance of these things for our own use but a large surplus as well." The population of the Juarez Stake is reported to have increased 23 % over that of 1922.

A sidelight on the conditions in the colonies is now introduced from the pen of an outsider—a correspondent of the Chicago Tribune. The letter is written from Colonia Dublan and bears the date of November 10, 1923. The writer explains the friendly feeling of the Mormons for the Indians, feeling as they do that they are of Israel. He graphically pictures the growth of the colonies prior to the exodus and asserts that, "The Mexican Mormons grew wealthy and their farms, gardens, homes and schools were by far the best and most striking of all the foreign colonies in Mexico. For the lands of Casas Grandes and the Juarez valleys they built reservoirs and dug canals to bring the water to irrigating ditches that carried it through the towns and over the prairies.

"The Mormon is sufficient unto himself. He provides his own amusements in accordance with his religious belief and conceptions of morality and civic duty. There is no religious law against smoking or drinking in the Mormon colonies in Mexico, yet during my five days' stay there I found neither an intoxicated man or a smoker among the Mormons. * * * No saloons, cabarets, or places of questionable amusement are permitted in the territory over which the Mormons have jurisdiction.

"The Mormon town of Dublan, for instance, has a magnificent centrally located campus for sports of all kinds. * * * Sports are encouraged throughout all the Mormon colonies. * * * The Mormons never indulge in sports on Sunday because they are trained to keep the Sabbath day holy, but the Mexican boys make use of the campus and no objection is raised, for the Mormons do not believe in gaining moral ends through physical restraint.

"For almost a week I was in close contact with the Mormon people and I never once saw a child disobey his parents or grumble at the parental decree.   Nor did I ever see a parent use force.

"The friendly relations between the Mormons and Mexicans was in evidence on every hand. Deserted, wrecked brick residenes in all the Mormon colonies attest the blighting effect of the revolution on them.   With the one exception of Dublan such ruins are so frequent they are to be found on every street.   Windows, doors, floors, fences and in some cases roofs were carried away to serve for firewood in a land where wood is scarce.

"In places like Colonia Diaz, Mormon lands have been squatted on and Mexican families belonging for the most part to the laboring class have taken possession of fine Mormon residences. Scattered about the town were palatial homes that once belonged to prominent leaders in the various colonies.   Some had become thoroughly discouraged over the Mexican situation; others were too old to return, and others were dead.   I had pointed out to me buildings, the construction of which had cost from $10,000 to $20,000 that had been recently sold for $3,000."

The prosperity of the Mormon colonies near the close of 1923 is announced in an article to the Deseret News. The largest and most profitable apple crop in the history of the colonies is reported, the bulk of them having been produced at Colonia Juarez, although Dublan will ship thousands of boxes.   Pacheco will market a carload also. Mr. Combs of Arizona, an expert cheese maker, is investigating the feasibility of establishing cheese factories in all the colonies.   He is much pleased with the outlook and will first establish the industry in Dublan. Saw mills are running full blast at Colonias Pacheco and Garcia.

The Juarez Stake Academy is stated to be in a very prosperous condition.   The largest enrollment since the exodus of 1912 is reported, with five new teachers added to the faculty.   The health of the people is good; the depression is lifted, and almost daily old settlers and new ones are coming to make their homes.

Again in 1925 Joel H. Martineau reports a bumper crop of fruit. From Colonia Juarez 19 cars of apples had been shipped and several more cars were to be graded and packed for shipment. The apple crop was valued at $50,000.

In the spring of 1925 a frightful tragedy was enacted and cast a deep gloom over the entire group of colonies, particularly Dublan. Two sons of Bishop Anson B. Call, Waldo, aged 21, and a younger brother but six years old were freighting lumber from Dublan to Carretas, a distance of about ninety miles, the latter place being near the border line of Chihuahua and Sonora. While enroute to Corrales they overtook a Mexican accompanied by a woman, possibly his wife, who were tramping across the country. The boys out of sheer pity evidently picked up the natives and bore them on their way.

Night fell and a camp ground was selected a few miles west of Ojitos, midway between there and Carretas. It appears that the Mexican had taken an axe, supposedly to procure some wood for the camp fire when without warning he stepped up behind the elder Call boy and struck him a death blow on the back of the head with the back of the axe. The terrified child of six was clinging to the body of his mortally wounded brother when the wielder of the axe split his head with the sharp edge, which must have resulted in instant death.

Following the tragedy, the murderer and the woman continued their journey but were overtaken by a posse of men who had been apprized of the gruesome deed by searchers, who, becoming apprehensive for the safety of the boys, had come upon the dead bodies. The slayer was arrested and was being conducted back to Casas Grandes for trial when vengeance overtook him. He was slain before reaching his destination, the claim being that he was trying to make his escape. It seems more reasonable to conclude, however, that he was a victim of the "ley fuga," then so commonly practiced in Mexico to expedite judgment.

The campaign against Church interference in the political affairs of Mexico waged by the Calles regime was obviously a blow aimed at the dominance of the Catholic Church in Mexico. Legislative enactment, however, as applied to clergymen, Church schools, etc., must react upon all churches alike. All were amenable to the law.

The law of August 21, 1926, requiring all religious teachers to be native born, was meticulously complied with by the Latter-day Saints in Mexico, as set forth in a report of President Joseph C. Bentley to the Presiding Bishopric of the Church. To meet the requirements of the law it became necessary to supplant the older existing bishops in the various colonies with young men born in Mexico, in the conduct of all religious meetings. Those selected were Helaman Judd called to preside at Chuichupa, Harvey H. Taylor at Dublan, Enos Wood at Garcia, Leland H. Martineau at Pacheco and Henry E. Turley at Colonia Juarez.

The schools of the Latter-day Saints in the State of Chihuahua were closed for one day under the order of government officials, but following an explanation submitted by President Anthony W. Ivins, President Calles ordered their re-opening. The explanation made by President Ivins was in effect that anyone may send his children to the Latter-day Saint's schools in Mexico by paying a tuition fee. The Mormon schools are not religious schools in the meaning of the Mexican constitution and therefore do not come under the category of the schools which the Mexican officials are attempting to close. From that time to the present there has been perfect accord between the Mormons in Mexico and the officials of that Government with respect to these religious matters.

In 1929 Joel H. Martineau declared a spirit of optimism to be still prevalent throughout the colonies. Only one death had occurred in Pacheco over a period of seven years. Millions of acres of fertile land were awaiting the magic touch of irrigation in the country. He deprecated the stories in the United States newspapers concerning disorders in Mexico and branded them as mere fabrications. Since the common people have been given homes there is no further need of revolution, he avers.

At the present time the colonies are at peace and the people abiding there are enjoying a period of prosperity perhaps not excelled since the evacuation in 1912. Five of the original colonies in Chihuahua have been re-occupied, as follows: Colonia Dublan with the greatest population, Colonia Juarez, Colonia Pacheco, Colonia Garcia and Colonia Chuichupa. The total population of all the settlements amounts to slightly few over twelve hundred. The principal sources for a livelihood are to be found in the soil and the livestock, though some manufacturing is carried on, such as lumber and shingles, cannery and leather goods and cheese. Several splendid mercantile establishments are owned and operated by efficient business men of the several colonies.

The educational interests of the people have not been neglected during the years of struggle and turmoil through which these people have passed since the Madero revolution. There has scarcely been a year in which elementary schools of a fine order have not been in continuous running, and the Juarez Stake Academy has furnished a high school education for the young men and women of the colonies second to none in the country. Each year a large percentage of the graduates from the Academy find their way to higher institutions of learning in the United States, and almost without exception they rank high in scholarship and in character they have no superiors.

The people are not wealthy so far as this world's goods are concerned but they are thrifty and industrious, and best of all they are God-fearing and virtuous and to a marked degree they live the golden rule. Ambitious young men whose economic opportunities are limited and who are not afraid of honest toil would do well to investigate care-

17

fully and then take advantage of the opportunities afforded in the Mormon colonies in Mexico.

The Church to which the colonists belong has always been solicitous of their welfare. Economically it has never permitted them to suffer where it was possible to help and in a spiritual way it has always been their faithful guardian. Soon following the return of a few families to the colonies the Church gave them a local Church organization that their spirituality might not be permitted to languish. As will be recalled, before the first general exodus the Saints in Mexico were closely knit together in a spiritual bond under a stake organization over which presided three high priests. Within this stake organization were wards presided over by a bishopric who acted as spiritual fathers to the members of the wards. With the migration of the Saints from these colonies to the United States there was a breaking up of the local ecclesiastical organizations under which they had lived. With the return of Mormons to the colonies a need was recognized for some sort of Church organization.

Joseph C. Bentley, the bishop of Colonia Juarez at the time of the exodus, was appointed by the First Presidency of the Church to have general supervision over those returning to the colonies. This appointment was made several weeks after the exodus when Bishop Bentley and a number of others returned to their homes. At a conference held May 9, 1915, Bishop Bentley was set apart to preside over the people of the colonies as well as those living along the border in Mexico and the United States. There was no further organization effected at that time. Slightly more than one year later, on April 10, 1916, Mr. Bentley was set apart to preside over the Juarez Stake of Zion. At a quarterly conference held in the Juarez Stake on May 13 and 14, 1916, John T. Whetten and Arvil L. Pierce were set apart as Counsellors to President Bentley. In 1918, with the resignation of Arvil L. Pierce as second counsellor to President Bentley, Albert A. Wagner was appointed to fill the vacancy in the quorum. It appears that until 1920 President Bentley was also stake clerk but at this time he was succeeded in that position by Theodore Martineau, who served until 1924, when he was followed by Ivins Bentley.

At a conference held on September 8, 1929, there was a reorganization of the Presidency of the Stake. Ralph B. Keeler was sustained as the President with Claudius Bowman and Moroni L. Abegg as his counsellors. The following day Joseph C. Bentley was sustained as Stake clerk.

On December 31, 1930, the Juarez Stake had a membership of 1263 souls, 2 Patriarchs, 687 High Priests, 30 Seventies, 75 Elders, 63 Priests, 55 Teachers, 80 Deacons, 537 lay members and 353 children. The High Council consisted of Orin N. Romney, John E. Telford, Ernest Hatch, Lorin L. Taylor, Robert C. Beecraft, Toribio Ontiveros, John T. Whetten, Albert A. Wagner, David M. Haws, Harvey L. Taylor, and Clarence Lunt. The Patriarchs were John J. Walker and Joseph C. Bentley. Neils Fredericksen was president of the High Priest's Quorum. Oscar E. Bluth president of the 99th quorum of Seventy and Frank Romney president of the 1st quorum of Elders. Officers in the Stake Relief Society were Nell Spillsbury Hatch, President, and Lucy M. Bluth and Gertrude Olsen Keeler as counsellors and Ida E. Turley, secretary.

The Stake Sunday School was presided over by Wilford M. Farnsworth as Superintendent with Harvey Taylor and Oscar E. Bluth as his counsellors and Theresa T. Wagner as secretary.

The officers of the Stake Y. M. M. I. A. were Velan D. Call, President, and Enos Wood and Mathias O. Skousen, counsellors, and Joseph T. Bentley, secretary.

Maud T. Bentley was the President of the Stake Y. W. M. I. A. and assisting her as counsellors were Mary V. Bluth and Della Taylor with Fluto Hatch as secretary.

The Presidency of the Stake Primary were Cecil S.

Young, President, with Belzora Foutz and Florence Wood as her counsellors and Ida Lake Turley as secretary.

The first conference held in the colonies after the exodus of July 28, 1912, convened in May, 1915. At this conference attended by President Anthony W. Ivins of the General Authorities, Joseph C. Bentley was sustained as Bishop of the Juarez Ward with John J. Walker and Daniel Skousen as his counsellors. Anson B. Call was called to be Bishop of Colonia Dublan and his counsellors were Ernest Young and Nephi Thayne. Philip H. Hurst was sustained as Presiding Elder of the El Paso Branch and Arvil L. Pierce and D. V. Farnsworth were appointed to assist him.

The other wards of the Stake came into being later.

At this conference a new organization was effected by President Ivins to take the place of the old Colonization Company to issue titles to undeeded land. Joseph C. Bentley was made the President and Manager of the company, A. L. Taylor, Secretary and Treasurer, with Anthony W. Ivins, S. J. Robinson and John W. Wilson, Directors.

The people of the Juarez Stake at the beginning of 1934 were firmly entrenched in their homes, with brighter prospects for economic independence than at any time since 1912. With a greater inflow of energetic, optimistic and forward-looking homeseekers, I see no tangible reason why the colonies should not again blossom forth into prosperity, peace and contentment such as they enjoyed before revolutionary bandits shook them up so mercilessly a quarter of a century ago.

The officials of the national government appear to have matters well in hand. A period of peace for Mexico both at home and abroad, such as the Republic has not enjoyed in many years has been inaugurated and bids fair to continue indefinitely. The problem of illiteracy is one of the greatest questions facing the country at the present time as it always has been. Steps are being taken by the present administrative officials to solve this problem by the introduction of a better public school system whose function will be to furnish opportunities for the intellectual improvement of the great masses of the people whose past is beclouded with intellectual and economic serfdom. With a population of about sixteen or seventeen millions, three-fourths of whom cannot read or write and seven millions of whom are full blood Indians, scarcely touched by conditions of civilization, the Government has a gigantic task before it. But the demon ignorance must give place to enlightenment if stability of government is to be maintained under a Republican form of government such as theoretically exists in Mexico. That such a condition will ultimately be attained I confidently expect. Mexico has everything else, water, land, timber, oil, minerals and climate to make it the envy of the world.

Spiritually the colonies have never been in a more healthy condition than now. All of the quarterly statistical reports issued by the General Authorities from Salt Lake City indicate that the Juarez Stake is well toward the front in all Church activities such as tithing payments, attendance at meetings, ward teaching, etc.

The list of Stake officers and Bishoprics in the Juarez Stake as they existed at the close of 1933 when the last report was given is as follows:

Stake Presidency are Claudius Bowman, President, with Moroni Abegg and Harold W. Pratt as his counsellors; the High Council consisted of Orin N. Romney, John Telford, Lorin L. Taylor, Toribio Ontiveros, Albert C. Wagner, David M. Haws, Harvey H. Taylor, Clarence L. Lunt, Ernest L. Farnsworth, Bryant R. Clark, Lester D. Farnsworth, Ralph B. Keeler with Joseph C. Bentley as Stake Clerk and Clerk of the High Council.

Patriarchs are Joseph C. Bentley and John J. Walser.

The Presidency of the High Priests' Quorum are Albert A. Wagner, President, and Orin N. Romney and Clarence F. Turley, counsellors, and Isaac Turley, secretary.

The Stake Board of Education contains the Presidency

of the Stake and the following named, Daniel Skousen, Miles A. Romney, Anson B. Call, Anthony J. Bentley, Clifford L. Whetten, Elmer J. Farnsworth, Moroni L. Wilson, Ella R. Farnsworth, L. B. Black, and Ralph B. Keeler.

The Stake Relief Society is presided over by Nellie S. Hatch as president with Lucy Bluth as her first and Rosena N. Farnsworth as her second counsellor, with Ida E. Turley as secretary.

The Administration officers of the Stake Sunday School are Wilford Farnsworth, superintendent, and Harvey H. Taylor and Oscar Bluth as his counsellors. Thressa Wagner is sustained as secretary.

The Stake Y. M. M. I. A. has as its superintendent, Bryant R. Clark and as counsellors, Henry A. Whetton and A. O. Call.

The Stake Y. W. M. I. A. is presided over by Maud T. Bentley, president, and Laura D. Call as her assistant, with Thelma Whetten as secretary.

The Stake Primary officers are Rita B. Clark, president, with Ella T. Bentley and Edith M. Farnsworth as her counsellors and Ida Lake Turley, secretary.

The Stake Genealogical Society is represented by Samuel J. Robinson as the Stake Representative and Ella R. Farnsworth, secretary, with the following aids: Gladys Romney, Joseph F. Mermott, Edward F. Turley and Fannie C. Harper.

The various Bishops and their counsellors and the ward clerks follow:

Anson B. Call, Bishop of the Dublan Ward, with Joseph F. Mermott and Jesse L. Cardon, counsellors.

The Bishopric of Garcia are Elmer I. Farnsworth, Bishop, and Stephen A. Farnsworth as his first counsellor. The second counsellor does not appear on the list.

Anthony Ivins Bentley is the Bishop of the Juarez Ward and his counsellors are Ernest I. Hatch and Velan D. Call. Clarence F. Turley is named as ward clerk.

Pacheco has as its Bishop, Marion L. Wilson, whose

counsellors are Heber M. Cluff and Glen C. Haynee. J. H. Martineau is the clerk.

In addition to these wards the stake has a branch of the Church located at Colonia Dublan. Orson P. Brown is the president and is assisted by Toribio Ontiveros and Juan Etrada. Pleasant L. Williams is the clerk of the branch. The membership of the branch totals 140, practically all of whom are Mexicans and Indians, converts to the Mormon faith.

As previously indicated, the Sonora colonies are no longer existent. The land upon which Morelos once stood was sold as announced by Orson P. Brown on December 15, 1921, in the following statement: "The lands of Colonia Morelos, Sonora, Mexico, have just been sold to the Mexican Government for $100,000. An order has been given by the government to restore lands of Colonia Diaz. Delivery is expected to be made January 1, 1922. There were about 800 Mormons in Morelos and 650 in Colonia Diaz at the time of the exodus."

A statement issued June 22, 1921, confirms the above announcement and adds some details that are important in this connection. "Squatters took possession of the land soon after the exodus. About six months after an effort was made to regain possession of or dispose of it to the Mexican government. At Douglas, Arizona, a meeting was held represented by most of the Morelos interests. Millard Haymore was appointed to take up the matter with the Mexican Government and effect some kind of settlement. He went to Mexico City. The Government agreed to take over the land and improvements and pay the owners $100,000 U. S. currency."

A committee was appointed at Douglas to consider the claims, consisting of L. S. Huish, Lynn Haymore, Joseph Lillywhite, William Beecraft, and Will Curtis. All claimants were advised to get in touch with the committee and to give all the details of their claims that a just and amicable settlement might be made.

Chapter XX

THE HUMAN PRODUCT

"Do men gather grapes of thorns or figs of thistles?" This question was put by Jesus to his auditors more as an argument in justification of the kingdom He had come to establish than with any apparent thought of receiving an answer to it, for there could be but one correct answer given. He was merely stating an axiomatic truth in the form of an interrogation. He continued the dialogue with himself by adding: "A corrupt tree cannot bring forth good fruit, neither can a good tree bring forth evil fruit."

There are two influences which determine the quality of a tree and the kind of fruit it will bear. The first and perhaps the more important is the influence of heredity and the other is that of environment. However well taken care of, a crab tree can never produce Jonathan apples. Heredity has placed bounds which objects in nature cannot transcend. This is true of the human species as well as of all other forms of animal and plant life. An individual having superior ancestral stock and reared under proper environmental conditions is most certain to achieve success and just as surely will evil results follow him of an inferior birthright and bred in an improper environment.

In the light of this reasoning what can be said of the human product of the Mormon colonies in Mexico? This question obviously cannot be answered in terms of mathematical precision. The best that can be done is to present a few generalizations based on personal observation and information gained through careful research.

An element which enters in to complicate the matter of human evaluation is the great disparity of opinions relative to human values. But it has ever been so. The Spartans of Ancient Greece placed the greatest value upon ability to function well in warfare. Stealing from the enemy was considered virtuous and praiseworthy if by so doing the cause of the fatherland was enhanced; the Athenians of the same period placed chief value on the beautiful in whatever form it might appear, while the Hebrews of Canaan considered most important in life the living of the law inscribed in the Pentateuch. With the devout Christian of today, chief emphasis is placed on the moral code and the observance of the religious doctrines announced by Jesus. If progressive in his thinking he gives due value also to the accomplishments in all legitimate fields of human endeavor, in science, in invention, in art, as expressed in literature, architecture, music, sculpture and painting, and to the ability required in the accumulation of material wealth. He sees in all these things if properly exhibited and wisely used, values that will help to establish the kingdom of God and bring about the brotherhood of man.

It is in this larger sense of values that I shall consider the younger generation produced by the founders of the Mormon colonies in Mexico.

The first generalization I shall make is that the young generations of the Mormon colonies inherited a rich legacy genetically, for the founders of the colonies, generally, represented some of the best blood of the Church. As was true of the great bulk of the Church membership they traced their descent mainly from the Nordic stock of northern Europe who were largely responsible for the introduction of democratic principles in government, first to find favor in England, and from thence made their way into Scandinavian and other countries of northern and central Europe. They came, not from the autocrats of Europe, nor from the lower ranks, but rather from the great yeoman class who have been responsible in all ages and among all races for the greatest advancement in all that goes for the betterment of the world.

These hardy pioneers came also from the very small minority (never at one time more than $4\frac{1}{2}\%$ of the male Church population) who embraced the doctrine of plural marriage. To them it was a God-given principle and like the pilgrim fathers before them who forsook the shady lanes of England to become exiles on the cold, bleak shores of New England, so these puritanic folk, rather than renounce a tenet of their faith became exiles in a foreign land.

Whatever the attitude of my readers may be relative to Mormon polygamy, I shall give them the credit for at least imputing to these people, generally, an unquestioned sincerity in its practice, and certainly they must admire the courage and pluck which would enable them to stand by their religious convictions at the peril of their freedom.

Several of them had been sent to the "house of correction" in the City of Detroit to serve a term of three years because they refused to abandon their plural families. No disciplinary measures at this penal institution were deemed too severe or even too degrading for its inmates. One of the most gruelling, because so nerve-racking, of the regulations imposed, was one restricting speech to a mere whisper. Any one found guilty of an infraction of this ruling had swift and severe punishment meted out to him. Only those who possessed constitutions of iron could endure these ordeals and retain a soundness of mind and body, during the period of a jail sentence.

Some others whose homes were in Arizona, had been condemned to spend a term at the State penitentiary, then in Yuma. It would have been punishment sufficient to have been retained at such a torrid place with a fair degree of liberty, but incarcerated, as they were, in cell-like rooms whose ventilation was poor and with a summer temperature of something like 110 degrees in the open, confinement must have been hell.

Offenders of Utah were generally confined in the State penitentiary in Salt Lake City and must suffer the indignity imposed in the wearing of stripes, and of shaven heads, being compelled to sit at the dining tables with murderers and others of the vilest of characters.

Facing the probability of such punishments or hoping

to evade a second consignment it seems not strange that these harrassed religionists should flee to a foreign land. Such a move in many cases involved the loss of the greater portion of the earnings of a lifetime and, in a few instances, men must disguise themselves against even recognition by members of their own families in order to escape the searching eye of the ever vigilant United States marshal who was always on the alert to bring the polygamist to judgment. Such were the conditions under which my own father went into Mexico after having been forced to flee from the confines of Arizona where he had been a resident for several years. With his numerous family in hiding in two of the states of the southwest he finally, after an all-night journey, had them brought together and with two wives and eight children all piled into one lumber wagon began a journey of several hundred miles to a place of safety. On Christmas eve we camped in the Kaibab forest in three feet of snow with father's hands so badly frozen that it was impossible for him to make a fire. Arriving finally in Saint George in Utah's Dixie, father left my mother and family to be cared for by her father while he, in disguise, and the other branch of his family fled to Mexico, leaving us to come later.

The conditions which confronted the refugees in Mexico, as I have pointed out in previous chapters, were of the frontier type, but such conditions were not entirely strange to the newcomers for most of them had been reared on the frontiers of western America and their fathers before them were frontiersmen. The free, open life lived on the frontiers had tended to develop in them an independence of spirit and courage that enabled them to conquer the difficulties common to a frontier environment. Their sustenance must be wrung chiefly from the soil, the timber and other virgin resources, and this necessity served to develop in them a resourcefulness not common to those cradled and nurtured in the lap of ease. Industry and thrift, so necessary in a land where economic existence is the reward of struggle, enabled them finally to conquer grinding penury and establish themselves in plenty.

On the plains and in the mountains of northern Mexico a miracle had happened. Where once was naught but the solitudes of a wilderness, arose modern villages whose beauty and comfort became the envy of the native population. In three decades these exiled Americans had erected settlements and established farms and vineyards the like of which could not be duplicated in any portion of the Southern Republic. They had done more in redeeming the waste places than had an equal number of Spanish blood since the Spanish conquest.

Best of all, the colonists banned all recreation of a questionable character. Saloons and all other places of doubtful repute were conspicuous for their entire absence from any of these Mormon settlements. Tobacco was also boycotted in harmony with the doctrine of the Church, and for many years it was an unheard of thing for one of the younger generation to indulge in the use of tobacco or strong drink.

With the exodus of the Mormons from their homes in Mexico, and with the sifting of their numbers among the different communities from Mexico on the south to Canada on the north, and their eastern and western infiltration being restricted only by the two oceans, what of the younger generations of the Mormon colonists? How are they behaving under a new order of things? Are they living up to the ideals and traditions of their immediate forbears? Have any of them become prominent in Church or in any of the professions or other vocations common to the communities in which they live?

These questions may be empirically answered with a large measure of accuracy in a generalization that, whereever found, the product of the colonies are known for their sobriety, their healthy outlook upon life, their religious fervor and for their unusual qualities of leadership. I am bold to make this observation after carefully weighing the evidence which has come to me first hand from Church and civic leaders in the many communities visited in almost every section of the country. Such a flattering eulogy to be sure, does not apply to all, for some still have clay clinging to their feet.

A general statement, however, unless backed by tangible evidence usually carries with it but little conviction. It shall be my purpose, therefore, to give a few detailed data in support of my thesis.

From the angle of Church leadership it is worthy of record that there is scarcely an official position below that of Presiding Bishopric of the Church in which representatives from the Mexican colonies cannot be found. Indeed, in one quorum above that of the Presiding Bishopric is a relatively young man, Antoine R. Ivins, a son of President Anthony W. Ivins, who holds the position of President in the "First Council of Seventy." Antoine was not a native of Mexico but went there with his parents when a mere child to make his home. For several years he had the distinction of managing the Church Sugar plantation on the Hawaiian Islands, having been released a couple of years ago to preside over the Mexican Mission and at the same time to fill a vacancy in the "First Council of Seventy."

Prior to the appointment of Elder Ivins to these important Church posts, another Mexican colonist had been similarly honored. Rey L. Pratt, a son of Helaman Pratt and a grandson of Parley P. Pratt (a member of the First Council of Twelve in this dispensation and a member of the first group of four missionaries sent to preach to the Indians), presided over the Mexican Mission for nearly a quarter of a century. During the last few years of his life he was also one of the Presidents of the First Council of Seventy.

Elder Pratt went to Mexico with his parents when but a lad at about the time when his father was concluding his term of presiding over the Mexican Mission, with headquarters at Mexico City. Rey continued to call Mexico his home until after the exodus, when, in 1913, he was asked by the Presidency of the Church to remove his elders from the Southern Republic due to the political disturbances. With their withdrawal the elders were assigned to labor among the Mexican population of several of the states of the West and Southwest. Elder Pratt directed the affairs of the mission from his headquarters in El Paso for several years, when the Mission headquarters was moved to Los Angeles, California, where it continued until recently. President Pratt was still residing at Los Angeles at the time of his tragic death resulting from a major operation performed in Salt Lake City while he was in attendance at a semi-annual conference of the Church. With his passing went one of the greatest preachers of the Gospel to the Indians that the Church has produced. He was instrumental in revising the Book of Mormon in the Spanish tongue as well as having contributed considerable literature both in prose and poetry in the Spanish language. It was his distinction, also, to have gone with Apostle Melvin J. Ballard and Rulon S. Wells to open a mission in South America, where he did yeoman service. Rey left behind him a devoted wife and a large family of splendid children to mourn his loss.

Within the past few months Antoine R. Ivins has been released from presiding over the Mexican Mission and has been succeeded by Harold W. Pratt, a young brother of Rey, now in his thirties, who was born and reared in Mexico. Young Pratt had filled a mission to the Lamanites (Indians) which, added to other essential qualifications possessed by him, admirably fitted him to carry on the great work initiated by his illustrious grandfather and in which so many of his family have participated. He has removed the headquarters of his mission from Los Angeles back to El Paso where it formerly had been.

Another mission President produced by the colonies is George S. Romney, son of Miles Park and Hannah H. Romney, two pioneers who functioned large in the building of Colonia Juarez. George presided over one of the foremost missions of the Church, known as the "Northern States Mission," with headquarters at Chicago. Before being called to this position he was engaged in the teaching profession which he had followed continuously since several years before leaving Mexico. He was graduated from the University of Utah with a B. A. degree and from the Stanford University with a Master's degree. At the time of his call to head the mission he was at the University of Chicago on a sabbatical leave of absence from the Ricks Normal College at Rexburg, Idaho, of which institution he was president. He was also serving the people of the Fremont Stake, Idaho, as their president. One of these two positions would have been sufficient for most men but Mr. Romney proved his ability to do justice to both.

H. Grant Ivins, the second son of President Ivins, while a mere youth, was sent on a mission to Japan in company with a few other Mormon Elders. This was a most difficult field in which to preach Christianity. The Japanese, like most Orientals, are loth to turn from the religions of the Far East, grown heavy with age and sanctified by the sacrifices of their forefathers, to an acceptance of a belief in Jesus of Nazareth. But while meager success attended the preaching of the Missionaries when measured in terms of converts, they achieved success in making friends and in the acquiring of the Japanese tongue—a great undertaking in itself. Young Ivins displayed rather unusual ability in the learning of the language and in qualities of leadership, resulting in his being selected to preside over the Japanese Mission for a term of years.

Martin Sanders, a resident of Colonia Diaz, and a son of one of its founders, presided with dignity and efficiency for several years over the Samoan Mission.

Another Mission President, William Sears, while not a product of the colonies, made Colonia Dublan his home for several years. Mr. Sears presided over the Samoan Mission where he had years before travelled as a missionary.

The highest position in the territorial divisions of the Church is that of Stake President. Those from the Mexican Colonies honored to fill this position in addition to Junius Romney and Joseph C. Bentley, one time presidents of the Juarez Stake, and George S. Romney of the Fremont Stake, all of whom have received previous mention, are Harry Lorenzo Payne, who for several years has presided with efficiency over the Saint Joseph Stake in Arizona. He still serves in that capacity and is greatly loved by the people over whom he presides. His home is in Thatcher, Arizona. President Payne spent nearly all of his life in Colonia Dublan until the exodus, when he permanently left Mexico to begin the struggle required to support a family in a new land. He spent several years as a teacher of music in the Gila Academy, Arizona.

Jesse Richins, formerly of Colonia Diaz, and where he spent the greater portion of his early life, is now presiding over the Twin Falls Stake. This stake is situated in a productive part of Idaho, its headquarters being at Twin Falls from which city it takes its name. Before leaving Mexico, President Richins held several positions of trust, chief of which was a counselorship to Bishop Ernest Romney of Colonia Diaz, a position he held at the time the colonies were evacuated in 1912. He is honored for his frankness and unadulterated honesty and serves well his people.

Claudius Bowman at the present time is president of the Juarez Stake, in which capacity he serves with efficiency. For a number of years he was first counsellor in the Stake presidency under the leadership of Fred B. Keeler. With the resignation of President Keeler some years ago, came the appointment of Mr. Bowman to fill the vacancy. The education of President Bowman was obtained in the schools of the colonies and at the Brigham Young University at Provo. He is the son of the late Henry E. Bowman, a one time distinguished merchant of Colonia Dublan.

Many others have served their Church with honor as

High Councillors and Bishops and in other positions of responsibility. Indeed, they are so numerous that even the mentioning of all their names is out of the question. I submit, however, the names of men who have served and are serving as Bishops in wards outside of Mexico.

Arvil L. Pierce, a prominent business man is presiding over the El Paso Ward; Manuel Naegle was one time Bishop of Cornish, Cache County, and now is a member of the High Council of the Benson Stake; Park Romney, a member of the High Council of the Granite Stake in Salt Lake City, was for a number of years, ante-dating the incumbency of Manuel Naegle, Bishop of Cornish. Gaskell Romney, who served a term as a Commissioner of Salt Lake County, was Bishop of Yale Ward in Salt Lake City for several years; Clarence V. Cardon, who for a number of years was a High Councillor in the Logan Stake, was later made Bishop of Glendale Ward upon his removal to California to make his home; Eugene Romney is Bishop of Duncan Ward in the Saint Joseph Stake, Arizona; Ernest Steiner, Bishop of Colonia Pacheco before the exodus, later became the Bishop of Oakley, Idaho; Adrian Haymore was for several years Bishop of the ward at Douglas, Arizona and Bishop McCall presides ecclesiastically at Mescal, Arizona.

In a professional way the progeny of the colonists have been equally outstanding. Every year witnesses a fine, large group of young people from the colonies enrolled at institutions of higher learning in the United States, principally at the Brigham Young Universtiy. Joseph C. Bentley has the honor of having graduated from the "great Church school" six sons, and Miles A. Romney, another resident of Colonia Juarez, has had an equal number of children take their degrees from the same institution. Several other families have done almost equally as well in this regard. These are remarkable records in view of the economic struggle of these people and bear witness to an insatiable thirst for knowledge. This record has been

18

equalled by the refugees who have never returned to the Mexican colonies.

Scores of the Mexico Mormon youth have taken their B. A. degrees; fewer have gone on for their Masters degree and a number have reached the doctorate. Among those to have had conferred on them the Ph. D. degree are: Harold W. Bentley, a son of Joseph C. Bentley, who claims Mexico as his birthplace and the country in which most of his life was spent. His home was in Colonia Juarez and here he received his training in the grade school and in the Juarez Stake Academy from which institution he graduated with honor. His thirst for knowledge led him from his native country to Utah, where he enrolled as a student at the Brigham Young University. The four years spent there were of inestimable worth to young Bentley. The economic stringency of his family made it necessary that he finance himself, which he did by teaching a class or two in Spanish, and in turning his hand to whatever else would assist in meeting the expenses incident to the acquiring of his education. After completing his work at the Church Institution he matriculated at the Columbia University where he received a doctor's degree in English. His record was such that he was employed, following his graduation, to manage the Columbia University Book Store, a position he holds at the present time.

Nathan Whetten, another native son of one of the colonies, after graduating from the Juarez Stake Academy, became identified with the student body of the Brigham Young University. His experiences in working his way through the University were similar to those of Bentley. Following his graduation he spent a couple of years at his Alma Mater as an instructor and, at the same time, he was completing the requirements for a master's degree in the field of sociology. He next enrolled as a graduate student at the University of Minnesota and while there he achieved the signal honor of receiving a national scholarship (of which there were only nine given in the United States) amounting to two thousand dollars. A bid came from Harvard University offering to add to the scholarship materially to have Whetten finish his doctorate there. The offer was accepted. After his graduation, Dr. Whetten received a position in one of the important colleges of the East, where he is recognized as an authority in his field. Dr. Whetten is a son of John T. Whetten who has been a prominent figure in the history of the colonies. For several years after the exodus he was first counsellor in the presidency of the Juarez Stake.

Carl F. Eyring, one of the first children born in Colonia Juarez and a son of President Henry Eyring, referred to in earlier chapters, has made an enviable record in the field of science. Since graduating from the Juarez Stake Academy he has been a student in several of the great universities of the United States at all of which he was known for his fine mind and splendid personality. He was a student of Dr. Milikan, America's outstanding physicist, under whose guiding hand Mr. Eyring obtained his doctor's degree. During the greater part of two decades Dr. Eyring has been a member of the faculty of the Brigham Young University. At the present time and for several years he has filled the position of Dean of the College of Arts and Sciences. For a period of two or three years he was away from the B. Y. U. on a leave of absence working for the Bell Telephone Company in New York City at a greatly increased salary. He could have remained in this new position for an indefinite period, but the memory of his happy associations at the Mormon school and in the Garden City of Provo, impelled him to return and take up again the work he had left off. Dr. Eyring is prominent, not only as an educator, but is outstanding as a civic and Church worker, as well.

Hyrum Harris, a son of Dennison E. Harris, an early and prominent educator of Colonia Juarez, completed his Ph. D. degree in the field of economics at the Leland Stanford University. Much of his advanced work was done at the New York University before he took up his studies at the former institution.   He was employed for a number of years to teach economics at the Utah State Agricultural College, at Logan, but finally discontinued teaching and established himself at Salt Lake City where he is employed as a tax expert.

Edward Eyring is at the present teaching in a college at Las Vegas, New Mexico. He was born in Colonia Juarez, Mexico, where he was reared until about nine years of age when he came with his parents at the time of the exodus, to the United States to live. The Eyrings made their home at Pima, Graham County, Arizona, where they still reside. In his eighteenth year while attending the Gila College at Thatcher Arizona, Edward was called on a Mission to the Central States where he did excellent service for the Church. Upon his return home he registered at the University of Arizona where he was known as one of the brilliant students of the school. Here he completed the requirements for a Master's degree meeting his expenses by teaching Spanish and waiting on tables.   From the University of Arizona he went to the University of California to continue his work for a doctor's degree.   During his sojourn here he was an associate in the language department by which means he was able, largely, to meet his expenditures. Several years ago he was awarded a Ph. D. degree from the great California University in modern languages.

Dr. Franklin Stewart Harris although not a native of Mexico, came to Colonia Juarez with his parents, Dennison E. and Eunice Stewart Harris while a mere lad in the early nineties. Here he received his early training in the grammar schools of Colonia Juarez and at the Juarez Stake Academy from which he was graduated with high honors. Soon after his graduation from the local academy he came to Provo to attend the Brigham Young University.   At this institution, very fortunately for him, he came under the tuition of Dr. John A. Widtsoe, perhaps the most outstanding educator Utah has produced.   Needless to say this contact proved to be of untold worth to young Harris professionally, and a bond of friendship was formed between teacher and student which has continued to grow stronger with the passing of the years.   Dr. Widtsoe left the Brigham Young University to become identified with the faculty of the Utah State Agricultural College at Logan, first as Director of the experiment station, and later as President of the College.   Chiefly through the influence of Dr. Widtsoe, Franklin S. Harris was drawn thither.   His brilliant scholarship coupled with his many other enviable qualities, enabled him to advance from one responsible position to another.   Finally, in the meantime having completed his doctorate at Cornell University, he became the head of the Agronomy department as well as the Director of the Experiment station.   These positions he continued to hold until in 1921 he was chosen to be the President of the Brigham Young University.   During his incumbency the school has grown from little more than a high school to one of the outstanding universities of the Rocky Mountain region.   When Dr. Harris came to his position the school had scarcely any recognized standing scholastically while today it is fully accredited by the "Association of American Universities."

Some idea of its growth numerically under the Harris administration can be gained from the books of the registrar which show that at the time President Harris came to the Presidency there were fewer than 400 matriculated college students enrolled while at the close of the school year 1937 the institution could boast of a cumulative enrollment of 2500 college students.

Since Dr. Harris came to the Presidency he has circumnavigated the globe.   His travels took him to nearly every great country of the world and among all races of mankind.   His itinerary covered a period of almost a year and during that time he was building a fund of information through study and observation that has given him a world view of things, so necessary for the head of a great university.

Later an unusual distinction came to him when he was invited by certain Jewish leaders, upon the approval of the Russian Government, to head a committee composed of several outstanding scientists of the country to make a study of the climatic, topographic and agricultural conditions of the Amur River Valley in Siberia. The investigation was to be made with the view to the planting of a Jewish colony in that region should the report be favorable. Ultimately it was intended to become an abode for several millions of Jews chiefly from Russia. Several months were occupied by the Commission in a thorough survey of existing conditions and a detailed report of their findings was submitted to the Russian government officials. The report was declared by them to be entirely satisfactory and the group of scientists were highly complimented for the efficiency of their investigation.

In addition to his many other accomplishments Dr. Harris is an author of no mean reputation, having written several books and numerous scientific pamphlets. Perhaps the best known and most widely read of his books is one dealing with the culture of the sugar beet. This is recognized as an authoritative treatment of the subject.

President Harris is relatively a young man having just recently passed the half century mark. With such a rich background upon which to capitalize and the probability of many years more of physical and mental activity before him even greater achievements would seem to be in store for him than he has yet experienced.

Dr. Henry Eyring, born in Colonia Juarez, Mexico, 37 years ago ranks as one of the greatest of the younger generation of scientists of America. He is of German-English extraction, his father, Edward C. Eyring, coming from a line of distinguished German ancestry and his mother, Caroline Romney Eyring claiming descent from equally prominent English forbears. His paternal grandfather, Henry Eyring, and for whom the young man was named, was prominent in the founding of Colonia Juarez, as was also his maternal grandfather, Miles P. Romney.

Young Eyring's first formal instruction outside of the home was had in the schools of the village in which he was born. He was not long to enjoy the sweet environment of his native home, however, for when a lad of eleven his parents experienced the necessity of fleeing with the balance of the colonists from their homes to become exiles in the United States. Crossing the international boundary line they found themselves in El Paso without food and with no visible means of support save that which would come to them through toil. Henry obtained a position in a grocery store where he served as a cash and grocery boy. Later the family moved, first to Safford and then to Pima, Arizona.

Henry completed his grade school work at Pima, graduating from the eighth grade at the head of his class and honored with the appointment of "class Valedictorian." He next entered the Gila Academy at Thatcher, an institution founded and supported by the Church to which young Eyring belongs. At the head of his class scholastically and as its president, Henry graduated in 1919. Upon his graduation from the Gila College he was honored by receiving a $500 scholarship contributed by Graham County to the most efficient graduate from the high schools of the country. The scholarship entitled him to enroll at the University of Arizona, where he matriculated as a freshman student at the beginning of the fall term. The expenses of the remaining three years at the University of Arizona must be met from other sources since the scholarship applied to the freshman year only. The problem of finance was met by Eyring by waiting on the tables of the dining room of the University during the winter months, and as a miner during the summers at the Miama and Bisbee mines, and as a smelter hand at Clarksdale, Arizona. With the completion of his work for a Bachelor's degree in mining engineering in 1923, the rising young scholar was given a scholarship which enabled him the following year to take out an M. A. in Metallurgy. With the beginning of the next school year he found himself a regular member of the faculty of his Alma Mater, but after teaching for one year he concluded it best to take another step higher up the ladder of learning. The lure of a higher professional standing among his fellows beckoned him on.

A fellowship was granted him to attend the University of California at Berkeley, where, in 1927, he graduated with a Ph. D. degree in chemistry. He had switched his major to chemistry feeling that this field of science offered greater opportunities for growth than could possible come to him in metallurgy. For two years after receiving his doctorate, young Eyring taught at the University of Wisconsin. During this time he met Miss Mildred Bennion, Professor of Physical Education at the University of Utah. An attachment sprang up between them which ripened into love and ended in a marriage in August, 1928.

While teaching at Madison, Dr. Eyring won a scholarship at the Kaiser Wilhelm Institute at Berlin, Germany. The amount stipulated in the scholarship was $200, each month, plus traveling expenses. The year spent at this great German University was to prove of inestimable worth to Dr. Eyring furnishing an opportunity, as it did, to engage in research work in a chemical laboratory with some of the most distinguished scientists of Europe. While abroad he wrote his first extended paper on quantum mechanics in collaboration with Professor Polyanyi a noted member of the University staff. This was the first of a series of such papers that have made young Eyring famous.

Returning to America, he accepted a temporary position on the staff of the University of California in 1930-31, and while here he received an invitation to go to Princeton and deliver a series of lectures, for which he received a salary of $100 per lecture. The result of this visit was a permanent position on the Princeton University Staff.

Henry has just completed his third year at the institution and each year has witnessed a growth in his popularity and a decided increase in salary.

Four years last December (1933) a science convention was being held at Atlantic City, attended by distinguished representatives in all the branches of science from far and near. A prize was being offered by the American Association for the Advancement of Science to the one presenting the "outstanding paper" of the convention. It happened that young Eyring one morning addressed his wife rather jestingly: "I think I shall go down to Atlantic City and bring back the $1000 offered for the outstanding paper of the convention." He went to the convention, delivered his paper and quietly left for his home.

The next morning Dr. Eyring awoke to find himself great. He had won the prize and streaming across the front pages of the leading papers of the United States were graphic accounts of this great achievement, by a youth from Mexico, still young in years but ripe in intellect. A few excerpts from leading papers of the country will suffice to tell the story.

On the front page of the San Francisco Chronicle, January 1, 1933, appeared the following:

"For a discovery that heralds a new science, the union of chemistry and physics, with practical human application outstripping past progress, Henry Eyring, Ph. D., 32, Princeton University chemist, was awarded today the annual $1000 prize of the American Association for the Advancement of Science for an "Outstanding paper." Eyring, a graduate of the U. of C. in 1928 (1927) is one of a group of youngsters in American Science who have been showing how physics can be combined with chemistry.

"His paper bears the forbidding title, 'Quantum mechanics in Chemistry with Particular Attention to Reactions Involving Conjugate Double Bonds.' * * * His friends here say that playing with chemistry is his major fun.''

Industrial and Engineering Chemistry of January 10, 1933, said:

"The prize of $1000 given annually by the American Association for the Advancement of Science for the *best* paper submitted at the winter meeting, was awarded at Atlantic City to Henry Eyring, research associate of the Frick Chemical Laboratory, Princeton University. Doctor Eyring's paper was an application of the principles of quantum mechanics to the laws governing the chemical bonds between the elements.''

Brisbane, noted correspondent of New York and other papers, in the columns of the "New York American" of January 2, 1933, said:

"Dr. Henry Eyring of the Frick Laboratory of Princeton, only thirty-two years old, has been exploring the sub-atomic world and brings up facts that amaze learned gentlemen concerning reactions involving conjugate double bonds.

"Theoretically, employing the new quantum methods, that would give most of us a headache, Dr. Eyring predicted conditions that laboratory work has confirmed. From him you learn why two atoms of hydrogen, each with a valence of only one, are held fast by one single atom of oxygen, which has a valence of two, thus giving us the combination H_2O necessary for our existence.''

Mail Report, Science Service, Washington, D. C., January 1, 1933: "Dr. Henry Eyring, 32 year old Princeton chemist, is working with mathematical equations of the new quantum mechanics to solve themical problems. Chemists in laboratories make experiments which check his theoretical problems. * * * Your chemistry text book says that hydrogen gas and fleurine react easily.   Dr. Eyring's calculations showed they should not and German chemists found that these two elements in pure state at ordinary temperatures had such great antagonism that they would not combine regardless of what the text book said."

Similar announcements, some of which filled two or three columns appeared in the New York Times, New York Herald Tribune, Philadelphia Inquirer, Kansas City Star, New York Evening Post, Berkeley Gazette and other leading periodicals.

In spite of the great publicity given Dr. Eyring by the Press throughout the country he remains still the humble, unobtrusive, sweet individual his friends and acquaintances have always found him to be, indeed, one marvels that one so simple in his habits can have achieved so much. I had the privilege of visiting Dr. Eyring last summer in his home, at his laboratory at Princeton, and at Church and was struck by his utter lack of ostentation. I found him presiding over a congregation of 26 Latter-day Saints—a position prized more highly by him than any professional titles he holds or any acclaim which has come to him as a result of academic achievement. Again this summer on a visit at my home, he paid a glowing tribute to the little group of Saints back at New Brunswick, New Jersey, and referred to them affectionately as the best people in the world.

Others from the colonies have done honor to their ancestry and their training, in the various fields of human endeavor, but the examples given will suffice to show the quality of the young generations reared in the Mormon colonies of Mexico.

As a conclusion to this topic it may be well to observe that the human product of the colonies have functioned large since the exodus in directing the thinking of the youth of the Church which they represent. Simultaneously, there were six colony men presiding over as many Church schools of which there were but twenity-one such institutions supported by the Church. Guy C. Wilson was President of the L. D. S. University at Salt Lake City; Franklin S. Harris presided at the Brigham Young University; George

S. Romney over the Ricks College, Idaho; Erastus Romney President of the Dixie Normal College at Saint George; Charles E. McClellan of the Millard Academy, Hinckley, Utah and Thomas C. Romney of the Oneida Academy, Preston, Idaho.

In the Seminary system of the Church at the present time, the following teachers hail from Mexico: Lucius and Ernest Clark, Newel K. Young, and Thos. C. Romney.

At the Brigham Young University in additions to President Franklin S. Harris are Guy C. Wilson, Carl Eyring, and H. Grant Ivins, and at the Utah State Agricultural College in Logan, Charles E. McClellan is Assistant Professor of Education.

In law, in business, and in other vocations the colonists have left their stamp upon the communities where they reside.

CHAPTER XXI

ATTEMPTED PROPERTY SETTLEMENTS

I have referred in a former chapter to a settlement made by the Mexican Government with the Mormons of the Sonoran colonies for vacated lands at Morelos and Oaxaca for the sum of $100,000. This amount was to be pro-rated in an equitable manner among those who had suffered losses.

Attempts have been made several times through the good offices of such men as Judge George W. Bartch and Attorney J. Reuben Clark of Salt Lake City, to negotiate an amicable and just settlement between the Mexican Government and American colonists who lost heavily in the state of Chihuahua and elsewhere. Their efforts apparently met with no success at the time but in recent months it is reported, authoritatively, I presume, that Mexico has agreed to compromise by giving a lump sum to meet such claims against the government.

The pathetic thing connected with the offer is that the proffered sum represents only a very small fraction of the total loss sustained. Any amount truly is better than none but such a huge financial loss certainly is anything but pleasing even to the most self-sacrificing individuals.

Any discussion or observation I may have to offer relating to the subject of property losses and attempts at settlement will have a bearing directly upon the Mormon colonies in Chihuahua.

When the colonists left their homes in a body in 1912, as previously pointed out, few there were who ever dreamed that the move would be more than temporary. It was thought that the trouble would soon blow over and that the people would return in a body to re-occupy their homes and enjoy otherwise the comforts of their hard-earned material prosperity. When, however, the days passed into weeks with no apparent abatement of the strife which had shaken the very foundations of the Republic for years, hope began to wane in the breasts of the exiles. Under these conditions they were counseled to submit a list of their holdings in the colonies with an itemized statement in figures of the actual value of each piece of property at the time the colonies were vacated.

It stands to reason that a sub-value estimate would not be placed on their properties since there is a tendency common to men to desire full values for their material possessions. Yet the fact that each one submitting a listing must do so under oath before a notary would tend to reduce to a minimum extravagant figures. Another safeguard against exaggerated estimates is the nature of the forms that must be filled out. These forms call for an itemized statement of properties, each item to have placed opposite it, its estimated value. Such headings ask, for example, for the number of fruit trees in bearing, young fruit trees, bushels of wheat, corn, barley, potatoes, beans, number of milch cows, mules, hogs, buggies, houses, city lots, acres of farming land, grazing land, number of out-buildings, saddles and many other similar items.

Any attempt at settlement would naturally be beset with difficulties. In the first place, there would most likely be a disparity of opinion regarding property values, since the loser of the property and the one to pay the damages would have contrasting interests in the matter. In the event of property suffering only partial destruction the extent of the damage would become a moot question; and again, the matter of culpability must be settled in order to fix responsibility.

As we have seen, robberies of all sorts were perpetrated against the colonists, from the stealing of their agricultural products and the killing of their cattle to the burning of their homes. In some instances the theft of horses and cattle and of the produce of the soil were accounted for by the issuance of receipts to the owners. These high-handed robberies, however, were most frequently committed, not by federal soldiers in the employ of the government, (although they were sometimes guilty of theft), but by those opposing the government who promised to pay on condition of being successful in the overthrow of the government and the establishment of themselves in power. More frequently they were detached groups of bandits whose chief purpose in traveling about was to obtain a livelihood by preying upon others. Of what value would receipts be from such as they? Obviously they would be of less value than the paper on which they were written.

To what extent a government shall be held morally accountable for acts of brigandage within its borders would justly be determined by the attitude of the government toward such actions. It is entirely obvious that if a government does all within its power to protect the lives and properties of foreigners within its domain, but fails to stamp out or prevent further acts of brigandage, it has done its duty and in justice cannot be held accountable for what has happened. If, however, it remains indifferent to acts of violence against either life or property, or still worse, if it encourages such nefarious actions, it is wholly culpable and should, as far as possible, be made to compensate for losses.

The degree to which the Mexican Government should be held responsible for atrocities committed against the colonists, may be difficult to ascertain. If, as Judge Bartch declared before the "Senate Sub-Committee to investigate Mexican affairs" that "officers of the Mexican government took part in the numerous ravages to terrorize the American people to leave the country so that their property might be confiscated among the Mexicans" and if, as he further pointed out that, "Generals of the Mexican army publicly proclaimed their intention to drive the Gringos out of the country and through speech and action encouraged the soldiers into still greater acts of violence then there is but one conclusion to be reached. Mexico should make restitution as far as possible for all losses to life and property whether suffered directly at the hands of federal troops or of bandits."

As to the reliability or the origin of Judge Bartch's information relative to this matter I am not prepared to say. It seems certain, however, that a man of his reputation and standing in public affairs would not present as fact evidence that had not been well sifted. I am inclined to the belief, notwithstanding, that the government officials of Mexico, generally speaking, did not encourage or even uphold acts of violence against Americans for the purpose of confiscating their properties to the native population. That there were some holding prominent national and local government positions guilty of such anti-American machinations there is no doubt, and from personal observation covering a period of years, I am certain that some of the local Mexicans were eagerly looking forward to the departure of the colonists that they might possess their homes and their property.

Since the exodus the government has shown a willingness to permit the colonists to return and re-possess their landed properties, by paying the delinquent taxes. Previous mention has been made of a statement made by the Presidente of Casas Grandes to citizen Joel H. Martineau of Colonia Pacheco that, "all lands that have been for years abandoned may be settled on by any American citizen. If the owner comes back later and pays all back taxes and expenses we will let him have his property back."

Joseph C. Bentley, representing the colonists in their property interests in northern Mexico, in an article dated October 3, 1921, urged all former colonists possessing lands in Mexico to pay the delinquent taxes lest the "owners lose unoccupied lands in the Mexican colonies." He stated that the Mexican Government was willing that Mexicans should cultivate unoccupied lands of the colonists, that they would cultivate the land for three years without rent, but that they could receive no title and if, after three years they continued to use the land, they must settle with the owners for rental.

Notwithstanding the favorable attitude of the Government for the return of lands to the colonists, but few have availed themselves of the opportunity to re-possess them. Several factors have entered in to create this lack of desire. In the first place, the disturbed conditions in Mexico were of such extended duration that many of the refugees, in the meantime, had purchased homes and other property in various localities of the United States, and an attachment had grown up for their relatively new environment that held them fast. Then, there were others who still had a longing to return to Mexico, even after a lapse of many years, but who were fearful to return lest another political upheaval should send them scurrying from the country again. Some there were whose properties had so depreciated in value through the permanent withdrawal of the population from the regions where located as to render them almost valueless and, finally, there were a number of instances in which the older members of the family had a desire to return but the younger members thereof had no such desire, they having been born since the exodus or being too immature at the time of the exodus to retain any fond memories of the land of their birth.

Rather than to wait on the delayed action of the Mexican Government to remunerate for losses incurred in the withdrawal from the colonies, or wearied over waiting for a return of peace, many colony property holders, not wishing to return, have sold their holdings to their returning brethren for paltry sums. In some instances homes and orchards have been disposed of for ten percent of their original value. Range lands bordering on the Bavispe River and adjacent to the colonies of Morelos and Oaxaca were in the heyday of Mormon colonial expansion of great worth. Thousands of cattle fed fat on its luxurious growths of grass and shrubs the year round, netting each year to the many owners thousands of dollars of easy money. But

19

the series of revolutions came on and in their wake came the slaughtering of these great herds of cattle by soldiers and other wandering nomads in quest of food, and revenues to be obtained from the unlawful sale of beef hides and tallow. The lands are still as fertile as ever and their titles are in the hands of the colonists but their value has crumbled.

Today these hills and canyons are solitudes whose stillness is broken only by the dismal howl of the coyote or an occasional intrusion of a ranchero in quest of an animal that has strayed from its moorings. From these deserted hilltops could be seen in years gone by, thrifty American colonies resting peacefully on the banks of the Bavispe whose waters reach the Pacific through the gateway of the Rio Yaqui. These villages, too, have disappeared and nothing remains to bear witness of their former glory save fast decaying dwellings and other mute evidences of that once industrious civilization. In the place thereof can be seen a few ranches dotting the landscape here and there and above the din of the cattle can be heard the voice of the vaquero as he swings his lariat in rhythmic fashion. This picture in a number of its aspects can be duplicated in certain localities in proximity to some of the Mormon colonies in northern Chihuahua.

Yet damage to such property resulting from forced isolation would be difficult to collect from the government. The land is still the same in extent, the streams of water continue to thread the same canyons and ravines and all other natural facilities are intact as of long ago. The same thing is true of the farm lands similarly damaged. The Mexican authorities guarantee to reinstate the owners in their rightful possessions. What more can be expected of a government? Nothing unless it can be established that the Government through negligence is responsible for permitting conditions to arise making it necessary for the population to permanently abandon their possessions. This responsibility the Mexican Government refuses to assume.

In the event of property being totally destroyed by fire or other violent agencies the question as to the extent of the damage done is not a difficult one to arrive at but the problem of placing the responsibility for the damage and of bringing the guilty to judgment is not so easy of solution. Especially is this true where large groups of offenders are involved. The total destruction of Colonia Diaz by fire is a case in point. It is well known that a band of revolutionists calling themselves "Red Flaggers" did the deed, but to convict them and compel them by law or otherwise to pay the bill, was out of the question. The only recourse left open to the owners of these once beautiful homes was to appeal to the Mexican Government for compensation. If, as has been charged against the Government, many of its leading officials connived at and even encouraged such outlawry, then in the name of justice it should make full restitution. But the Government has refused to assume any responsibility in the matter except to guarantee to the colonists their lands in and around Diaz in case they wish to return.

A few of the Mormons who have returned to the colonies have fared well financially at the expense of those who, for various reasons, refuse to return to their homes. These adventurous spirits endowed with unusual business acumen have monopolized for the most part the orchards and farm lands as well as the industrial facilities of certain of the colonies. This was made possible by the inordinate eagerness of many of the refugees to dispose of their holdings if for nothing more than a mere pittance. Others of the returned exiles have benefited by having the free use of range and irrigable lands whose titles are held by those indifferent to the uses being made of them.

CHAPTER XXII

HAZARDS OF A RELIGIOUS BOYCOTT IN MEXICO

In the preceding chapter I called attention briefly to the difficulties encountered by the colonists who returned to Mexico, resulting from the war of government officials on religion. I pointed out that the colonists met these difficulties in a judicious manner with the result that but little friction exists between the Mormons and the Mexican officials. It is to be hoped that these amicable relationships may continue indefinitely, but who, less than a prophet would dare forecast what the future may hold in store for any group of religionists in a situation so delicate. True it is that the anti-religious enactments of Congress backed by the relgious pronouncements of recent Mexican Presidents were aimed directly at the Roman Catholic Church, yet no group of professed Christians has any assurance that sooner or later its freedom in worship may not be jeopardized.

The purpose of this chapter is to point out the precarious situation that obtains in Mexico with respect to worship, in the hope that those who now enjoy a large measure of religious freedom may not through ignorance of the law or through unwise actions incur the hostility of the Government.

The fight now on against religious worship is not new in Mexico—the conflict between church and state has been waged for three-quarters of a century. But at no time in the history of this warfare has the state been more vigorous in its attempts to crush the church than at the present.

An attempt to analyze the causes of this strife is fraught with untold difficulties, since there is scarcely any agreement among the witnesses to the controversy as to the historicity of reputed facts bearing up the subject.

No historian can deny the fact, however, that much of the persecution being waged against the church results from an attempt on its part to usurp authority in the past which rightfully belonged to the state. No less an

authority than Dr. Macfarland declares that, "The church
has used other than spiritual weapons; to a great extent its
own procedures have brought it into its present condition.
Had the church begun earlier and carried out farther its
more recent and present plans for social reform the result
might have been very, very different." The present Secretary of Foreign relations says that the church "by reason
of its moral and physical enslavement of the masses, made
it impossible for any political organization to undertake an
energetic program of government." He continues by
charging the church with having "entirely selfish aims of
swelling the fortunes of the clergy, of enhancing their
political power and of freely allowing undue traffic in the
acts of religion." Much of this accumulated wealth, he
asserts, is sent out of the country to "uphold an alien
sovereign." "To the church has now come the hour when
its responsibility will be exacted from it; the Mexican
State cannot in any way permit a renewal of criminal interference by any religious group."

Sr. Portes Gil, ex-President of the Republic, makes
the charge that, "The church was an institution fundamentally devoted to the exploitation of everybody: Span-
iards and Indians, rich and poor."

Back of these statements there is a likelihood of some
bias, but nevertheless, history bears record to the dominance
of the church over affairs in Mexico over a period of three
hundred years in all things secular as well as spiritual.
During that period the wealth of the country flowed into
the coffers of the church, making it fabulously rich. One
prominent writer has affirmed that during the rule of
President Diaz the wealth accumulated by the clergy
amounted to more than eight hundred million pesos. During
the period of Catholic rule nearly half of the land areas
of Mexico fell into the hands of the church; the education
of the masses showed little improvement and the economic
conditions, except among the favored few showed but
little advancement. From these untoward conditions was

born the Constitution of 1857—a document designed to separate the powers of church and state and to establish the supremacy of the state throughout the republic.

Naturally enough the church exerted all of its power against the enforcement of the Articles of the Constitution. In a defiant attitude Pope Pius IX in a mandate declared:

"Thus we make known to the faith in Mexico and to the Catholic universe, that we energetically condemn every decree that the Mexican Government has enacted against the Catholic religion, against the church and her sacred ministers and pastors, against her laws, rights and property and also against the authority of the Holy See. We raise our Pontifical voice with apostolic freedom before you to condemn, reprove and declare null, void and without any value, the said decrees, and all others which have been enacted by the civil authorities in such contempt of the ecclesiastical authority of the Holy See."

If the Constitution of 1857 was full of dynamite for the church, what shall we say of the Constitution of 1917, a product of the revolution.

Article 27 of the Constitution of 1917 declares that, "Places of public worship are the property of the nation as represented by the Federal Government, which shall determine which of them may continue to be devoted to their present purpose." It further states that all places of public worship which may later be erected shall be the property of the Government. Likewise "Episcopal residences, rectories, seminaries, orphan asylums or collegiate establishments of religious institutions, convents or any other buildings built or designed for the administration, propaganda, or teaching of any religious creed shall forthwith vest, as of full right directly in the nations to be used exclusively for the public services of the Federation of the States within their respective jurisdictions."

Article 130 says that "The State legislatures shall have the exclusive power of determining the maximum number of ministers of religious creeds, according to the needs of each locality. Only a Mexican by birth may be a minister of any religious creed in Mexico." Still farther, "no ministers of religious creeds shall, either in public or private meetings or in acts of worship or religious propaganda, criticize the fundamental laws of the country, the authorities in particular, or the government in general; they shall have no vote, nor be eligible to office, nor shall they be entitled to assemble for political purposes." There is a further stipulation that "no minister of any religious creed may inherit either on his own behalf or by means of a trustee or otherwise, any real property occupied by any association of religious propaganda for religious or charitable purposes."

About 1927 a decree of the President makes it unlawful for a foreigner to take part in religious propaganda in public. This pronouncement raises a bar against foreigners exercising any ministerial functions. Still later we have President Cardenas, the present chief executive of Mexico, prohibiting the use of the mails for publications containing religious information and even private letters dealing with religious matters.

Restrictions on ministers are not confined to religious activities, but are effective in the fields of education and politics, as well. Article 3 of the 1917 Constitution specifies that, "No religious body, nor a minister of any religious sect will be allowed to establish or direct schools of primary education." Article 55 states that, "a deputy of Congress may not be a minister of any religious sect" and article 59 places the same restriction upon a Senator. Article 82 expressly forbids the President the right to belong "to an ecclesiastical body nor can he be a "minister of any religious sect."

The extent to which these laws are enforced in the various Mexican states is determined by a variety of factors such, for example, as distance from the Federal District, economic conditions and the strength of the Roman Catholic Church. Dr. Macfarland in his recent book entitled

"Chaos in Mexico" asserts that in about thirteen of the Mexican states religious institutions have been either totally or partially wiped out, including such states as Sonora and Chihuahua on the north and Tabasco and Yucatan on the south. The states are grouped by Mr. Macfarland under three headings, extreme, mediating and liberal. Listed under the first heading are such states as Tabasco, Sonora, Sinaloa, Chihuahua, Chiapas, Queretaro, Oaxaca, Veracruz, Zactecas; in the mediating states he names Yucatan, Durango, Michoacan, Nuevo Leon, Puebla; and in the liberal group are Aguascalientes, Jalisco, Hidalgo, Morelos, Tamaulipas, San Luis Potosi, Mexico and the Federal District.

In Tabasco there is no church nor saloon; jazz music and saxophones are forbidden and marriage is regarded as being merely a social contract. The schools are anti-church and absolutely anti-religious. To get a position in one of the schools of this state one must sign a document declaring that he is an atheist and belongs to no church.

The pledge required of the teacher in Yucatan is in part as follows:

"I declare that I am an atheist, irreconciliable enemy of the Roman Catholic religion, and that I will use my efforts to destroy said religion and to do away with all religious profession, and that I am ready to oppose the clergy wherever and whenever it may be necessary.

"I declare that I am ready to take a chief part in the campaign against fanaticism and to attack the Roman Catholic religion wherever it manifests itself.

"At the same time, I will not permit any religious practices of any kind in my home, nor any images, and I will not permit any of the members of my family under my authority to attend any service of a religious character." Jan. 23, 1935.

While the pledges in the different states vary in form they appear to be sponsored by the Director of Education who is subject to the authority of the Secretary of Public Instruction.

Perhaps the most liberal of all the Mexican states is San Luis Potosi. Private schools, both Catholic and Protestant, have to a large extent continued. The Governor in the presence of President Cardenas ordered a chapel restored which had been taken by the Government.

In Monterey, the principal city of Nuevo Leon, Protestant schools still operate and a principal of one of these private schools is also teaching in a public school. The Catholic schools are closed here because of failure to accept the conditions regarding teaching. Catholic churches, however, are open.

Some of the newspapers of Mexico are decidedly atheistic and manifest a rabid spirit toward all forms of religion. Macfarland cites the Cristo Rey, a weekly newspaper supporting the Government, as having on its front page a caricature of Jesus as being in an intoxicated condition and "wearing a crown at a rakish angle, suggestive of ribaldry." In another issue of the same paper the crucifixion is represented with a donkey as the central figure. This picture was distributed throughout the schools.

Even some of the paintings of the most distinguished artists of Mexico, and occupying prominent places on the walls and ceilings of Federal Buildings, are strongly anti-Christian in tone. A mural painted by Jose Orozco reveals the figure of Christ "swollen and bloated almost to the bursting point, a tiny crown of thorns resting upon a luxurious growth of hair. It would be impossible to imagine a more repulsive figure, and the leer in the protruding eyes is not likely to be forgotten."

Another mural represents God the Father as a wicked old man with cross eyes and in an angry mood.

Some of the text books used in the school rooms contain stories and dialogues most damaging to the church and destructive of morals. I am indebted to Dr. Macfarland for the excerpts culled from text books which follow:

"Sometimes I go to the library: What a beautiful

building! Formerly it was a church, but now books take the place of the saints and I believe that that is better. Books do us good service.

"Mama believes that the strike can be settled by prayers. If the boss knew this, how he would laugh! Then mother confessed and told the priest all about the strike. The Curate is not in our situation and, as he does not know the indignity of being paid a miserable salary, and since he never worked with his hands, he counselled my mother, resignation and to bear everything in the love of God. A beautiful formula. Very convenient. But it did not convince my mother.

"If the owner throws you out: resign thyself.

"If the boss fires you: resign thyself.

"If the boss kills you with hunger: resign thyself.

"And all for the love of God, who permits the bosses to exploit the working man. This is all that a man who is called a shepherd of souls and who gives his hand hypocritically to be kissed, could counsel. I am going to find a more practical formula."

"When thou takest up the rifle, may it be to put an end to all those who even yet exploit us."

"The church—When the Spaniard conquered our Indians he erected by the side of the police jail, the jail of the church. In the church they taught meek resignation, the sort which was carried out in life the law of the conqueror. Think, country child, how much churches are worth and what you could do with that gold in your hands: schools for the children, hospitals, dispensaries, tractors,— yes, many tractors. In place of churches: high schools or gymnasiums."

From this brief review of conditions in Mexico the reader can see how difficult it is to hazard a guess as to what the outcome will ultimately be. The weel or woe of religionists will be determined largely, no doubt, by the extent and direction of the influence exerted by the Governors of the several states and the attitude of President Cardenas and those who shall succeed him as the chief executive of this Southern Republic. And let me here add that the attitude of these officials will in a measure, at least, be influenced by the reaction of the church toward the Government.

A recalcitrant attitude breathing a spirit of retaliation, or an appeal to a foreign ecclesiastical power for aid, will never profit a church in the least degree in Mexico. In this observation I do not justify the political officials of Mexico in their harsh and even unjust methods of attack upon religious organizations. Ends desired could be achieved by a policy of non-interference in matters wholly spiritual and which are of no concern to the state. It is paradoxical in the extreme, and highly unethical, for the state to impose intolerant restrictions upon the church and to exercise an unjust dominion over it as a retaliatory measure against an institution, for injustices it may have perpetrated in the past upon the people, and for its usurpations in government.

Better would it be for all concerned and in the interests of peace and prosperity in Mexico, if both church and state would learn each its proper places and in a Christlike spirit, "Render therefore unto Caesar the things which are Caesar's and unto God the things that are God's."

This is the spirit that has actuated the Latter-day Saints from the beginning of their settlement in Mexico. They have played fair with the Government and at no time in their history have they attempted to usurp political authority that did not belong to them, nor have they meddled in affairs of no concern to them. At the same time they have upheld and sustained in a spirit of loyalty the laws and institutions of the land to a marked degree. Such a policy continued will do more than anything else toward insuring them against political irritations and vouchsafing to them permanent peace and prosperity in the land of their adoption.

CHAPTER XXIII

CONDITIONS IN THE COLONIES IN THE
YEAR 1938

As I write these lines, a revolution is on in Mexico but the quick action and firm hand of President Cardenas are fast dissipating the strength of the rebels and it will be only a short time, apparently, when the revolution will be crushed.

The unsettled condition in Mexico, together with the expropriation of the oil properties of American and English capitalists have led many to fear for the future welfare and prosperity of foreigners in Mexico. What further discriminations may be enacted against them can only be conjectured in the light of what has already taken place. In the Mormon colonies within the past four months I have been reliably informed that certain hateful indignities have been imposed by local Mexicans against certain of the law-abiding citizens of these settlements. A Mrs. Bluth, whose home is in one of the colonies was subjected to the heart-breaking experience of seeing her home entirely stripped of every piece of furniture while she stood helplessly looking on. Another colonist, the water master, was placed behind the bars for venturing to do his duty. A native Mexican had refused to release the irrigation water to an American farmer who was entitled to it whereupon the latter complained to the water master. The water was taken from the Mexican and given to the American and this resulted in the water master being placed behind the bars. If such acts of injustice and intolerance continue no one but a prophet can foretell what the future may develop.

The economic condition of the nearly one thousand Mormon colonists in Mexico is none too flattering though there are a few of the more prosperous ones who are in fairly good circumstances. Particularly are the few colonists located in the mountains in an impoverished condition. Their poverty is reflected in the shabby appearance of their public buildings, the unkept streets and highways as well as in the dilapidated aspect of the private dwellings and tumble-down fences. At the present there are three Mormon settlements in the mountains, Pacheco, Garcia and Chuichupa.

The colonies of Juarez and Dublan show signs of greater prosperity but even in these settlements is not to be seen the economic prosperity that once was theirs. Many of the houses are inhabited by the native population and homes that have been unoccupied since the exodus have gone into decay.

To the honor of the honest, God-fearing people of these communities be it said, however, that in the face of all these discouragements they still look forward with hope toward the future. All of their earthly possessions are there and these material interests have been sanctified and rendered dear to them by the sweat and blood of long years of toil and hardship. When some out of pity have suggested the abandonment of these colonies and the immigration of the colonists to more favorable regions within the confines of the United States the suggestion has been met with stout disapproval. Many of them feel that they are on a mission in the interests of the Church and would prefer to die than to prove recreant to a trust reposed in them. Others, still, there are, who prefer to remain and brook the uncertainty of the future than to pull up stakes and begin anew the work of re-establishing homes.

Although financially poor the majority of these people are rich in spirit and in good works. No communities of Latter-day Saints in any part of the world are attending to their religious duties with a greater degree of enthusiasm and efficiency. The statistical reports of the Church show them to be among the most faithful of its membership in the payment of tithes and other offerings and their sincerity in the worship of God on the Sabbath has become proverbial.

In the matter of education I know of no people who have put forth greater efforts than they to give their children the opportunities offered by institutions of higher learning. In their poverty scores of young people have been sent from the Mormon colonies in recent years to attend colleges and universities of the United States and in most cases these young men and women have made the most of their opportunities. The Brigham Young University, the parent Church school, has profited most by this influx of students from the Mexican colonies. One father alone has sent to her well nigh a dozen children and several other families have furnished her with from four to six students apiece. The only regrettable feature for the colonies is that nearly one hundred per cent of these young people never return to Mexico to make their home.

After graduation from college they usually find employment far more profitable in the United States than could be obtained in Mexico. It is interesting to note, also, that these young people almost invariably find their mates while at college and while still attending college, or soon thereafter, assume the responsibilities of the married state. Instead of returning to the colonies in Mexico, where there is little inducement for ambitious young people to settle, they establish homes in the United States. As a result of this practice the population of the Mormon colonies is gradually falling off. Up to the present time there have been but few marriages between the Mormon and Mexican population but as time goes by there is danger of these mixed marriages increasing unless measures are taken to stop the migration of so many young people from the Mormon colonies.

An attempt is being made by the colonists to build up some industries that will help to stabilize the people by giving them a feeling of economic security. Among the institutions established in recent years are a cooperative poultry business established by a number of enterprising citizens of Dublan. Thousands of well-bred chicks have been imported from the United States and a man trained in the poultry business at the Brigham Young University at Provo, Utah, has been employed to manage the business. A cheese factory, established some years ago in Dublan, is turning out a fine product and each year the output increases to meet the growing demand both at home and abroad. Saddles, shoes and harnesses are manufactured in the colonies and are in considerable demand in certain parts of the country. Two flour mills are in operation which serve well the needs of the people at home and in addition supply a limited demand for these mill products outside of the colonies. The fruit growing industry is of no small moment at Colonia Juarez particularly. Apples, pears, peaches, grapes and berries are raised in considerable quantities and find ready market at Mexico City and elsewhere in the interior of Mexico. Dublan has never emphasized fruit growing for commercial purposes but within the past few years a number of young orchards have been planted looking toward that end. The experiment is too young to predict with any degree of certainty as to its outcome but I see no reason why the project should not succeed. The land is fertile and appears to be well adapted to the growing of fruit. The water supply under the Dublan reservoir system should prove to be adequate during normal years and the climate is good except for occasional late frosts in the spring which sometimes prove disastrous to the fruit.

The cultural outlook for the masses throughout the Republic of Mexico was perhaps never better. Under the aggressive administration of the young Mexican President, Cardenas, the public school system has grown apace. New methods of teaching are being introduced and the importance of an education for the millions of illiterates in Mexico is being stressed as never before. The aim of education in Mexico seems to be to produce an enlightened and loyal

Mexican citizenry such as the country has never known. All schools throughout Mexico are subject to Government inspection even though they be supported and operated by private concerns. The law insists that all elementary schools must emphasize the Spanish tongue as well as subjects relating to the best interests of the country. Such subjects as Mexican history, Mexican civics and the geography of Mexico must be taught and at least half of the daily curriculum must be presented in the Spanish language.

A Spanish department must be maintained in schools of higher learning and all students attending such institutions must take at least two years of Spanish. The teachers are required to attend annually the conventions appointed by the functionaries of the Government and are constantly subject to Government inspection. School holidays must conform to those of the country and in every way the school must inculcate in the minds and hearts of the children and of the youth a respect for the institutions of the Mexican Republic.

As a result of these stringent regulations it has been no easy matter for the Mormon colonists to harmonize all requirements of the Mexican school law with their own ideals appertaining to a Church school education. Yet Principal Keeler and his colleagues of the Juarez Stake Academy have made a fine job of it, all things being considered. Thirty thousand dollars are appropriated annually by the Mormon Church for the support of its educational system in Mexico which consists of the Juarez Stake Academy and the elementary schools in the several colonies. The law requires them to admit all classes and kinds into their institutions of learning and hence there is a large sprinkling of Mexican youth to be found in the student bodies of both the Academy and the elementary schools.

The Presidency of the Juarez Stake, consisting of Claudius Bowman, Moroni Abegg and Wilford Farnsworth, are doing all they can to advance the welfare of the people over whom they preside and at the same time to prevent any unpleasant relationships between the two races of people—Mexican and American. Associated with them intimately in an ecclesiastical way are the bishops of the five wards and other officers of the wards and stake, all of whom are loyal and dependable.

I have previously called attention to the attempted property settlements as applied to foreigners in Mexico but the progress made in this direction during the past few months requires me to refer to the matter again.

Over a period of twenty-two years, from 1912 to 1934, repeated efforts were made through the medium of a mixed claims commission consisting of an American, a Mexican and a neutral member to arrive at a settlement of claims between the two countries. These attempts, however, were futile largely because the neutral committeeman who was of Latin origin invariably sided with the Mexican member in denying American claims. Finally on April 24, 1934, a treaty was entered into between Mexico and the United States wherein it was provided that Mexico should make a lump settlement of all of her liability on claims which were under the jurisdiction of the Special Mexican Claims Commission, on the basis of 2.65% of the amount claimed. This was the percentage granted British, Germans and nationals of other countries by commissions concerned with the adjudication of claims over a period of twenty-odd years. The amount to be paid by Mexico to the United States was approximately $5,500,000.00 to be paid at the rate of $500,000.00 per year beginning with January 1, 1935, with interest on deferred payments. The whole number of claims filed by Americans, coming under the jurisdiction of the Special Mexican Claims Commission was 2822, totalling $218,365,-065.76. In addition to this there are 11 claims totalling $636,743.78 later found to be under the jurisdiction of the commission. The Special Mexican Claims Commission was strictly an American Commission consisting of three members, Edgar E. Wirt, J. H. Sinclair and Darrel T. Lane.

20

A total of 385 residents of the seven American Mormon Colonies of northern Mexico filed formal claims for loss of property, aggregating approximately five and one-half million dollars. Total gross awards of $1,104,037.00 were awarded the Mormon colonists who had settled in the states of Chihuahua and Sonora between 1885 and 1912, for their losses from uprisings between 1910 and 1920. Seventy-two of the colonists' claims were disallowed in their entirety due to inability to substantiate their claims. Many of the colonists failed to file claims due to lack of faith in obtaining any recovery. Such were barred from any participation in the settlement. The total gross claims allowed all American claimants including the Mormon colonists was approximately $10,000,000.00. Since Mexico agreed to pay only $5,500,000.00 the result was that of the gross award allowed each claimant, he could hope for ultimate payment of only about 55%, payable in annual instalments as Mexico pays, unless the American Congress sees fit to appropriate enough to pay in full these claims and then reimburse the U. S. Treasury as payments come in from Mexico annually. Such a bill has been introduced and is now pending in Congress and stands a fair chance of being passed.

Those to whom credit is chiefly due for presenting the claims of the Mormon claimants before the commission were J. Reuben Clark, Jr., originally attorney for a number of the claimants; later Ambassador to Mexico and a counselor to Heber J. Grant, President of the Mormon Church; the Honorable George W. Bartch, former Chief Justice of the Supreme Court of Utah, who acted as attorney for a number of the claimants; Preston D. Richards, of Los Angeles, California, formerly a law partner of J. Reuben Clark, Jr.; Mr. Don P. Skousen of Phoenix, Arizona, and Vernon Romney, prominent attorney of Salt Lake City, who represented a large number of claimants.

Mr. Romney was particularly well fitted for the part he took in this matter, having been born and reared in the

Mormon colonies and driven from Mexico with the other refugees. This, coupled with his three years' experience in the Department of State at Washington from 1919 to 1922, especially qualified him to assume the chief responsibility in the matter of assembling the evidence, briefing the law and acknowledging these cases before the commission. In 1927 Judge Bartch died and Mr. Clark withdrew from active participation in the matter when he became Ambassador to Mexico. Mr. Richards moved to California.

After more than twenty years of futile effort to obtain some settlement and when most of the claimants had abandoned all hope of receiving any compensation for loss of property, Mr. Romney refused to admit of defeat. At heavy expense he travelled extensively over the states of the southwest assembling evidence, briefing the law and finally arguing the cases before the commission. The recent unsettled conditions in Mexico; the confiscation of American and British oil properties and other similar acts have led many to wonder if Mexico will default in making the payments she has agreed upon, but Mr. Romney states it as his personal opinion that Mexico will make her payments according to schedule.

Referring to the present status of affairs in Mexico Mr. Romney had this to say, "A number of acquaintances and clients who have recently visited in northern Mexico, have returned with the impression that things are too uncertain and hazardous there to justify any Americans who can possibly avoid it remaining there to live at present. The colonists who still remain are experiencing much difficulty in holding their land under the existing Agrarian policy of government; are being deprived of irrigation water rights which they have enjoyed for years and their personal property is being taken from them on many occasions without reimbursement therefor. While the country is blessed with remarkable natural resources which deserve development, American capital is reluctant to risk itself in that country."

Elder Melvin J. Ballard, a member of the Council of the Twelve, has been the chief sponsor of the Mormon colonies since the death of President Ivins. To him especially, the colonists look for advice in matters temporal as well as spiritual. He is in constant touch with conditions in Mexico and frequently visits the colonies. He is, therefore, one of the best informed on matters pertaining to the Latter-day Saints in that country.

In an interview with Apostle Ballard, recently he expressed pleasure at the treatment accorded his people in Mexico by the Federal Government. While admitting that some indignities may be perpetrated against the Mormons by local Mexicans, they are done without the sanction of the Federal or State Government. Every concession possible under the law is being tendered the Mormon people as an inducement to have them remain and build up the country. As an illustration of the friendly attitude of the state, Elder Ballard pointed out that the Dublan reservoir is to be doubled in capacity by increasing the height of the dam; that the cost of enlargement will be met by the state and the local Mexicans whose land will come under the reservoir, the state to pay one-half and the local Mexicans the other half. With the completion of the project, the Mormons and Mexicans will share equally in the profits. Such a project will tend to create harmony between the two races with respect to irrigation rights in this section of the country.

There is a general upward trend in salaries paid in the colonies and the surrounding territory and the industrial outlook is improving considerably. The American Smelting and Refining Company, with headquarters at Chihuahua City, is offering inducements to Mormon youth of college training to seek employment with them, and already a few of the outstanding young men from the colonies have obtained lucrative positions.

The cheese industry, Elder Ballard declares, has expanded to the point where it has become necessary to move the head plant to Chihuahua City. The factory is under the supervision of a son of Bishop A. B. Call, who received special training in cheese manufacturing at the Iowa State College in Ames, Iowa.

Elder Ballard is constantly reminding the colonists of the necessity of improving the appearance of their homes and surroundings, and he feels that many of them are heeding his advice.

The Latter-day Saints are fulfilling a great mission in Mexico, says Elder Ballard, in supplying missionaries for the Mexican Mission. Only citizens of the country are permitted to engage in missionary work in that land. At the present time there are 26 young men from the colonies laboring as missionaries in the interior of Mexico. No other group of people in the Church, of equal size, is furnishing so large a number of young men for the ministry. Apostle Ballard is encouraging all of the colonists in Mexico to become citizens of that country.

CHAPTER XXIV

THRILLING EXPERIENCES

THE TEMOCHE REVOLUTION

Highly emotional and with an inborn love for adventure, the natives of Mexico, for centuries, have been embroiled in martial conflict, much of it guerrilla in character. Grievances, in the light of Mexican philosophy, usually must be atoned for in physical combat. In the absence of actual grievances the elasticity of the Mexican mind has but little difficulty in hatching imaginary ones.

The intermittent fighting of a century overthrew Spanish rule in New Spain but did not end some of the iniquitous practices introduced here by the Spanish conquistadores. Class distinction and political and economic inequalities continued to thrive as in the days of Spanish glory. Lack of leadership and organization tended to hold the poorer classes in subjection to their masters and beneath the placid surface embers of hate were but awaiting the opportunity to burst forth into a lurid flame. Under the Diaz regime concerted action against these abuses seemed impossible before the Madero Revolution, although spasmodic and somewhat localized outbreaks occurred during the decades ante-dating that event.

I well remember just such an outbreak in 1893, when a group of eighty Temoche Indians from the mountains of northern Mexico inaugurated what is known as the "Temoche Revolution." The initial step taken in the revolution was an attack on the Customs House at Palomas near La Ascencion in northern Chihuahua. The raid was successful and netted the raiders considerable loot. Fired with their success the Indians contemplated an attack on other towns in Chihuahua and with that intent had begun a march toward the southwest. Directly on their line of march was Colonia Juarez, situated about seventy miles from Palomas.

Hearing of their approach and fearing an attack the colonists prepared to defend themselves through the agency of a local police force to consist of all able bodied men within the colony. The general command of the group was committed to Miles P. Romney, a man of some knowledge of military tactics and whose later life had been lived among the dangers of the frontiers. Associated with him as officers were three men known for their courage and reliability, John C. Harper, Orson P. Brown, a son of Captain James Brown of Mormon Battalion fame, and Brigham H. Stowell. President George Teasdale of the Mexican Mission counselled against the shedding of blood if possible, but in the event of an attack, he felt the colonists would be justified in defending themselves even to the point of taking life, if necessary.

Pickets were placed at all strategic points around the town with orders to fire if the Indians refused to halt. At the same time Orson P. Brown, Amos Cox and Carl E. Neilson were sent out as spies to ascertain the location of the enemy. On November 21, 1893, three of the Indians had made their way into the colony on a tour of inspection followed at a distance by Carl E. Neilson who was keeping watch of their movements. Several of the important business houses, including the "Union Mercantile," would likely have received their careful scrutiny had they not, in the meantime, become suspicious that their identity had been disclosed. Hastily they left the town followed by the intrepid Neilson.

While this scene in the drama was being enacted scouts Brown and Cox unexpectedly had come within the limits of the camp of the Temoches and before they made the discovery three of the sentry had their guns drawn on them and, in a commanding tone of voice, had ordered the Americans to raise their hands high in the air. Quick as a lightning flash the scouts reciprocated the act of the Indians and threatened them with death should they make one false move. What a tense moment this must have been! One unwise move on the part of either side and dire tragedy would have taken a frightful toll. Later, in speaking of the event, Brown acknowledged that as he looked down the muzzle of the gun aimed at him he felt it was in the hands of a man who knew no fear and would stand his ground to the last ditch. A policy of mediation was therefore decided upon, the Americans agreeing to withdraw with the promise that the Indians would not fire upon them. As they retreated, the scouts were careful to keep their faces toward the enemy, fearful lest the proverbial treacherous nature of the Indian should assert itself. The Americans pushed on toward Colonia Juarez with all speed possible and reported their experience, resulting in a small company under Stowell being ordered to join Brown and Cox to watch the movements of the enemy.

Meanwhile the Temoches had broken camp and were pushing farther up the Piedras Verdes River. At night a strong guard was placed about the town and the following morning a company of seven men consisting of Brown, Cox, Stowell, Judd, Taylor, Neilson and Wood were sent to locate the Indian camp. A few miles brought them to a point where the raiders had paused to kill a beef to augment their food supply. From here they journeyed on with moderate speed and with a degree of caution lest they be trapped again by the wily outlaws. Near the hour of noon they had reached a secluded spot in the Sierras and off in the distance, not to exceed one hundred and fifty yards, they beheld the camp of the enemy. Imagine their horror, however, when the scouts discovered that they were almost entirely surrounded by picket guards who had placed themselves at stratgeic positions behind rocks and trees. Annihilation seemed to be inevitable. Their retreat was cut off and the only possible way of escape was along a rocky steep in view of the entire force of the Temoches. A race for life began with the bullets of the Revolutionists falling like hail around them. The horse ridden by Judd stumbled and fell, the signal for a blood curdling yell from the throats of eighty Indians. But neither horse nor rider was injured and with a mighty effort the horse recovered himself and was again racing at break-neck speed. Finally the gauntlet had been run—the enemies' camp had been left in the rear and the line of the sentinels had been passed; a place of comparative safety had been reached and from an eminence the scouts poured forth a deadly fire from their long-range rifles with telling effect. They saw seven of the enemy fall, several of them to rise no more. Neilson was sent in haste to bear the news to the anxious colonists, while the remaining scouts kept vigil from their vantage ground. That night there were few who slept within that little Mormon town nestled near the foot of the Sierras. From the west side of the river the colonists were removed to the east and a line of guards was placed along the river front. All night long the watch was maintained, and as the hours dragged by these men of the frontiers listened and waited but the enemy came not, and the only sound that reached their ears was the murmur of the stream and an occasional cracking of a twig as the anxious guards paced back and forth along the shadowed path.

Fearing that the Temoches would yet seek revenge, it was decided in council to seek help from the municipality of Casas Grandes. At that point a Federal troop was garrisoned and it was felt that if the officers in command were solicited they would send reinforcements to strengthen the threatened colony. It fell to my lot, a youth of seventeen, to carry the message to Casas Grandes, twelve miles away. I had never prided myself on being courageous, but to the contrary had always felt to shrink from danger, yet, having received a commission I felt I would rather die than to shirk the responsibility. I shall always remember the emotional complex I experienced as I set out on a journey that seemed to me then to be fraught with danger. I was not without fear, but I recall also my feeling of pride as I passed down the principal street of our beautiful city and received from the little groups along the way tokens of good will and a hearty wish for a safe return home.

My trip was without incident and I arrived at my destination none the worse for my hurried ride. I presented my message in the form of a document and received from the proper authority an assurance that a portion of the garrison would return with me to the colony and that I was to act as the guide. Night fell before the troops were ready to move, but finally the command was given to march and toward the west we made our way. What a rabble those dirty troopers were! I wondered if my life was any safer in their hands than it would be at the mercy of the wild Temoches. All of the soldiers were footmen except those in command, and a sorry looking lot they were. Barefoot or with nothing on but sandals, they were compelled to travel at double quick time to keep up with the horsemen. Liquor had been imbibed freely even by the officers and its effects were manifest in a spirit of boisterousness and levity that made me wish for the journey to soon end. It was a welcome sight to me when finally we reached the winding dugway and saw beneath us in the narrow valley below the hundreds of electric lights flashing at us a welcome to the village. I had left in the early hours of the day. The soldiers were stationed for the night within the walls of a residence under construction and the next day, not wishing to meet the Indians in combat, returned to Casas Grandes leaving the colonists to fight their own battles. But the Temoches did not return, they had gone on to greener pastures.

THE SAVIOR OF NACOZARI

One hundred and fifty miles from Douglas, Arizona, in the state of Sonora nestles deep in a canyon the city of Nacozari, one of the important mining camps in northern Mexico. It was built by the Moctezuma Copper Company, a branch of the Phelps-Dodge Company, as a center for their extensive mining interests throughout a large area in northern Sonora. Here they built one of the finest concentrating plants in the world to process the ore from several mines, conveyed there by the company's system of railroads. When I was there more than thirty years ago there were about two thousand inhabitants made up chiefly of Mexicans and Americans most of whom were in the employ of the company. Like many others I went there to retrieve a small fortune lost in mine speculations and found employment in the building line. The majority of the houses at Nacozari were company built and company owned and to the credit of the company be it said they paid their employees well.

In 1908 I was acting foreman for the company in the construction of their buildings and as such was on my way from a row of tenement houses under construction to the planing mill when I observed a train of cars winding its way over the circuitous route leading up the steep acclivity east of town. There was nothing unusual about such an event, for trains were constantly going back and forth from the mines, except that in this instance the train seemed to be on fire. I watched it with interest and with considerable curiosity until the last car had passed over the summit of the hill when almost immediately there occurred the most terrific explosion that I had ever witnessed. The force of the concussion was so violent that it seemed to me my head would be blown from my shoulders and as if by instinct I found my hands locked over the top of my head to keep it from being blown into space. After the the shock was over I went at top speed to the summit of the hill to discover if I might, what had happened. The sight I beheld beggars description and like Banquo's ghost, it haunts me still. The first tragic scene in the picture was a dead man lying on his back with the warm blood from his body flowing down the hill in a small rivulet. Passing on I observed that the warehouse which had stood by the side of the track had been so completely demolished that not one particle of evidence remained to confirm the fact that such a building had ever existed. Even the solid shelf of rock on which the building once stood had received a scar fully three feet deep. Off to the left three hundred yards from the track had stood a tenement house that had sheltered several familes. To my astonishment the structure had been blown to atoms. Not one stick of timber was in its original position. Several of its occupants had been blown into eternity but worst of all my eyes fell upon the forms and features of two women, a mother and daughter, who had been gazing out of the window at the approaching train when the explosion occurred. The glass from the window was hurled with such terrific force into their eyes that they were literally torn from their sockets, and nothing was left but great gaping, hideous cavities where once the eyes had been. And those sightless women could not die but were destined to live on in a world of total darkness, subjects of charity until a kind providence should see fit to end their sufferings. I then looked about to ascertain the damage to the train, and saw that the engine had been dismantled, and learned that the body of the engineer had been blown from the cab and was lying horribly mangled by the side of the track.

Anxious to learn the cause of the disaster, I interviewed a group of men standing nearby and received from them a detailed account of the accident, the essential features of which I now pass on to my readers.

The train had come from the mine loaded with ore and was to return laden with an assortment of merchandise for those employed at the mines. On one car was loaded six thousand pounds of giant powder taken from a great stone magazine situated at the foot of the hill and in another car several tons of baled hay had been placed. When all was in readiness the engineer gave the signal, the engine began to puff and the train started to climb the hill. When less than half the distance had been reached the engineer cast a backward glance and to his consternation he saw the

sparks from the engine had set aflame the bales of hay and
that the burning hay, in turn, was being blown into the
midst of the tons of powder contained in the open car immediately in the rear.

"Run for your lives!" shouted the youthful Mexican
engineer to the train crew and a dozen passengers on their
way to the mines. No second command was needed, and in
a moment Juan was left alone. His Gethsemane had come.
He, too, might escape but what of the thousands in the town
below? Should the powder explode at this point the jar
would be sufficient to set off the hundreds of tons in the
magazine below and then what? Not one of the thousands
would live to tell the tale. Great beads of perspiration protruded from every pore and with a heavy groan he opened
wide the throttle and the train sped on. Scarcely had the
summit been reached when the powder exploded, but the
courage of the engineer had saved the town.

Six months had passed. The sun was about to sink
from view behind a serrated peak when a train of cars was
seen coming down the steep declivity east of town. It was
crowded with men, women and children on their way from
the mines. They had come to witness a solemn event, the
unveiling of a monument to the memory of Juan Garcia,
the youthful Mexican engineer. Multitudes had assembled
—Mexicans and Americans—social differences were cast
aside and all were blended into one great throng to pay
homage at the shrine of the hero who died that they might
live.

Words of eulogy appropriate for the occasion were
spoken and strains of soft-toned music floated out on the
evening air in heart-breaking loveliness only as a well-train-
ed and emotional Mexican orchestra can produce it. Then
as a hush came over the assembled multitude a veil was parted disclosing to view a polished granite shaft on whose base
was inscribed a glowing tribute, the spirit of which was as
follows: "To the memory of Juan Garcia, the courageous
youthful engineer, the savior of Nacozari, who died that

we might live. 'No greater love hath any man than this, that he should lay down his life for his friends.' "

Years have passed since then but those intervening years have not dimmed the memory of that courageous deed nor the sorrow of that widowed mother and orphaned sister as we tenderly placed in the casket the broken body of that heroic youth to whom honor and service were dearer than life.

FROM ALFALFA TO VENISON

The year had been a hard one. The crops had practically failed and there was little work to be had. Our family was an unusually large one and to feed and clothe them was a problem not easy to solve. My father was a hard worker and possessed considerable financial ability, and all members of the family had been trained to industry and economy, otherwise our lot would have been a pitiable one. Under the most favorable conditions possible, the living was scant, consisting merely of the bare necessities and at times it was a matter of deep concern lest the supply of food would not be sufficient to go around.

The different branches of the family were considerably scattered. My mother and her children were located in the tops of the Sierras at a picturesque spot bearing the designation "Cliff Ranch." Our only means of sustenance was a small patch of irrigable land and a few head of range cattle. The other branches of the family were having a similar struggle in the Casas Grandes Valley forty miles below.

For months not a pound of white flour had been known to enter our door. Our only bread was made from the corn, home grown and ground into meal on a hand mill in the house. In the summer time when the rain was abundant our food supply was measurably increased by the luxurious growth of red roots and pig weeds that sprang up as if by magic on every hand. These made delicious greens and served to break the monotony of our simple and meager diet. When the weeds became toughened with age rendering them unfit for use and the meal in the bin was running low, Mother cast about for something to supplement the decreasing store of food. Her woman's instinct finally suggested to Mother that the tender alfalfa plant must be nutritious since animals and fowls thrive on it, and so, for the next meal, we had as the principal article of our menu, alfalfa greens. Truly, Mother was forty years ahead of her time for in those days who ever heard of alfalfa being good for man? But today the best authorities in the field of dietetics have confirmed my mother's judgment as evidenced in the fact that alfalfa is recommended as being one of the best of salads. I had always been fond of red roots and pig weeds, but to my dying day I shall never forget that mess of alfalfa greens. In an effort to please Mother, I struggled hard to gulp them down but each attempt proved futile. Finally in desperation I blurted out that I had no objection to competing with pigs in the consumption of weeds but in the eating of alfalfa I must draw the line. I regretted greatly this expletive when I later glanced across the table and saw the pained look on my mother's face. My ingratitude had nearly broken her heart and no more alfalfa greens were ever seen on our table while I was present.

A short time after this painful incident Mother approached my brother and me about going hunting for wild game. Strange we hadn't thought of it before for the mountains were full of wild animal life of nearly all varieties. Likely we had not considered hunting before because of our youthfulness. I was but twelve years old and my brother only a year and five months my senior, and as I recall, neither of us had ever so much as fired a gun. Under these conditions I am certain mother would never have suggested such a thing were not starvation right at our door. With light hearts and filled with the spirit of adventure we set out in quest of food.

It was a matter of small moment which direction we should take, for game was as likely to be found in one place as another but we had chosen to try our luck up Spring Creek, a rugged canyon that entered Cliff Ranch from the north. Having but one gun, a 44 Winchester rifle, the question must be decided relative to the order of firing and since George was my senior, we agreed that he should have the first opportunity to shoot and that I should have the second shot. As a mere lad I recall vividly the feeling of exaltation experienced as we made our way up the winding canyon lined with jagged cliffs and forest of pine and other varieties of timber. At each turn in the canyon our emotions would soar in anticipation of seeing something to shoot at, but each time we were disappointed until we had branched off into the north fork of Spring Creek, distant from home about three miles. At this point as we emerged into a fairly open space among the pines we sighted a large buck deer standing broadside to us and not more than seventy-five yards away. Feverish with excitement my brother drew the bead on the animal and pulled the trigger but with no apparent results but a loud report that echoed and reechoed far up and down the canyon. The animal did not budge but stood looking at us after a quizzical fashion as if trying to discover what the racket was all about. It was my turn to shoot but George pleaded so hard to be given an opportunity to retrieve his ill fortune that I finally consented to let him try again. The second shot took effect, the bullet centering the forehead between the eyes and the giant of the forest, as he appeared to us, came down in a heap. I have always felt that providence guided that bullet to its destination or that the killing was accidental for my brother undoubtedly would not have taken chances on losing the deer by shooting at its head when its whole body was exposed to his view. As I recall, however, the matter did not come up for debate. Perhaps it was because I felt it would be unethical to argue such a delicate question with an older brother.

Be that as it may, both of us thrilled at the sight before us and down deep in our hearts was a feeling of deep gratitude, for we had a happy vision of changing our diet from alfalfa to venison.

We rushed to the deer lest he recover from the shock and escape in the forest of pines but when we reached him he was dead. Imagine our feelings when we reached for a knife to sever his jugular and remembered we had left it at home. A moment's consultation and it was decided that George should run home for a knife which would leave me to stand guard over the deer. My job would not have been a disagreeable one but for the fact that the day was cold and the gray clouds overhead portended a snow storm, and there I was with feet as bare as they were the day I was born. Soon the snow began to fall in great flakes and my feet must have frozen had I not kept them in motion. Presently over my head I heard the flutter of wings and looking up I saw a big flock of wild turkeys winging their way across the canyon. When they hit the ground they were within fifty yards of me. Full of excitement I leveled my gun on a huge gobler but before I could pull the trigger he had disappeared behind a bush. I tried it on another and still another but each time with the same results. Not a shot did I get and when finally the flock had disappeared and I was left alone with my emotions and the deer, I fell down in a heap and literally bawled. How long my brother was gone I had no way of knowing but to me the time seemed almost interminable. When he did arrive he was accompanied by my mother and a younger brother who had come to assist in transporting the buck to our home. When the animal had been prepared each of us seized a leg and began our homeward journey, but our progress was slow as it was all some of us could do to manage our load. With difficulty we would carry it a few rods when some one would call time out. We were all but exhausted when to our joy we were met by our neighbor, Helaman Pratt, who, having heard of our success, had come with his pack mule to give us a lift.

That evening there was a happy group of children while Mother was preparing the evening meal as they inhaled the odor from the frying venison and a still happier group when they sat down to the table and had a real fill of the sweetest meat any of us had ever eaten. Once or twice during the repast I thought I saw a tear drop glistening in her eyes and once I fancied I heard her mutter a praise to God for his bounteous gift.

THE THOMPSON TRAGEDY

Nestled away in the top of the Sierra Madre four miles northeast from Cave Valley and thirty miles west of Colonia Juarez is a little valley called Cliff Ranch. Appropriately named, surrounded as it is by rugged cliffs and lofty peaks, it occupies a position at a point where Spring Creek, flowing from the north, empties its crystal stream into the waters of the Piedras Verdes.

Flowers of almost endless variety cast their perfumes into the mountain air, while from overhead gorgeously plumed parakeets screamed and screeched as they winged their way through the leafy boughs of the graceful pines. This little valley for ages lay wrapped in seclusion save for the song of the bird and the tread of the wild animal and perchance for the occasional visit of the roaming Apache until the advent of two typical Mormon families, the Pratts and the Romneys, who came from the valley below to take up their abode. There were forty in all. For three years the cry of children was heard and the song of youth and maid echoed from cliff to cliff as gaily they roamed the meadows and steeps of their adopted home. No thought of fear marred their peace of mind as they strolled through the forests of virgin timber. In the seclusion of this mountain fastness they felt secure. There came a time however when the social and economic voice from afar called them hence and the picturesque spot again lapsed into silence except for its original sounds. But soon human voices again were heard. This time a Scandinavian family, Thompson by name, had come to till the soil and graze their cattle on the luxuriant growths of grass and shrubs. There were five in all—father and mother—two sons, Hiram and Elmer, 18 and 14 respectively, and a grand-daughter, Anna, six years of age.

Sunday morning, September 19, 1892, dawned clear and bright. Apparent peace and security hovered over the little valley. There was nothing in the environment or in the minds or hearts of this happy family prophetic of the dire calamity that was soon to overtake them. Early in the morning the father parted with his family to go to Pacheco, eleven miles away to work on a threshing machine, for the grain was ready to harvest.

Monday morning came. The boys must be off to their work in the field but before leaving they would carry the feed to the hogs to lighten the burden of their mother. Anna would accompany them to return the pails to the house. Hiram arrived first at the pens and while in the act of pouring the feed a report of a rifle shot rang out sharp and clear. The youth fell mortally wounded. Another shot echoed through the pines and Elmer, who was on his way to the pens, likewise fell to the ground. He had been shot through the hips. In agonizing pain the boy lay still, afraid to move lest another bullet should end his life. Until now the source of the shooting was a mystery to the youth but suddenly from behind the outbuildings several lithe dusky forms sprang forth and ran to the house. In the meantime the mother hearing the shots rushed to a door facing the cook house that stood a few feet away and immediately her body was pierced by a bullet fired from without. With the blood pouring from her wound, the woman fled from the house and unwittingly ran into a group of savage redmen who had concealed themselves at the rear of the cookhouse. In mortal agony she pleaded for mercy but her cries were answered with a shower of stones that crushed out the life from her pain-wracked body.

While this horrible tragedy was being enacted at the house, the wounded boy dragged himself into a chicken coop nearby hoping to escape further detection by the savages. Presently as he peered from his hiding place he beheld the fleeing form of his terror-stricken niece. The little girl had witnessed the death of her grandmother and thinking that her two uncles had shared a similar fate she was fleeing to escape what seemed to her most certain death. Several efforts were made to attract the attention of the child when finally the youth succeeded in beckoning her to his side and within this seclusion, the two remained until the savage fiends had collected the spoils and their retreating forms had disappeared in the distance. The physical and mental agony of the boy as he lay there critical-ly wounded, and the terror of the little girl in the presence of death are appalling, but the courage of the two is a worthy theme for an abler pen than mine. Something must be done or soon the fate of the lad would be as tragic as that of his heroic brother and sainted mother. Drop by drop his life's blood was ebbing away. No time must be lost. The nearest neighbor was several miles distant. The journey must be a painful one and very tedious for the nature of the wound was such as to render the lower limbs comparatively helpless. Progress was possible only on hands and knees, yet the lad must steel himself to the ordeal. Slowly and painfully the boy crawled along, each moment adding to his already pent-up agony when finally, from sheer exhaustion his limbs refused to move. A deathly feeling crept over him; then all became black; he had fainted from the loss of blood. Frantically the girl ran forward. She must get help before it was too late! How her little heart pounded as she made a turn in the road, to see a man coming toward her. Was he friend or foe? She was about to turn and flee when she discovered that the approaching figure was a friend of the family. To him she poured out her tale of sorrow. In haste the two made their way to the nearest settlement to report the awful tragedy and to make arrangements to care for the dead and wounded, the dead to be tenderly laid to rest in graves beneath the pines and the wounded boy to be nursed back to health and vigor.

Eight years had passed and the tragic fate of the Thompson family had well nigh been forgotten when reports became current that a band of Indians were still infesting the Sierras in proximity to Cliff Ranch. At the same time reports were given out at Williams' Ranch, two miles west of Cliff Ranch, that fields of growing corn were being entered nightly by marauders who were stripping the stalks of their ears and bearing them away on the backs of horses. To escape detection the feet of the animals were muffled with what appeared to be gunny sack. Their patience exhausted, the owners of the corn, Harris and Allen, decided the thieving must cease. Accordingly one Sunday very early in the morning, the two mountaineers picked up the trail at the point where it left the field and with difficulty followed it for a short distance when it was lost to them entirely in an area of rocky ground. By this time they were quite certain that the trail was headed for the upper waters of Spring Creek, off to the north. A brisk walk of two or three hours brought them to a high point overlooking a little valley on the north fork of Spring Creek in which they saw a volume of smoke curling upward from a camp fire. The men were convinced from appearances that the campers were Indians and that they were preparing to leave for other quarters. Cautiously they made their way into the valley a short distance below the camp where they secreted themselves behind huge boulders that had fallen from the ledge above. Here they felt they would be safe from detection and at the same time would be able to watch the movements of the Redmen. The savages were not long in collecting their equipment and placing it upon the backs of the ponies. When all was securely tied, they mounted their saddle horses and in true Indian style began their march. The pulses of the secreted men beat faster as they saw the Indians coming but they saw no avenue of escape. As it was, there was nothing to do but to let matters take their course and to breathe a prayer that Providence would blind the eyes of the Redmen to their presence. But in this they were to be disappointed. Ever alert for dangers in such mountain fastnesses, the keen eye of the squaw on lead of the procession, fell upon the Americans and immediately she gave the signal in a war cry that sent a chill down the spinal cords of the hiding men that nearly froze the blood in their veins. They saw the chief, quick as a flash reach for his gun but before he could draw it from its scabbard two shots rang out from behind the boulders and the chieftain and a small boy fell from the same mount never to rise again. Bullets flew thick and fast but only for a brief moment. The Indians fled in terror leaving their slain upon the field of battle. When the smoke had cleared away three savage forms were seen stretched out in death while the men who fought to save their lives escaped without a scratch, but not without regrets that even in self defense they had been compelled to shed the blood of men.

No time was lost in reporting the event to the proper authority with the result that a local investigation of the affair was made. Harris and Allen were commended for their courage and self-control in a situation that would have terrified less heroic men while the three Indians were carefully laid to rest in the primeval forest. No one knows, but it seemed most probable that after a lapse of years retribution had finally come to a band of savages responsible for the massacre of members of the Thompson family.

THE HOG-TIED COW

The range land surrounding Colonies Morelos and Oaxaca was individually owned but, since it was unfenced, cattle and other live stock could wander at will. This condition led to an admixture of animals of the various brands thus necessitating semi-annual "round-ups," one in the spring and the other in the fall of the year.

A fall round-up was in process when I happened to be driving a team and wagon from Morelos to Oaxaca, a distance of twenty-six miles. As I approached a large corral on the outskirts of Oaxaca I observed that it was being emptied of a big herd of cattle. The branding and ear marking of the calves and long ears had been attended to and all had been released from the enclosure except a long-horned cow and she was lying hog-tied in the middle of the corral. As I drove up I noticed a group of cowboys standing around the animal and being of a gregarious nature and curious to learn what it was all about I jumped the fence and joined the crowd. Presently all left the corral but a fellow by the name of Scott and myself. Scott remained to untie the cow's legs but my motive for remaining behind is inexplicable even to this day unless it was that I courted a little excitement. But whatever the motive I was soon to experience the thrill of my life.

I stood by watching with interest the loosening of the bonds that held the cow fast and then followed the cowboy in haste to a snubbing post not far away. This was to serve as a place of refuge in case the animal should show fight which, from all appearances, seemed most probable. Deliberately she rose to her feet, looked about the corral scrutinizingly and the moment her eyes fell upon us she made a mad rush for us with head bent downward in a hooking position, and with mouth opened wide from which she emitted a sound that fairly raised my hair to a standing position and increased my heart beat perceptibly. Scott seized the post with both hands and I grabbed the top band of his trousers with the strength of an octopus. As the infuriated beast would make a lunge at us we would fly to the opposite side of the post from her, thus around and around we went. Observing the tenacity of the animal and fearful of getting winded Scott suddenly broke loose from the post and in so doing swung me directly between him and our pursuer, at the same time tearing my hands loose from his trousers.

Frantically we ran for the fence, being hotly pursued by the cow. Fear added speed to my limbs but with each bound the beast lessened the distance between us. Never in my life had I been known as a speedy man but the distance from the snubbing post to the fence was covered in record time. Then with the spring of a panther I raised myself from the ground and leaped wildly into the air just as I felt the hot breath of the critter on the seat of my pants. I had hoped to balance my body on the top pole of the seven foot fence but imagine my surprise when I found myself lunging headforemost toward the ground on the opposite side. The impact dazed me but it was only for a moment. Sheepishly I arose, dusted myself and amid the roar of the crowd I sauntered back to my wagon a wiser and saner man.

A DAGGER IN THE MOONLIGHT

Two of my older brothers, Miles and George had leased a portion of the Williams' ranch adjacent to Cave Valley in northern Chihuahua, hoping to find ready market at the mines for all the vegetables they could produce. The mines were situated along the backbone of the Sierra Madre range which formed the boundary line between the adjoining states of Sonora and Chihuahua. The trails through the region leading from western Chihuahua into Sonora were rather difficult of travel since they traversed mountain passes and box canyons rendered almost inaccessible because of being hemmed in by jagged cliffs. In company with others the journey was a trying one but when taken alone it was almost intolerable due to its utter loneliness.

To add to the income it was agreed that Miles, when not otherwise engaged, should purchase cattle for certain companies, he to receive his compensation in the form of a commission. One of these business trips took him through the mountain passes and rugged canyons of the Sierra Madre far off into the valley of the Bavispe where the Sonoran cities of Baserac and Bavispe were the chief centers in a rich agricultural and stock raising territory. From residents of these communities he made his purchases and reimbursed them with bank checks deeming it unsafe to carry on his person large amounts of currency. As he moved about from place to place his attention was called to a strange Mexican dog that was following him in a friendly fashion. Having a fondness for dogs he reciprocated the animal's advances of friendship, with the result that the dog refused to leave him.

With his purchases made and with the sun still two hours above the western horizon my brother decided to begin his homeward journey. Twenty or twenty-five miles at most would bring him to a good camp ground in the midst of the pines where water and pasture were abundant and where the bracing air of the mountains would insure him a night of refreshing sleep. With a light heart and a song on his lips he passed out of the region of the mesquite and cat claws, where the air was warm and sultry into the higher altitudes where the air was crisp and where a variety of timber grew. As he jogged along he cast backward glances and saw that the strange dog was following him. He tried to drive him back but all in vain. Long before the projected camping ground was reached the sun had sunk beyond the horizon at his back and dark shadows had cast their mantle on the forests of pine and oak. Presently to his delight, he saw the moon appear above the summit of the peak in front of him for now he knew he would experience but little difficulty in following the winding trail. At last the arduous journey of the day was over. In a delightful spot he pitched his camp. The two faithful horses were unsaddled and unpacked and put out to graze, and then the weary traveler took from his bag a cold lunch that had been prepared for him in the valley below and fell to eating.

His supper over, he spread out his blankets and with his gun by his side he was soon wrapped in slumber.

How long he slept he could not conjecture when the strange Mexican dog with a fierce and prolonged growl awoke him from his sleep. With a start he opened his eyes to behold a Mexican in a crouching position coming toward his bed and clutching in his hand a huge dagger with which he expected to strike the deadly blow. The years of training among the dangers of the frontier had taught my brother well the lesson of self protection. As if by instinct he seized his rifle and with a steady aim he drew it on the approaching form and in a clear cut Spanish tongue commanded him to retrace his steps or he would pull the deadly trigger. The native, with bated breath, lost no time in argument, but hastily withdrew to a more congenial clime. The click of the rifle had unnerved him. As for Miles, when he was left alone with the dog he gave him a fond caress while tears of gratitude glistened in his eyes there in the moonlight. The attempt of the bandit had been frustrated and a life had been saved by the growl of a dog.

How strange that in times of crises men have nerves of steel but in the aftermath, when the danger is passed their nerves become limp as the strings of an unstrung bow. Such was the condition of my brother. During the long hours of the unfinished night he shook with fear while his tired eyes sought sleep in vain. With the break of dawn he was on his way and still following him was the dog. A few hours passed and this time when he cast a backward glance to his astonishment the dog could not be seen. For several miles he followed back the trail but his faithful friend could not be found. As mysteriously as the animal had come into the life of the traveler did it pass out again. Surely, thought my brother as he pushed on toward home there is an unseen power protecting the lives of men from dangers of which they are unaware and even dogs are made to serve good ends.

The Rushing Waters of the Bavispe

Bill Jarvis and I were on our way to the "Cane Brakes," a point midway between the colonies of Morelos and Oaxaca on the Bavispe River. We were to attend a fall round-up at which all the cattlemen for many miles around would be present. The day was clear but the air had a tang about it that betokened the passage of the warm days of summer and the approach of the cooler atmosphere of autumn.

To shorten the journey we decided to follow the trail that led up the narrow canyon of the Bavispe rather than the regular highway which, though much easier to travel, would require several more miles of riding to bring us to our destination.

With light hearts so characteristic of youth on the frontier we set out on our journey each mounted on a fine pony "raring to go." The tortuous trail up the Bavispe was followed without difficulty for a distance of several miles when to our great disappointment we found that, owing to the narrowness of the canyon and the precipitous nature of the mountains, it would be impossible to proceed further without crossing to the opposite side of the river. To attempt this was hazardous due to the swollen condition of the stream. An unusually heavy rainy season had left great deposits of moisture in the mountains which was now rapidly making its way to the canyon below to join the waters of the Bavispe. At the point where we must cross, the river ran diagonally from one side of the canyon to the other and narrowed to about half the width of the stream elsewhere. Like water pouring through a huge funnel the angry waters splashed and roared and beat against their banks with a maddened fury that bode ill to any who might be so foolish as to venture into the flood.

For a brief moment Bill and I paused to consider what was to be done and hastily decided that rather than turn back we would attempt to get over to the opposite side. Conscious of the danger of such an attempt, I urged Bill to remain where he was and let me make the experiment and should I succeed without accident, then he could follow after. I alighted from my mount and garment by garment I removed everything from my person except my B. V. D.'s and my top shirt, feeling that this precaution should be taken to insure against drowning in case I should be swept from my horse. Even though a fairly good swimmer, I feared the result should I attempt to battle the raging torrent clad from top to toe. With a mighty swing I sent my shoes hurtling through the air to the opposite side of the stream and then proceeded to make fast the balance of my clothing to the horn of my saddle. With everything in readiness I struck my horse and with a terrific lunge he pushed into the stream.

The muddy waters beat violently against his side and the swishing torrent almost tore me from the saddle. The faithful animal fought valiantly but the ever deepening channel and the increasing fury of the waves were too much for his failing strength. Suddenly his feet were swept from under him and down went horse and rider to the bottom of the stream, with a desperation born of fear, I tore myself loose from the saddle and with a mighty effort, I brought myself to the surface of the water just in time to seize the end of a cottonwood limb that protruded from the opposite bank far into the stream. Like a drowning man that I was I clung desperately to the limb as the writhing water gurgled and hissed about me to threaten to snap the branch and hurl me to destruction. Inch by inch I pulled myself in the direction of the bank fighting desperately to keep my head above the water, but with all that I could do there were moments when I was entirely engulfed and I felt I must die of strangulation. I recall vividly as if it were but yesterday the swirl of the mud and the roaring of the waters as I struggled to free myself from the grip of a monster that seemed determined to drag me down to certain death. Likewise I live again in fancy that feeling of deep gratitude I experienced when at last I emerged from the angry flood and found myself on dry ground and contemplated that I had been spared to again behold the faces of my little flock at home who would be anxiously awaiting my return.

As for the horse, he managed to extricate himself from the dangerous predicament in which I left him and had made his way back to the bank of the stream from which we had started.

I shouted to Bill to meet me at the cane brakes and then pulled on my shoes and began my six miles journey on foot. I missed my trousers more from a sense of lack of comfort than from a sense of conventional impropriety for the cool autumn zephyr was fanning my wet limbs to a numbness that made traveling slow and somewhat painful. Far above the noise of the water I wound my way around the steep mountainside where it would be difficult in places even for the mountain sheep to keep his footing. At last when the evening shadows were about to disappear and night had begun to cast her black mantle over the face of things I entered again the canyon of the Bavispe at the cane brakes and found awaiting me my faithful friend Bill and my much needed wearing apparel. Bill joked me some but I didn't mind that for I would soon be warming myself before the crackling flames at the camp of the round up.

INDEX

Bentley, Joseph C., bishop of Colonia Juarez, 258; president of Juarez Stake, 258; report of, 235.

Bible, record of Israel in eastern world, 22.

Book of Mormon, parts of, translated into Spanish, 38; record of Israel in western world, 22, 23.

Brown, O. P., appointed as first bishop of Colonia Morelos, 122.

Call, Anson B., experience of, with rebels, 223-228; leader in making settlements, 31; sons of, slain, 255.

Casas Grandes, parley of Mormons and Mexican officials at, 161, 163, 164.

Cave Valley, associations organized, 104; first presiding elder, 104; first settlers, 104; location of, 103; United Order attempted, 105; why named, 103.

Celestial Marriage, meaning of, 49.

Chihuahua, Mexico, services held in, 41.

Chuichupa, associations organized, 113; first bishop of, 113; first called Mariano, 113; location, 112; meaning of name, 112.

Church of Jesus Christ of Latter-day Saints, driven from homes, 25; doctrines of, 34; history of, 21-26; moves westward under Brigham Young, 25-34; organization of, 23.

Colonia Diaz, education provided, 80; first bishop, 76; first dwellings at 76; first mill, 81; first permanent settlement, 74; growth of, 81; murder at, 83; purchase of land at, 75; recreation at, 78; social life of, 77.

Colonia Dublan, church auxiliaries organized, 100; first bishop, 100; first meeting house erected, 100; Huller tract, 96; location of, 97; purchase of land, 96; settlement of, 95; store and mill built, 99.

Colonia Juarez, bishop appointed, 91; center of Church activity, 128; church and school building erected, 129; dam built, 90; fertile soil at, 86; first death, 85; industries established, 92, 93; Juarez Academy established, 129, 141, 142; location of, 85; railroad to, 143; roads and mills erected, 91; schools at, 88, 141.

Colonia Morelos, deserted by colonists, 200; erection of church and school house, 123; farming district, 124; first settlers, 121; game district, 120; land cleared, 123; location, 120; social life, 125; survey of townsite, 122; trouble with outlaws, 125, 126; ward organized, 122.

Colonia Pacheco, bishopric organized, 109; named for Mexican, 108; purchase of land, 109.

Dagger in the Moonlight, story of, 328.

Diaz, Porfirio, conditions in Mexico under, 14-19; ruler of Mexico, 13; sketch of life, 13-19; welcomes Mormons to Mexico, 59.

Dilworth, Mary J., first school teacher in Utah, 33.

Education, earliest, in Utah, 33; Mormons believers in, 33.

Edwards, T. D., American Consul, 156.

Exiles, conditions of, 189, 190, 206; U. S. Government renders aid to, 212; homes of, burned, 242.

Exodus from Mexico, causes leading to, 144-148, 195, 214, 215; conditions of colonies at time of, 182, 183, 192; deaths caused by, 198.

Garcia, associations organized, 111; industries at, 111; location, 110; settlement of, 110; ward organized, 111.

Garden Grove, Mormons make station at, 27.

Grant, Heber J., makes exploring trip in Mexico, 54; visits Mexico, 53.

Harvey, James D., assassination of, 168, 169.

Haws, George M., first bishop of Chuichupa, 113.

Haymore, Edward, kidnapping of, 199.

Heaton, Christopher, assassinated by Mexicans, 145.

Hog-tied cow, story of, 326.

Huerta, interviewed by Junius Romney, 207; Mexican General, 207.

Immorality, of Mexican Troops, 196.

Irrigation, introduced into Great Basin, 28.

Ivins, Anthony W., advice to returning colonists, 218; appointment as president of Mexican Mission, 47; explains plan of settlement, 69; first president

of Juarez Stake, 130; letter reporting conditions in Chihuahua, 246; life sketch, 132-139; reports from, 235, 239; visits General Castillo, 175.

Juarez Stake, organization of, 130; leaders of, 129, 139, 140; reorganization of, 259; statistical report, 259.

Juarez Stake Academy, conditions at the, 257; Guy C. Wilson, first president of, 141.

Johnson, William D., first bishop of Colonia Diaz, 76.

Keeler, Ralph B., appointed president of Juarez Stake, 259.

Kidnapping, colonists suffer, 199.

Land, purchase of, 62, 65; prices of, 62-64, 66, 67.

Lewis, Frank, killed by Juan Sosa, 163.

Lunt, Edward, experience of, with rebels, 228, 229.

MacDonald, A. F., conditions of colonies described by, 64; reports findings of trip to Church leaders, 58, 59; visits northern Chihuahua, 55.

MacDonald, Agnes, assassinated by Mexicans, 144, 145.

Madero Revolution, history of, 150, 151.

Mariano, See Chuichupa.

Merchandise, prices of, 68, 70.

Mexican Colonization and Agricultural Company, conditions of settlement under, 69; organization of, 63; purpose of, 63-68.

Mexican Government, relations of Mormons to, 149-181.

Mexican Mission, organization of the, 43.

removes to Missouri and Illinois, 24, 25; visit of Angel Moroni to, 21.

Smith, Joseph F., advises colonists to leave Mexico, 237; views on colonists returning, 216.

Smith, Jesse N., Jr., first bishop of Colonia Pacheco, 109.

Stevens Family, tragedy of the, 220, 221.

Sugar Creek, camp of Mormons at, 26.

Teasdale, George, head of Mexican Mission, 57; leads company seeking sites for settlements, 56, 57.

Temoche Revolution, story of the, 310.

Tenney, Ammon M., Indian interpreter and missionary, 48.

Thatcher, Moses, appointed president of Mexican Mission, 43; arrives in Mexico City, 43; dedicates land for opening of mission in, 44; second appointment as president of Mexican Mission, 47.

Thompson Tragedy, history of the, 322.

Thurber, A. D., appointed leader of colonist army, 193.

Union Mercantile Store, robbed by bandits, 157, 158.

United Order, attempted at Cave Valley, 105; described, 105-108.

University of Deseret, first university west of Missouri River, 33.

Villa, Pancho, rebel leader, 238, 241.

Wayside Stations, made at Garden Grove and Mt. Pisgah, 27.

Whetten, John T., appointed first bishop of Garcia, 111.

Wilcken, August, appointed president of Mexican Mission, 46.

Wilson, Guy C., first president of Juarez Stake Academy, 141; visits Madero on behalf of colonists, 164, 165.

Winter Quarters, history of Mormons at, 27, 28.

Young, Brigham, leads Mormons to Utah, 25-34; makes plans for colonization, 30.

Young, Brigham, Jr., accompanies Heber J. Grant on exploring trip, 54; visits Mexico, 53.